The I AM America Collection

BUILDING THE SEAMLESS GARMENT

*Revealing the Secret Teachings of
Ascension and the Golden Cities*

ALSO BY LORI TOYE

A Teacher Appears

Sisters of the Flame

Fields of Light

The Ever Present Now

New World Wisdom Series

I AM America Atlas

Points of Perception

Light of Awakening

Divine Destiny

Sacred Energies

Freedom Star Book

I AM America Map

Freedom Star Map

6-Map Scenario

US Golden City Map

BUILDING THE
SEAMLESS GARMENT

REVEALING THE SECRET TEACHINGS OF
ASCENSION AND THE GOLDEN CITIES

LORI & LENARD TOYE

I AM AMERICA PUBLISHING & DISTRIBUTING
P.O. Box 2511, Payson, Arizona, 85547, USA.
www.iamamerica.com

© (Copyright) 2017 by Lori Adaile Toye. All rights reserved.
ISBN: 978-1-880050-10-1

All rights exclusively reserved, including under the Berne Convention and the Universal Copyright Convention. No part of this book may be reproduced or translated into any language or utilized in any form or by any means, electronic or mechanical, including photocopying, recording, or by any information storage and retrieval system, without written permission from the publisher. Published in 2017 by I AM America Seventh Ray Publishing International, P.O. Box 2511, Payson, Arizona, 85547, United States of America.

I AM America Maps and Books have been marketed since 1989 by I AM America Seventh Ray Publishing and Distributing, through workshops, conferences, and numerous bookstores in the United States and internationally. If you are interested in obtaining information on available releases please write or call:
I AM America, P.O. Box 2511, Payson, Arizona, 85547, USA. (928) 978-6435, or visit:

www.iamamerica.com
www.loritoye.com
www.loritoye.org

Graphic Design and Typography by Lori Toye
Editing by Dawn Abel, Elaine Cardall, Felicia Megdal, and Betsy Robinson

Love, in service, breathes the breath for all!

10 9 8 7 6 5 4 3 2 1

"Down with death, conscious immortality arise!"

~ SAINT GERMAIN

Contents

FOREWORD by Susan Liberty Hall   XXIII
PREFACE   XXVII

CHAPTER ONE

Emanation • 33

    The Earth Is Absorbing Light Forces 33
    Transmuting Genetically Held Fear 34
    Cellular Acceleration of Light 35
    Ray Forces and the Cellular Awakening. 35
    Law of Harmony 36
    The Astral Body 36
    Ever Present Now 37
    The Color Rays 37
    Lord of the Ray 38
    A Ray Emanates 38
    Emanation 39
    Choice and Evolution 40
    The Cell of Perfection 40
    Interplay with the Astral Body .41

Emanation of a Master Teacher 42
Lifetime to Lifetime. 43
Emanation in a Golden City Vortex 43
Qualification of the Ray 44
Conductivity and Sacred Geometry 44
Through the Kundalini. 44
Golden Cities Duplicate the Ray Forces 45
Enhancement of Ray Forces. 45
Use of Crystals and Gems 46
Sound and the Violet Flame. 46
Liberation through the Flame 47
The Alchemy of the Flame 48
Spiritual Fusion 48
Conducting the Ray Forces 49
The Vibration of Freedom 50
Focus and Intention 51
Discipline and the Flame 51

CHAPTER TWO

Behind the Interplay • 55

Service Lifts Karma. 55
The Planets Flow with Light and Life. 56
Service of the Planets 56
The Difference Is the Experience 57
Personal Balance 57
The "HU" Completes and Intensifies 58
Seal the Energy 59
Discover and Activate Your Sound. 60

CHAPTER THREE
A New Day • 63

Humanity's Evolution and Ascension 63
Shattering Old Beliefs............................64
Down with Death..................................64
Unification of Self..............................65
The Role of the Golden City......................65
Illusion and Spiritual Deterioration 66
The New Consciousness 66
Release Fear 66
Identify Intention 67
The Internal Spark 67
First Steps 68
Birth of Conscience..............................68
"Equal To" 68
Declutter Your Consciousness.....................69
Live Life for Life...............................69
Simplicity and the ONE 70
"We Take Form at Will" 71
Self-Evaluation..................................72
Collective Illusion 73
The Gift of the Flame 73
Be Specific 74
Forgive Yourself 75
Know Thyself 76
Constructive Change..............................76
Golden City Energies.............................77
Union of Body, Mind, and Soul 78

The Inner Change 78
Working with the Master.........................79

CHAPTER FOUR
Golden City Rays • 81

Spiritual Evolution and the Rays 81
The Rays and the Human Aura 81
Gobean, the Blue City.............................82
The Blue Ray.....................................83
Malton and the Ruby-Gold Ray 84
The Process of Purification 85
Orchestration of the Rays 86
Wahanee and the Violet Ray 86
Shalahah and the Green Ray 87
Ascension Valley..................................88
Interdimensional Travel 88
Abundance and Prosperity 89
Klehma and the White Ray........................89
United States Capitol 90
Venusian Energies.................................90
Cooperation and Community 90
White Fires of Ascension 91
Golden City Mantras..............................91

CHAPTER FIVE
Blue Illumination • 95

Golden City Network..............................95
Shamballa's Provenance...........................96
The Crystal Cities.................................96

The Great Immortals............................96
Disharmony and War 97
Shamballa Is Moved and Rebuilt..................97
Perfection Is an Emanation 97
The Second Demise of Shamballa 97
The Ethereal Shamballa 98
Shamballa and the New Times 98
Exercise of the ONE.............................99
Shamballa and the Golden City of Gobi 99
Heaven and Earth 100
Gobi and Gobean are ONE.......................100
The Deathless Body 101
Golden City Doorways..........................101
Infusion of Truth...............................101
Akhenaten and Serapis Bey......................102
Ancient Gobean 103
Quetzalcoatl the Christ..........................103
Shamballa's Hall of Wisdom 103

CHAPTER SIX
Template of Light ◆ 105
The Star of Gobean 105
The God State..................................106
Higher Frequency 106
A Beckoning...................................107
Let Go 108
Ray Forces Enter the Star........................108
The Inner Sun 109

Qualification of Light 109
Light unto Light..................................109
Ripples of Light and Sound 110
Light Joins Sound.................................110
Evolution and the Violet Flame....................111
OM Shanti...111
Mastery of the Physical 112
Step-down Transformer.............................112
At-ONE-Ment 112
Violet Flame Assists the Oneness 113
Elixir of the Heart 113
Family, Love, and the ONE 114
Blue Flame Meditation 114
Alignment of the Will 115
Union...115
Regeneration 116
Suggestions for Spiritual Practice 116
The Higher Chakra System 117

CHAPTER SEVEN

Time of Testing ✦ 119

Accept Perfection 119
The Perfected Cell and Its Lighted Stance.........119
The Forgetting....................................120
Compassion 120
Swift Changes.....................................121
Crossing the Threshold 121
Intervention of the Golden Cities 122

Awakening 122
The Assimilation Process 123
Star Energies 124
Choosing a Star 125
On Community. 126
Prophecies of Change 127
A Valley. 127
Sacred Architecture 128
A Temple. 129
Remember the Rhythm of Cycles 130
Planetary Schoolrooms 131
Spiritual Memory 131
A Family of the Rayces 132
The Twelve Adepts 133
Twelve Sacred Teachings. 133
Spiritual Lineage 134
Loss, or a New Way? 134
The Ascension 135

CHAPTER EIGHT

Memory Is Freedom ♦ 137

Transmutation and Transformation 137
Time and Perception. 137
The Law of Love. 138
Law of ONE 138
Memory and Liberation 139
Removing the Death Consciousness. 139
True Memory and Immortality. 140

Time of Testing 140
The Oral Tradition. 140
Recall Your Divinity 141
"Listen with Your Heart" 142
A Thousand Eyes 142
The Seamless Garment 143
Your Journey 144
"Within the Wave" 144
The Limitless I AM. 145
Beyond Illusion 145
Service and Blessings 146
"Debt Is Doubt" 148

CHAPTER NINE

Golden Ray Compassion • 151

The Gold Ray 151
Prerequisite Use of the Violet Flame 152
Preparing the Body for Ascension 152
Purification in the Star. 153
A Divine Inheritor 154
The Path of the Heart 154
Compassion and the Fire of Alchemy. 155
Surrender to Victory 156
"Two Shall Come Forth". 156
Complement of Energy. 157
Meeting through the Ascension 157
Remove Limitation and Bondage 158
Separation and the Web of Illusion 158

Reuniting through the Gold Ray .159
Ascension and the Golden City Star 159
An Alignment Process. 159
It Is Vibration and Frequency 160
A Gentle Nudge 161
When the Student Is Ready. 161
"You Are All a Oneship" 162
Development of the Will. 162
One Mind. 163

CHAPTER TEN
Ascension Valley ♦ 165

Unity and Healing in Shalahah .165
Alignment and Preparation. 166
Enlightening Your Cells 167
Hierarchy of Consciousness. 168
Atlantis and the Sun God 168
The Darkness of Kali 169
Cells, Citrus, and Energy. 170
Vortices of Acceleration 170
The Feminine Nurtures Our Perfection 171
Lord Sananda 171
The Crystal Points of Ascension Valley 171
Ascension and the Sacred Fire .172
The Ascension Areas. 173

CHAPTER ELEVEN

Ascension of Consciousness • 175

Cause and Effect...................................175
Alignment and Harmony 176
"Love in Action" 176
Healing and the Ascension.......................177
Spiritual Education 178
Karmic Patterns..................................178
"The Reward Is Immeasureable"..................179
Review Your Patterns 179
The Heart and Sacred Fire 180
Beyond Illusion 180
Invoke the Flame 181
Taming Emotions 181
Growth through Experience 182
The Mighty I AM Presence.......................182
The Awakening Point 183
Beyond the Physical 184
The Ascension Process 184
Ascension and Diet 185
Divine Love 186
Action and the Violet Flame 187
Emotional Attachments 187
Energy for Energy 188
Emotions and the Violet Flame 189

CHAPTER TWELVE
Ascension through the Dimensions • 191
The Spiritual Training of the Mind. 191
Ascension of Souls. 191
The Open Heart 192
Preparation through the Golden Cities 192
Parallel and Paradox. 193
A Unified Body of Light 193
The Unseen Kingdoms. 194
Translation between the Dimensions. 194
Life Beyond. 195
Golden Cities and the Fourth Dimension. 195
The Fourth Dimension and Earth Changes 195
An Exponential Leap. 196
Energy Fields of the Fourth Dimension 197
A Range of Ray Forces. 198
When the Time Is Right. 198
Babajeran and the Elemental Life Force 199
The Divine Oneship of Nature .200
Opening the Divine Cell 200
Change and Choice 201
Interconnectivity. 201
Sound Frequencies 202
Perception 202
Divine Chamber of the Heart. .204
The Ascension Process and the Master Teacher 204

CHAPTER THIRTEEN

Finer Bodies of Light • 207

Violet Flame Angels of Protection 207
Exercise the Light Bodies........................207
The Inner Mind 208
Dream World 208
The Greater Spiritual Body 208
Candle Meditation 209
Overlapping and Nightmares 210
Breath Techniques 210
Nature and the Physical Body 210
New Energetics 211
Attention and the Flow 211
Building Blocks................................212
The Lights of Creation 212
Darkness Defines Light..........................213
Harmonic Concordance of Light and Sound 213
Instinct, Feeling, and Emotion 213
Reinvigoration of the Chakras....................214
Consciousness Grows 214
Awakening to Light.............................215
Dare to Dream.................................215
Golden Cities of Light 216
The First Spiritual Body 216
Embrace Life...................................217
Golden Age of Kali Yuga 217
Nourishing Soul................................218

    Spiritual Preparedness..........................218
    The Masses....................................219

SPIRITUAL LINEAGE OF THE VIOLET FLAME	221
GLOSSARY	223
APPENDIX A: The Candle Meditation	249
APPENDIX B: Saint Germain, the Holy Brother	251
APPENDIX C: El Morya	255
APPENDIX D: The Violet Flame	257
DISCOGRAPHY	259
INDEX	261
ABOUT LORI AND LENARD TOYE	279
ABOUT I AM AMERICA	284

Foreword

Greetings in the name of that Mighty Christ I AM, and I would like to share with you my experience with Lori Toye and the *I AM America* body of work that she has received from the great Ascended Masters, and in obedience, has given it to all the world.

First, I want to share a little about myself. I am a seventy-two year old grandmother, and I have been in service and devotion to Saint Germain, the great Aquarian Master of the Violet Flame, and later to Mahatma Morya El, Hierarch of the Golden City of Gobean and the Will of God, since 1973. I have what some may call a, "colorful past." I was always a spiritual seeker, but I did not understand *exactly what* I was seeking. So, I traveled the world. I was a Playboy Bunny at the New Orleans Playboy Club, as well as the London Casino, and there I learned a great deal about what I *did not* want. Later, I would become a dancer and model, and looking for adventure, I moved to Japan and for five years I loved my life, but I questioned my purpose.

In Japan I was kidnapped by a godfather of the Japanese Mafia, and I learned that I would have to marry this gangster, or face the consequences. I recognized that I had attracted this violence into my life, so I fervently prayed that I would find the way to change my vibration. I told God that I would devote my life to HIM, if I could just be rescued from this dire situation. Three days later, the godfather was arrested and jailed for a prior offense. I was free, and I had to keep my bargain with God. So I began to search for HIM, and the teachings that would change my life in a profound and amazing way.

After I left Japan, I was guided to meet Keith Rhinehart, the world's most scientifically tested physical adept medium. Reverend

Rhinehart was able to manifest apports though his body, mainly his eyes, chest, and solar plexus. Soon, I would witness thousands of beautiful crystals apported through his mediumship. (An apport is a physical object that is dematerialized from one place and rematerialized to another through a medium, in this case, through Keith.)

The crystal stones and other apported gems are programmed by the Ascended Masters. First, for a world mission, and a secondary personal mission for any chela who sacrifices through a tithe to earn them. In this way, I aggregated an amazing collection of these precious stones. Some of them are specifically for the Ascension; many are for spiritual growth and healing. A few are very specific like the *Karma Explosion Stone* that accelerates and transmutes karma, the *Miracle Healing Stone*, the *Atlantean Mental Body Stone*, the *Peace Stone* for the entire world, a unique stone to protect one from all natural disasters, a *Master Contact* stone, a *Shamballa Contact* stone, the *Auric Protection Shield*, the *Star of Life Happiness* stone, and many, many others.

Most skeptics think this is trickery, but one time I saw thousands of stones appear. No, this is not a scam, this is the real deal. Sometimes, truth is stranger than fiction.

I returned to California, to visit my mother and to see a doctor. Earlier that year I had noticed several lumps in my breasts and they were painful and worrisome. This was the seventies and at that time doctors were so afraid of breast cancer that they handed out mastectomies like candy. My doctor examined me, and without a mammogram or any other kind of test to verify his findings, he recommended a double mastectomy as soon as possible. Of course I was devastated and filled with fear. Later that evening I heard the phone ring. Then I realized that the ring was *not* the telephone. The ring was telepathic, an ethereal ring, and it was continuous. I finally decided to pick up the phone – the real telephone – and over its receiver I heard: "Greetings in the name of that Mighty Christ, I AM, this is Count Saint Germain!" I was astonished, and he continued, "We of the great Karmic Board are not allowed to interfere with the karma of our chelas, but I have received a special dispensation for you. We are aware of the doctor's recommendation to have a mastectomy. We ask that you get a total of three opinions . . . if all three opinions agree that you should have this surgery, then we say, 'Have it.' But, we of the great Karmic Board do not believe that you will find three consenting opinions."

At that moment I knew I did not have cancer. Saint Germain spoke to me about our personal friendship and that he would never forget me. As I hung up the phone, my pain was entirely gone. Again, my prayers were answered; but more importantly, I realized that I was Saint Germain's chela!

After I was guided to the Ascended Master Saint Germain and the teachings of the Ascended Masters, my life was changed in the twinkling of an eye. Very quickly I learned about the Ascension, and what was necessary for me to achieve that goal in this lifetime. I immediately realized the importance of the tithe, as taught by God in the Holy Bible. It was just something that I knew would bless me, and I did not question where my money went, or if I would receive a blessing from the gift that I would give to God. I had no expectations, but I did know this law and its teaching: "It is in giving, that you receive."

I had no idea how that would impact my life, as I always struggled to make money and to support myself. That would change! I built an astounding *Young Living Essential Oils* business, and although the great multi-level marketers that I knew had made fortunes in this work, I was not such a good business person. This would not matter, because I had the Count Saint Germain working beside me. Through our joint spiritual efforts, I now enjoy a comfortable lifestyle and I am free to pursue the two goals of my life: service to the Ascended Masters, and to obtain my Ascension.

I met Lori about twenty years ago, after I heard her speak on television. The moment I heard the words, "I AM America," I instantly knew that she was also in service to Saint Germain, his teachings based on the I AM Presence, and the importance of the I AM Race, freedom, and democracy.

The *I AM America Map* captured my attention, and I wanted to be a part of Lori's work, to help create Cities of Light, where, "The Masters have pledged that there will be no unbearable cataclysmic changes in the Golden City areas." (From the Freedom Star World Map.)

So, I determined that I would buy some land in the Golden City of Gobean, and build a cabin that could be a source of happiness as a getaway second home; but also, as a place of safety in the event of Earth Changes and the prophesied political, social, and financial changes. I now have a beautiful cabin on two and a half acres with ponderosa pines. My cabin is more than just a home to me, it is my spiritual retreat and a base for my ongoing spiritual practice, personal joy, and inner peace.

I've studied Lori's work, and we are also good friends. When the *Freedom Star World Map*, (this map depicts the locations of the fifty-one Golden Cities world-wide), was almost readied for publication and release, I wanted to help. Since service and the tithe are the ways that I choose to make my own Ascension, I assisted financially with the final costs necessary to release this important map to all the people of the world. I did this with gratitude to Lori and through HIS GRACE.

Most importantly, I would like to divulge what I believe is the most important action to assist anyone who is determined to achieve the Ascension. It is the study of the Ascended Masters, and applying what you learn. That is why Lori's new book, "Building the Seamless Garment," is so timely and a rare treasure for those who can see, hear, and understand.

I hope my words are helpful and assist your journey to enlightenment. I recognize Saint Germain through Lori's channeled works, and I pray that you will also realize that the *real gift* is now in your hands. Ascension is a, "do it yourself project," and there is no time to waste.

Always Victory,

Susan Liberty Hall

Susan Liberty Hall has recently released the book, "Ha, I Laugh in the Face of Cancer." This is Susan's true story of overcoming breast cancer, when through prayer, she was given the way to overcome cancer by herself - without a Doctor - through the herbal remedy, "Two Feathers Healing Remedy." Remarkably, she was cancer free in less than three months. She now helps others who have been diagnosed with cancer. She asks the Masters to, "Send me their chelas who have cancer, so that they can be healed," and assists their healing process through prayers, decrees, calls, and of course, the tithe.

Preface

The series of lessons featured in this book focus on the hidden teachings of Ascension—that is, the spiritual and mental processes, and the spiritual techniques that can free us from the confines of the need to reincarnate, yet again, back into a physical body. Yes, I have no doubt that this knowledge, if properly understood and applied, can free you.

Certainly these teachings are not conventional and I doubt you will find this type of spiritual wisdom anywhere else. The following pages are a rare collection of valuable transcripts from channeled sessions with two of the most profound spiritual teachers that I have had the privilege to know and work with for the last thirty years, Saint Germain and El Morya. They are definitely qualified to teach and comment on this topic. After all, they are ascended and have freed themselves from the confines of terra firma. You can read their condensed biographies in the appendices of this book.

My first exposure to the idea of Ascension came through a conventional Christian upbringing. As a small child I would view the magical depictions of Jesus Christ floating in the heavens, surrounded by choirs of angels. Later, as a young adult, I heard the term "Rapture" from a friend of evangelical faith. This spiritual process seemed similar to Ascension, but not only for the spiritual elite. Apparently, this spiritual anomaly could befall even a common, everyday believer. I wanted to learn more, but for some reason, I was missing details.

My quest for this unknown teaching concluded to some degree when I discovered Ascended Master Teaching in the late seventies. Through this amazing wisdom my beliefs and attitudes transformed; but the practical, everyday explanation regarding Ascension was still missing.

In the early nineties when my relationship with the Masters significantly deepened through channeling, small details began to emerge. It was apparent that a novice would not be given all of the Ascension teachings at once. In fact, details on this subject seemed sparse and shared in small, baby steps. As we (Lori and Lenard Toye) became familiar with one spiritual exercise, we would ask more questions and hopefully receive answers that could expand or develop our practice.

Ascension is the process of Mastering our individual thoughts, feelings, and actions that balance both negative and positive karmas. When applying this instruction, please place your emphasis on action. These teachings contain many spiritual disciplines and practices that help one to achieve higher states of consciousness. There is a thin line that delineates Ascension from Rapture. In this material, the Masters view the Rapture as a soul-liberating event that is completely faith based and assisted by the Celestial Brotherhood—a hierarchy of Angels. In contrast, the Ascension is a spiritual process that is based on applying, practicing, experiencing, and Mastering different states of consciousness that liberates our soul from this Earthly plane. According to Saint Germain, some can obtain the Ascension in just one lifetime! For most, it is a spiritual path that, once committed to, drives personal experience and spiritual education to new planes of consciousness during and after this lifetime. This is the nexus of spiritual development. The Master Teachers refer to this growth as "Building the Seamless Garment."

According to the teachings in this book the soul-nourishing light of the Great Central Sun (Galactic Center) is on the rise. This quasar type of light induces a collective Spiritual Awakening of humanity on Earth while simultaneously activating the energies of the Golden Cities—specific sites that can expedite our spiritual growth in this important Time of Change. Golden Cities can increase the effectiveness of many of the techniques shared in these teachings, including the purifying Violet Flame, the Oneness of the Candle Meditation, and the soul-commanding Gold Ray. The Seamless Garment—a metaphor for the light bodies of Ascension—is woven thread by thread through the soul's initiation in Cellular Awakening, the activation of our innate perfection through the Eight-sided Cell of Perfection, the spoken command of the HU, alongside the conscious cultivation of True Memory. The details of these soul-freeing techniques and spiritual disciplines await you in these pages.

Since these lessons were first given to us individually, they naturally contain personal lessons. The chapter on Ascension Valley was transmitted in a hotel room, just before we ventured into a nearby project where Saint Germain led us to alchemic, dimension-piercing minerals that can be used specifically for Ascension. Some of this information scientifically correlates with David Hudson's groundbreaking work with ORMEs (Orbitally Rearranged Monotomic Elements). ORMEs are transitional metals and minerals and can appear naturally in specific environments. It is alleged by esoteric researchers and scientists that preparations from these elements assist longevity, immortality, and movement into the Fourth and Fifth Dimensions by causing the DNA to become a superconductor. So in essence, Ascension Valley literally is Ascension Valley!

Most serious students of Ascended Master teaching know that a Master Teacher will never tell you what to do. The Spiritual Masters know not to interfere with our individual choices or to become entwined in our personal karma. However, Spiritual Teachers will often suggest how *you* may overcome a difficult problem or enact a natural, spiritual law that can assist your situation. Occasionally, my husband, Len, would ask for input regarding business endeavors, and particularly for assistance in locating the perfect site for a Golden City community. This question and answer is included in the chapter "The Time of Testing." Based on Saint Germain's specific description in this teaching, we discovered a unique parcel of land in the Star of the Golden City of Gobean, where a spiritual community is currently being planned for development. I mention this because all too often we interpret this type of information as metaphor when, indeed, it is entirely literal.

Since this information is layered with nuance and subtlety, I suggest that you read and reread these words in order to fully comprehend its enlightening message. This material is a living text; that is, it is alive as you are. The words will morph, adjust, and calibrate to fit your level of spiritual comprehension. Students often comment,

"I know I read this before, and now the meaning is completely different!"

More importantly, read and reread "Building the Seamless Garment" as you begin the soul-transcending journey of building your light bodies of eternal freedom and Ascension. Reflection and contemplation on these spiritual passages can alchemically incite the necessary removal of the death consciousness that has been programmed through countless lifetimes. Let Saint Germain's words lift you to self-determined victory: "Down with death! Conscious immortality arise!"

      Yours, in the Light of God that never fails,

            Lori Toye

CHAPTER ONE

Emanation
Saint Germain on Ray Forces.

Greetings, Beloved in that Mighty Christ, I AM Saint Germain, and I stream forth on that Violet Ray of Mercy and Forgiveness. As usual, Dear hearts, I request permission to come forth.

Response: "Please, Saint Germain, come forward."

THE EARTH IS ABSORBING LIGHT FORCES

Dear ones, it is most important that you observe the energies that are moving now upon the Earth Plane and Planet. For, remember, we told you there would come a time when those with the eyes to see and the ears to hear would place their hands into action. You see, beloveds, it is very important we continue our work upon the Earth Plane to increase light upon the planet. The increased value of this light is that the Earth Changes, or, cataclysmic geological changes are held back, and those who have the eyes to see and the ears to hear have the opportunity to assimilate the higher energies at this time. These higher energies are coming forward through the Golden City Vortices and also through those areas that are known as the ancient Vortices. There are also many Portals of Entry, so to speak, as we have taught before in other discourses. All of these are sensitive points upon the Earth Planet, beloved Mother Babajeran, and indeed are taking in light forces at this time. Many among humanity absorb these light forces. This great cosmic force, as it works upon the planet as a great wave in the same way that the ocean tidal system exists upon your planet, has the ability, to speed up consciousness into a greater evolution, into a greater consortium of the ONE. It is important for you to understand that it is this Unity Consciousness that we are speaking of, and it is important, as the light energies increase upon the planet that you understand its ability to affect all humanity— to affect all in a much better way.

TRANSMUTING GENETICALLY HELD FEAR

For you see, Dear ones, there are those who live with great fear, those who live with the fear of impending doom, those who would live, shall we say, seeking only protection and safety from fear which resides within themselves. Now, this fear has occurred for many generations and lifetime after lifetime, and, you see, it can adhere to the genetic structure and is passed on from one family to the next and to the next. When an opportunity like this occurs, this allows one to transmute, even genetically, lifetime after lifetime of genetic-held fear—Cellular Fear. The light that emanates from the Great Central Sun is the light that shall free you all. It is the Light of Awakening. When we gave you instruction of the Cellular Awakening, this is, too, what we were referring to, and the increase of light is available for all to partake of. There are many opportunities that will come to accelerate this light process upon the Earth. It is indeed an acceleration of the light process, an acceleration of love, and an acceleration of Unity Consciousness. This is the only solution that can stop cataclysmic change and heal all as ONE.

Prophecy, as you know Dear beloveds, has been brought forward, to expedite this process, to bring forward the unconscious fear within yourself. Facing fears enables purification and redemption; then one is able to face the future with hope and love and a willingness to create for the good of all. Indeed when all are in this Consciousness of Light then—truly then, and I say this from a firmness of knowledge—all benefit; all are then received as ONE. So you see, during this process you spin off the past; spin off the karma of many lifetimes of fear, of war, of poverty, deceptions, betrayals, and the little hurts that occur to one. Now we see the results of past dharma and your purpose is connected to letting go of fear, letting go of the little wants, letting go of the little trappings that can keep you trapped within the world of your perception.

CELLULAR ACCELERATION OF LIGHT

We have discussed perception many times. But perception, Dear hearts, Dear chelas, is indeed a pivotal point when one has the choice to how they shall see something; the choice of how it will be contained within their being, and how it will create in their worldly experience. This Time of Acceleration, of Cellular Acceleration and of genetic acceleration is a Time of Light and Bliss. This is the time in which the purpose of the Mighty I AM is revealed to all. This purpose is revealed at an individual level and then released as to the many. So you see, beloveds, it is important to firmly hold this vision of light for all upon the Earth, to not see that it should go to just a select few, but light is to go to all. For all will gain through this experience and through this acceleration. The upliftment of the Earth is of the utmost importance and this upliftment is through the medium of consciousness. Also, the medium of conscience and many choose their greater purpose, and a greater way that will serve all. For you see, beloveds, the future is always in your hands. It is held in the power of your choice.

RAY FORCES AND THE CELLULAR AWAKENING

Let me get to the work at hand. I have come forward to give further instruction upon Ray Forces, as this has been the topic of many conversations between the two of you, and also conversations between many of the chelas who request information on Ray Forces and how Ray Forces color light, and sound vibration which activates one toward greater harmony, greater understanding of unity and a greater understanding of the current time, the Cellular Awakening. There are indeed seven Ray Forces that work in the HU-man, the man who is to be God, the man who is to be realized through self-understanding. As I have taught before, the Rays are indeed anchored within the heart, and emanate through various kundalini points along the spine with various meridians and points upon the body. The Ray Forces arc out of the bottom of the feet as well as through the hands. Also Ray Forces arc through various chakras situated along the spinal cord. Ray Forces carry the encoding. They carry the information of who and what you are as substance. They carry the past. They carry the present, and they carry the future. The Rays come under the direction of the Great Central Sun. This is a force emanating throughout your universe and acting like a collective consciousness to unite one purpose to the next, one karma to the next, one dharma to the next. Do you understand?

Answer: "Yes."

LAW OF HARMONY

Unity brings all together into a greater harmony. One would think at times that they are being punished for an experience they may experience, but indeed this is not so. There is harmony in all things. You must seek to see it. And when one understands the Ray Forces, they understand that the grand conduction of energy is only working through Law, and the Law is based upon the first Jurisdiction, Harmony. So you see, Harmony pervades all activities upon the Earth Plane and Planet as it comes under the conduction of the Great Central Sun.

THE ASTRAL BODY

Many of the Ray Forces that emanate from the Great Central Sun arc off of other planetary forces as they travel toward the Earth. Known as astrology, this science has been studied for many ages and is indeed true. It is the subtle science of the Astral Body, the first Body of Light that can be viewed by a HU-man, a God-realized man. This is the emanation, or the light-field force. This magnetic and electromagnetic force-field is indeed the emanation of the energies of the Rays in their commingling of experience. And this experience is indeed broad. It may vary, shall we say, from one Ray to the next in a current lifetime, but, you see, in as much as one event is committed, as you have learned in the Point of Perception, indeed it becomes a point of departure for another event, and so on, and so on, and so on. That one event is never dissolved—it is continuous. It is always an experience. So, all history, as you would perceive, is indeed always accessible.

EVER PRESENT NOW

There is truly no past, there is truly no future. There is only the Ever Present Now. So that you may understand . . . this—as your brain, as your intellect, is a binary system—one that relates more to duality—and I will explain it first from a more dual perspective. First, there is the perception that time exists as wasting away into nothingness. Yet, there is the present when time is potential, shall we say, much like a spore or an egg that has the ability to expand and grow into the future. Now do you understand this?

Answer: "Yes."

THE COLOR RAYS

I will proceed so that you may gain even a broader understanding of Ray Forces and how they work. You know the Seven Ray Forces, as they exist, identify and relate to a color. Each color is a particular harmonic for the Earth Field and Planetary Field of Experience. Each harmonic creates through various experiences for the individual. For instance, one who is imbued with the Green Ray is more apt to have more experiences with one's own physical body in relationship to disease or disorders that exist within the physical body. The Green Ray, then, naturally brings one to seek his own healing. So, through the experience of one's own healing, one comes forward to help many others on the path of healing. The experience of the Green Ray may be one that is not totally understood within the context of one lifetime. But often there have been many lifetimes in which one has suffered or one has had diseases that appeared to be incurable. So in a predominance of the Green Ray Force will provoke one to seek greater Harmony. The harmonies will first come through aligning the light-bodies, and that alignment sometimes comes through artistic and musical expression, but is primarily used as a force-field to bring healing to others, and to ease suffering and develop compassion. This is just one explanation of a Ray Force. My intention is to not go into great detail of descriptions of Ray Forces, for these are contained in many other materials, and also can be found in many Ascended Master teachings. Most of them are quite accurate. For those who are requesting greater accuracies on these, I will be willing to concord and provide such information. But for now, I would like to stay with the work at hand so that you may understand how Ray Forces work together.

LORD OF THE RAY

There is always a Chohan (Lord) of a Ray. This is a Master Teacher of that particular Ray Force. This Master Teacher is responsible for the way in which the energies of a Ray Force from the Great Central Sun is utilized upon the Earth Plane and Planet. Now, you understand in the science of Astrology that there are planets that arc certain energies, and the force of this particular Chohan resides as a consciousness between that planet and the Earth. For instance, the Chohan of the Green Ray resides as an energy force, a force of consciousness that is timeless and perpetually immortal between Mercury and the Earth.

A RAY EMANATES

The energy exists simultaneously not only as a light force and a sound force that is recognizable to one upon the Earth Plane and Planet, but as a Ray Force that is a resonance, a harmonic, so to speak. Those of science often identify this as a laser Ray or as a life force that can be sensed, measured by an existing scientific principle—but a Ray Force does not work in a direct current. Indeed, it emanates like a coal in a fire. It emanates a certain warmth that later ignites the fire, and so a Ray Force is as an emanation, an emanation a quality, and it brings this quality to the painting of the greater picture. Do you understand?

Answer: "Yes."

This emanation is an important factor in understanding Ray Forces and how they work together. For instance, take your hands and rub them together. As you rub them together, do you not feel a heat?

Answer: "Of course."

EMANATION

The heat is indeed the emanation of friction. This is how a Ray Force indeed works. It emanates, radiating and generating a greater and greater energy as it travels throughout space or time. And so, as one begins to recognize the workings, the qualities of a Ray Force through lifetime after lifetime, it begins to emanate a greater and greater surgence throughout the being. We have explained before that once the emanation exists, and if you were to measure this along a mathematical line once it is functioning above fifteen percent within the HU-man being, it may then be qualified. Again, an emanation may be qualified in several ways, for good or for bad, as the Earth Plane is dual. Things are hot; things are cold. Things are up; things are down. Again, Dear hearts, beloveds, it is perception as to how the emanation is realized and understood. This emanation, travels forward from lifetime to lifetime, and is qualified in this same manner. As it is qualified by the grand conductor and it is of course given as a free gift to the HU-man. For the HU-man, indeed, has the choice of how to utilize this energy for experience. For instance, referring back to the Green Ray, one may use the Green Ray for greater harmony to bring forth a great compassion and understanding of scientific knowledge, which frees another from suffering—this creates compassion in the world. But if there is not complete understanding of the emanation, the Ray Force is expressed as dual. You may meet one whose life is emanating, the lower qualities of a Ray, choosing only to produce or manifest the energies in this dualistic quality. When this occurs, the invidivual becomes overly analytical and scientific, and relies more upon the processes of the Ray, and not upon the results of the Ray. Have you not seen this many times?

Answer: "Very true."

CHOICE AND EVOLUTION

So one has a choice concerning how to utilize a Ray Force as it arcs from the Great Central Sun and gives each of you the life of Co-creation. The HU-man develops this faculty of choice. Within choice lies the ability to make the Earth a heavenly paradise or filled with the torments of hell. The darkness that has covered the Earth oddly, is but a choice—a choice of the qualification and utilization of emanation. When one speaks of the Ages of Darkness that have covered the Earth, do you now understand with greater wisdom and knowledge how the darkness had to exist in order so one could begin to understand and experience how Ray Forces are qualified and used for greater and further evolution?

Answer: "I see what you're saying."

It is not a matter of judging a time and saying that it must not exist, or it is of a darker or of lesser quality. It fully serves the function of reason. It fully serves the function of choice. Choice is indeed the wholistic pivotal process of how the Rays work, and how the Rays send their emanation.

THE CELL OF PERFECTION

Now, let us talk about the interplay of the Rays. Again, I have mentioned there are Seven Ray Forces that are utilized for the education of the soul and the enfoldment of the incarnation. These Seven Ray Forces, as I have stated before, enter into the Eight-sided Cell of Perfection. The Eight-sided Cell of Perfection is activated upon the first breath upon the birth of the child. That is why many upon the Earth Plane and Planet record a specific time of birth, but it is not so much the birth process itself, but the intake of the first breath. This breath activates the Eight-sided Cell of Perfection, the kundalini along the spine, and all of the Chakra Systems. You know that a chakra spins in a clockwise or counter clockwise position. The spinning utilizes the Ray Forces. This spinning can indeed tell you how the emanation of the Ray Force is conducting its karma or dharma within that particular individual system. So, when you see, for instance, a chakra spinning in a counter clockwise motion, producing, a cloudy Green Ray color, like a muddy green, you know the individual is still learning through the lower energies of the Green Ray and yet to qualify into the higher energies. This emanation sets up many experiences through the light and energies of the aura.

INTERPLAY WITH THE ASTRAL BODY

Now, you begin to see that the Human Aura is an interplay of the many Ray Forces as they interact along the Golden Thread Axis and emanate through the Chakra System. When you encounter a life force, at times you may meet one from whom your destinies are very different, from whom your experiences are very different, from whom your beliefs are very different. Upon meeting and greeting one another, you feel a sense of repulsion toward one another. Now, you have experienced this, and many others have experienced this. It is not a matter of judgment, of good or evil, it is a matter of understanding emanation. It is a matter of understanding the science, the Astral Body. This science of the Astral Body may be utilized in many forms. As one, we begin to understand the greater harmony and the greater working of mind, soul, and body. Now, this Astral Body that you carry with you at all times, your first light force, so to speak, the first interplay of all Rays coming together, also to some extent controls the field of experiences that you may have. For you see, Dear ones, as you carry this light field and force with you, it carries, shall we say, the programming of the Ray Forces so that throughout your day it can control the types of experiences you will have, the type of people you will meet, the types of interactions that you will have. Too, it sets up a force-field for your co-creative abilities. At night, when you sleep, there is a type of detachment from the physical body, and the greater light force is then freed up and allowed to explore the worlds that exist beyond that of only physical understanding. Many of you have had these dreams. Sometimes the dream experiences end up actually bringing forth a creation in your world. That is because the imprinting of that was already contained through the Ray Forces. Now do you understand?

Answer: "Yes."

This is very important to understand the emanation of Ray Force and how it works for creation, how it works to bring all forward in a greater harmony. And now I will open the floor for your questions.

The Master momentarily leaves the teaching, and then returns.

EMANATION OF A MASTER TEACHER

Greetings, Dear ones. Now I shall continue on this discourse of emanation. Did you feel the disconnection of our energies?

Answer: "No, not really."

What you felt was the continuing emanation. Now, for instance, when a Master Teacher enters a room, before that Master Teacher enters into the room do you not first feel the emanation?

Answer: "I hear your sound, I smell a fragrance and I see your light."

That is indeed an emanation, and when a Master Teacher leaves the room there is still a heat. There is still a fragrance. There is still a sound and a vibration within the room. This, too, is emanation. As you can see, emanation, much as the coal has been lighted to fuel the fire, is an energy that builds. That is why, whenever we come in to bring discourse, we build an energy. We build an emanation. This is very important so that people understand that the Ray Forces of the subtle Astral bodies are built lifetime after lifetime after lifetime. There may be one life force that comes forward into a very strong incarnation. The strengths of those Ray Forces within that individual have been built lifetime after lifetime after lifetime. One is not born with a strong Ray Force without, of course, putting the work forward, without having effort.

LIFETIME TO LIFETIME

So, you see, all comes together in a perfect harmony. This harmony, of course, is the result of actions that you have taken and choices you have made in previous incarnations. So, you see how important the Ever Present Now is, for this, too, will create your future, create the lifetimes that you will have in the future, create the experiences, the types of friends, and so on and so on. And so, Dear hearts, as you can see, emanation is indeed an important understanding when you begin to understand the work of Ray Forces and their conductivity within the human body.

EMANATION IN A GOLDEN CITY VORTEX

Now, Dear ones, when you understand how a Ray Force is gathered, in this case an individual lifetime after lifetime, when we begin to understand the Golden City Vortices and that each of them is part of an individual Ray Force, now you can understand that they, as new planetary Vortices, are building energies, their emanations starting, of course, and building and building and building. And so in the beginning to birth of a new Vortex, it may be difficult at first to feel the energies of a Golden City, to feel the emanation of that Ray Force. However, over time the emanation builds. And in the same way that a Ray Force emanates throughout the Astral Body of an individual, that Ray Force in the beginning may only be functioning, maybe at a low rate of five percent, seven percent, 10 percent, but then as this grows, shall we say, in its force-field, the Ray Force is then able to start giving its subtle indications. Remember, as I have taught, indeed this is a dual system, and so very often in the beginning of development of Golden Cities the more lower energies of that Ray Force will then exist. For instance, in the Golden City of Gobean, where you are dealing with transformation, harmony, all indications of the higher use of the Blue Ray, you may get shortsightedness; you may get coldness; you may get disharmony.

QUALIFICATION OF THE RAY

You see, it is a matter of qualification of taking the energy forces as they exist and using them at the higher level. This requires an understanding of perception, an understanding of your choice as we have always taught. Is the glass half-full? Is the glass half-empty? Again it is a matter of your perception of how do you utilize a Ray Force. This is known as qualification. These two principles, emanation, qualification, need to be understood so that the chela, the student of these teachings, may move forward in understanding how to utilize the energy of Ray Forces within their own being.

CONDUCTIVITY AND SACRED GEOMETRY

I should like to discuss the idea of conductivity. In the same way that we have described the pyramidal structures of the Golden Cities and outlined its circular motion, shown you the apex of a Vortex, the doorways of a Golden City, and the parameters in miles and kilometers, we must also explore this within the human body. You are all well aware of the idea of pressure points and meridians within the body. Many of you are also exposed to the idea of kundalini currents of this force moving within the spinal system, activating the Chakra System. Conductivity relies upon geometrical structures, each geometrical structure peculiar to each planetary system. The conductivity is carried out, of course, through this sacred geometry. Remember, Dear hearts, when we brought forth the teachings of sacred geometry so that you would understand its language, its purpose, and its intent?

THROUGH THE KUNDALINI

In the human body, most of the movement of conductivity occurs upon a circular motion. Sometimes this is also seen as a wave. This is why the kundalini current is sometimes known as the snake energy, as it mirrors the movement of a snake in the sand, but this is ideally a circular motion. That is why, throughout your life, you may have periods of time when you feel that two ends of a circle now meet. However, you also feel, through the series of experiences, that you have had a higher perception, a higher knowledge, in the closure of understanding a completed lesson. This spiral of energy is indeed circular when viewed from certain perspectives, but this is also how the Ray Forces work in their conductivity in your present field of experience.

GOLDEN CITIES DUPLICATE THE RAY FORCES

Within the Golden Cities, this sacred geometry, or shape, is based on a triangular system. As you were taught in previous discourse, triangular forces duplicate energies—duplicate them again and again—whereas, circular forces expand energies. The Golden City Vortices have been placed upon the planet to duplicate the Ray Forces, the Ray Forces of the higher emanation, qualification of understanding of their teachings. So, do you see, Dear ones, this harmony working together, the expansion of the HU-man, the God-man, the triangular forces duplicating the higher end of these energies so that they may be given to many others upon the Earth Plane and Planet at this time, and to move humanity into a greater evolution and understanding of its manifested destiny? Now I shall open the floor for questions.

Question: "Can Ray Forces be enhanced?"

ENHANCEMENT OF RAY FORCES

Ray Forces are enhanced through your understanding. When one begins to understand the force-field of the Ray Force itself, the existence of the Ray, the intention of the Ray, its higher and lower usage, indeed it is enhanced perceptibly by the individual, the HU-man. Then it is utilized in its greater understanding, in its greater workings for choice, and for the greater capacity for love, compassion, service and charity. Many of these higher forces are understood in the Twelve Jurisdictions, but then one is moved to utilize, to make the choices, with these Ray Forces for greater understanding. Enhancement may occur in many ways. Of course, the one method that we recommend for enhancement is meditation upon the Ray Force itself to gain an understanding of that Ray Force in your life. To simply meditate upon the Green Ray and its existence in your life will, of course, bring the Green Ray to a greater force-field within your experience. But it is better to bring it to the element of mind and to choice, consciousness, and conscience so it can be utilized at its greater understanding. It is recommended that you meditate upon the greater use of this force-field as a Ray, as an emanation within your life, in this individual's lifetime, to bring forth the desired result. Meditation, when used along this line and with this complete understanding, can be very beneficial to the chela.

USE OF CRYSTALS AND GEMS

Forces indeed exist within the Mineral Kingdom, these coming from beloved Babajeran, herself. Ray Forces can be increased through certain Golden Cities. These Golden Cities have been brought forth to help and assist those who would like to take a particular focus with a Ray Force or a Ray energy. The crystalline forces also contain many different emanations of the Seven Ray Forces, and it is best for the chela to choose one that they feel drawn to and that they feel magnetized toward. For, you see, Dear ones, it is always choice. So, Dear hearts, yes indeed, Ray Forces can be significantly strengthened throughout the body, throughout the mind, throughout the soul.

SOUND AND THE VIOLET FLAME

But perhaps the strongest of these, in terms of forces, is through the use of vibrational sound. Now you have known that when the Vibration of OM is given that it snaps the kundalini, or, shall we say, that Golden Thread Axis, into complete alignment with the Sun and with the Earth, and then there is indeed a sense of grounding, a sense of purpose, an expansion of the solar forces within the Astral Body. I have given you many decrees that vibrate to the Violet Flame. "Violet Flame, I AM, Come Forth. Violet Flame, I AM." You see, the Violet Flame forces help to aid one in overcoming especially trying circumstances. The Violet Flame is an emanation of the higher use of your karma. It allows the trying circumstances, suffering, tears, problems and anxieties that surround the release of karma of the misuse, or the lower emanation of a Ray Force. It drives the energies of that Ray Force up into its higher use, so that one is then freed, liberated, so to speak, from the lower understandings, from the lower emanations, of a planetary force. So, Dear hearts, it is entirely and absolutely recommended that the use of the Violet Flame is always of the utmost importance in strengthening any condition that may seem trying. It is sound vibration that comes forth within the Chakra System. It is sound vibration that comes forth within the consciousness. It is sound vibration that allows the conscience to have the clarity to choose the right way at the right time. That is why I have repeatedly recommended the Violet Flame to my students and my chelas, as this is the clearest, the quickest path to liberation and to understanding the Ray Force of emanation, and to allowing a greater field of experience. Indeed, it does expand your Astral field, your field of experience, the force-field that you have come to live through and to experience through. Questions?

Question: "Since the Ray Forces come together to make the Astral Body, or the Astrological Body, and that is the conductive control for the experiences or the life that a person leads, what attracts to them, what repels from them. If there are certain Rays that are functioning at smaller percentages than others, is the Violet Flame the best usage for, I would say, the neutralization of any of the afflictions of the Rays of Light?"

LIBERATION THROUGH THE FLAME

The Violet Flame has been brought forth to free, or liberate one so that they may understand the higher use of energies. When one has achieved a certain understanding of liberation through the use of the Violet Flame being used, of course, as sound vibration, then one may begin to explore the use of other vibratory forces through the use of sound to actually enhance or increase the force-field in another direction. But until that moment has happened, it is, of course, always best to free the individual first. It is through freedom that one is allowed to expand, until one is able to see that they can see it from a whole other viewpoint. This is the freeing of perception. And it is, of course, recommended that all sounds be used to bring healing forth for the individual, but the Violet Flame, as you can see, is, of course, the one that is used, shall we say, at the first levels so that consciousness is freed and ready to explore other harmonies that exist within them.

Question: "So what you're saying is that the Violet Flame is, of itself, also a transmutating Ray and that is the first focus?"

THE ALCHEMY OF THE FLAME

It is Alchemical, as well, as it fuses in an interplay of the Rays, allowing each of the Ray Forces, for instance, a Yellow Ray, a Pink Ray, a Blue Ray, to come together in greater harmony. These forces, at times, are not in harmony at will within the individual, for that individual had chosen to allow the Ray Forces to war against one another, to be in disharmony with one another. It is the Violet Flame, indeed, that allows the Ray Forces to work together. Have you ever seen a team that seems to have all the strengths and all the qualities to achieve its goals, but yet the individuals within that team war among themselves and are not able to cooperate to achieve one thing?

Answer: "Yes, I have."

SPIRITUAL FUSION

This is the same metaphor for understanding the Ray Forces within the Astral Body. One may have a great quality and another great quality, but they are not able to bring them together, to make them work together. The use of the Violet Flame brings, through sound vibrating, a lessening of the karma and a lessening of the disharmony; and it brings together a fusion of cooperation between the Ray Forces, that one may now work together. If you would begin to view the Seven Rays as a team force that is working for you, through your choices and through your consciousness within your Astral Body, then you begin to understand how the Violet Flame, and use of this mighty Violet Ray, will bring you to a greater freedom for you to achieve your goals.

CONDUCTING THE RAY FORCES

Question: "Can you give us a decree, specifically, to harmonize the Rays?"

> Violet Flame,
> come forth in harmony of the Seven Rays.
> Transmute the cause and effect and all records
> that have been genetically inscribed within me,
> genetically used by me.
> And now, Violet Flame,
> blaze forth in greater harmony to the
> Divine Plan and the Divine Will.

It is as simple as that: decreeing this unto yourself as a prayer. Let the Violet Flame be poetry to your soul. Let the Violet Flame come forward to bring greater harmony between you and the Seven Rays, so that each of the Ray Forces becomes a team player within you.

> Mighty Violet Flame,
> come forth in the Light of God that never, never, never fails.
> Mighty Violet Flame,
> come forth and heal all that ails me.
> Mighty Violet Flame,
> come forth and bring cooperation in, through and around me.
> I seal this forth in the name of the
> Divine Plan and Divine Will.
> Mighty I AM!

So, you see, Dear hearts, decree this unto yourself and it is so. It is the affirmation of your divinity. It is the affirmation of your Co-creatorship. Yet, this prepares you for a greater conductivity of the emanation and the qualification of the Ray Forces within you. As the Great Central Sun is the grand conductor of these Rays, do you see how you now become as a conductor of the Ray Forces?

Answer: "By pronouncing the decree, yes, we actually enhance the conductivity, and you harmonize that conductivity."

This is the idea of liberation and freedom so that one is then led to become as ONE with the forces of the universe. This leads one naturally to the Consciousness of Unity in Unana. This is the principle that we apply. This is the principle that we utilize.

Question: "Truly, this is most enlightening. To consider that for all the embodiments and all the eons, we can, at this moment, transmute much of that. How often would you suggest that this decree be done and at what time of day?"

THE VIBRATION OF FREEDOM

It is, of course, based upon each individual need. It is best, of course, that the individual prescribe this for himself, for only he would know the discomfort he is feeling. Only he would know the harmony that he is seeking. It is best for an individual to choose this for himself. Perhaps for one individual to use the Violet Flame once a day is all that is required. And yet, for another, whose discomfort and suffering is so great, perhaps he should use the Violet Flame a thousand times a day. Of course, this depends upon the person and his choices. But you see, Dear heart, when one begins to vibrate totally to this concept of the Violet Flame, to this concept of liberation and freedom, to this concept of greater unity within the self, one may speak this as a mantra and say it all day, throughout his being. It is not spoken, of course, through that spoken word but emanated through actions, emanated through choices, emanated through interactions with others. They carry this like a force-field, as part of their Astral Body, incorporated within their being. They carry it forward each day. This is just as sacred as sitting in front of your temple and shouting these decrees for all to hear. You see, Dear ones, it is possible to carry the mighty Violet Flame in, through and around your being all the time.

Question: "And how does one achieve this?"

FOCUS AND INTENTION

Through focus and through the focus of one's intention through imbuing these qualities within oneself and bringing them forth into actions and choices. Do you see, Dear one, how the emanation is built? Like the coal, fueling the fire, the Violet Flame is present and builds a greater and a greater energy. This is the concept again of emanation.

Question: "Through this focus, what is it that you would suggest or direct anyone to visualize or out-picture or focus upon?"

DISCIPLINE AND THE FLAME

It is individual choice, but if I were to recommend a program, perhaps it would be to say the Violet Flame seven times seven, forty-nine times. This would assure that a momentum would be gained for each of the Ray Forces within the being. Again, this is only a recommendation, and this is only brought forth in reference to your question so that you may begin to understand. The Violet Flame is then used forty-nine times per day, and from there the individual notices a lessening of the burdens within his life. Then perhaps he would like to bring forth an element of the Violet Flame, actually an act of forgiveness, an act of mercy, an act of compassion as an intention of the demonstration of the Violet Flame. We know that intention and demonstration carry this forth into the physical world, and there we have an expansion, of the emanation of the Violet Flame. Do you understand?

Answer: "Yes, it is a step-by-step process."

It is a step-by-step process. There is no formula or exact way for this to work. It is about the chela's union and harmony with the Seven Forces, the Seven Rays. It is the chela's choice, and this choice is revealed through action.

Question: "I understand. The number seven, or the Rays of Light and Sound, are really as far as our consciousness can perceive, aren't they?"

Let us start one step at a time, and as our consciousness emanates and grows into that Mighty Flame, that Mighty Light of God that never, never fails, then one is ready to be introduced to greater light, to greater understanding and to greater endurance in the Unity of Consciousness.

Question: "So, in the use of the Violet Flame, when you asked us to decree for peace, we could ask for the harmonization of the Rays of all governments, all businesses, all global consciousness, could we not?"

This is the ideal use of the Violet Flame: what moves beyond selfish motive and into a motive that serves the greater good. As I stated before, when suffering is lessened for your neighbor, indeed is not the suffering lessened for you?

Answer: "True, that is truly compassion. So this would probably be the most useful pivotal point for all types of healing. Yes, your personal challenges, but for the Earth Changes themselves."

Of course, beloved, this is the intention of the Violet Flame, to free and liberate one from fear, to free and liberate one from all that would inhibit the greater union with that Mighty Light of God. So, Dear heart, as we seek completion of this lesson, if there are no more questions I shall take my leave.

Answer: "No, I have no further questions, but, as usual, much more work to do."

> In that Mighty Light of God that Never Fails,
> I AM the Ember of the Violet Flame
> burning through all desire,
> burning now to seek the ONE service,
> the mighty union of all.

So be it. Hitaka.

Answer: "So be it, and thank you."

Unless you have further questions, I shall take my leave from your realm and will be glad to return with further Prophecies of Peace. Hitaka!

CHAPTER TWO

Behind the Interplay

*Saint Germain gives further instruction on
Ray Forces and sound.*

Greetings, Beloveds, in that Mighty Violet Flame I AM Saint Germain, and I request permission to come forward.

Response: "Please, Saint Germain, come forward."

SERVICE LIFTS KARMA

Dear ones, at this time I would like to speak to you about service. Service comes forward to release you from your own Karmic burden, your own Karmic debts. However, Dear ones, service, as you well know, is an expression of the intention of your own soul. And that intention is sometimes clouded with the ego, other yearnings and other desires. You have known at times those who have come forward offering to help you, yet they have come forward wanting only something of their own desire, and expressing their own desire. Service in its purest form is without desire. It gives only for the want of giving. Service lifts your Karmic debt. It can release your bondage to the wheel of life. It is another opportunity for you to free yourself, to be spiritually liberated. Service is another way that your life is lifted into spiritual light. Service allows one to see things from a more detached perspective, so that you may qualify the Rays of Light within your (astrological) chart to a higher understanding, to a higher learning, so that you may free the Rays of Light functioning within your aura to a higher qualification. Service also is again very much like the coal in the fire; it brings a greater emanation, and builds energy. But it is always intention that will determine how and when the emanation shall occur. So, it is important to scrutinize your intention. It is important for you to understand the motive behind all that you do and the reason for so doing. For service, you see, can create karma within itself. That from which you set out to free yourself can indeed turn around and create more. You see, Dear ones, the chelas upon the path, when they offer themselves to be of service, may indeed encumber themselves with even more karma in their own web of ego demand. It is important to understand desire, the working of desire, and where desires may lead you. Clarify your intention in all offers of service; also clarify your intent before offering yourself of service. Do you have questions?

Answer: "Not at this time."

THE PLANETS FLOW WITH LIGHT AND LIFE

Light continues to flow within the Human Aura; light flows at its highest intention to fulfill the demands of the cosmos, the Great Central Sun. The light emanates from the planetary life forces, and you see, Dear ones, planets also are life forces. Life streams through a planet in the same way life streams through your body. We have explained this before in the teachings of Beloved Babajeran, but this teaching is congruent within this planetary system, such as Mars, Venus, Jupiter and Saturn, and so on and on. Even your Moon contains a life force unto itself. Although it may seem to be a more collective life force, or a collective being. But, in the same way you contain many harmonizing systems—a circulatory system, a respiratory system, and an immune system within your body, the planets work similarly. They contain systems that must come together and harmonize for them to properly arc energies to planet Earth.

SERVICE OF THE PLANETS

Planet Earth at this time, Beloved Babajeran, is the ONE schoolhouse where HU-mans are learning. This learning is a very important process. It requires many lifetimes and allows the soul, the HU-man soul, to evolve through the course of experience. Experience is the only teacher from which one develops the idea of one's will, choice, and conscience. So, Dear hearts, it is indeed many lifetimes that you spend here on planet Earth learning and growing through the many experiences contained within these lifetimes.

The planets, the greater servants, and Beloved Babajeran, a greater servant unto herself, offer themselves to be of service to you during this your evolution. They offer themselves, arcing light and sound to you, and bring forward throughout your own Astral Body a multitude of experiences that create an evolutionary and experiential understanding. It is the apex of each experience that leads you to greater understanding, greater force, and a greater will for you to choose. Choosing seems to be the vehicle for the HU-man to begin to distinguish one experience from another.

THE DIFFERENCE IS THE EXPERIENCE

When one begins to understand the Ray Forces and how they work and orchestrate the many experiences throughout one's body, one begins to understand how to differentiate the various experiences. It is the Ray Forces that give us the multitude of experiences throughout the solar system. And on planet Earth a variety of experiences are afforded through the Ray Forces. As the Ray Forces arc themselves from the Great Central Sun to the planets who are indeed of service to this force greater than themselves, they, in turn, arc the energy to Beloved Babajeran. It is here that the energies are picked up through the Astral Body, and human experience unfolds. History is created, and the whole drama, the whole play is then set forward for learning to gain ever important experience. Beloved Sananda has said in past discourse, "What is the difference between you and me?" What the difference is indeed, Dear ones, but *experience.* And it is the Rays, through the interplay of the harmonies of the spheres, that light and sound blend and create your all-expanded awareness.

PERSONAL BALANCE

Intention exists behind the interplay of the Rays. This intention is orchestrated, not only through your will and through your choices, but also by your karma and your past; karma is one action for another, and seeks the balance within and the balance without. Many upon the Earth Plane and Planet define karma to be a punishment, the meter of judgment. But it is not, Dear one, for judgment and punishment exist only within yourself and the way in which you view circumstance, through your beliefs and your choices; and the way in which you deal with any given situation, or the actions in those situations, and how you create balance. The Higher Self is ever-present through each incarnation, and ever-present through all experiences, is there as the guiding angel, the guiding force, to see that balance is kept and restored within all situations. This allows for a greater harmony in the interplay of the Rays and for the interplay of sound within the Astral field. You see, Dear ones, it is almost as if the Astral Body is a grand book to be read, a grand book with an ever-changing plot, an ever-changing beginning, and an ever-changing end. It is this book that you must learn to read and begin to write for yourself, page by page, your own script, your own part, to achieve Mastership of the Ray Forces and the forces of sound.

THE "HU" COMPLETES AND INTENSIFIES

It is important that you begin to understand each Ray Force is also complemented by a great sound. Many cultures have brought forward the various sounds that they resonate to in terms of light. I have given to you the "HU" sound. The "HU" sound vibrates to the Mighty Violet Flame of Mercy and Forgiveness. When I give you the "HU" sound to use as a vibration, or to use as a mantra, it is used to bring a completeness to all that you do. All is held within that vibration of finer tuning, with respect to forgiveness, mercy, and Divine Intervention. The Vibration of "HU" is used so that you may be brought into a greater understanding, into a greater Oneship with all things. It is the "HU" vibration that vibrates to the higher levels of the Violet Flame. The Violet Flame is birthed out of the Blue Flame, the Blue Flame of Will and Conscience, the Blue Flame of Choice, that Blue Flame of Direction and Directive Power. But it is indeed the Violet Flame, when it is blended with the Pink Flame of Love, that Divine Compassion becomes a higher qualification of this force. And it is the "HU" vibration that you shall use alongside it to intensify its work.

SEAL THE ENERGY

For instance, when you practice a Violet Flame decree:

"Mighty Violet Flame blaze in,
through, and around all my past karma.
Mighty Violet Flame blaze in,
through, and around all of my present choices.
Mighty Violet Flame blaze in,
through, and around me,
raising me into the glory and the life of the Ascension."

Then repeat, "HU, HU, HU" three times three. This commands the Law of the Trinity and seals the energy. The sealing is very much like a seal that exists upon a chakra. Those who have developed their Auric Vision can see, when they work on an energy field or when they view their own energy field, a seal exists at the end of every chakra or center where light is taken in and released. This seal is of vast importance, for sealing the Chakra System enveloping the Human Aura seals the intention of a new creation. This allows the intention to carry through from the point of creation, the choice and the conscious will of the Co-creator. So, you see, sound acts as a complement to light and sound, and light, like best friends, create harmony similar to the Seven Rays and their work in the interplay of light. Sound comes, seals, and delivers the essence of the lighted command. Sound sets the intention, allows, and creates its manifestation or action. Do you understand?

Answer: "Yes, I do."

Dear one, do you have questions?

Answer: "Not at this time."

DISCOVER AND ACTIVATE YOUR SOUND

So, sound within itself is of major importance to bring forward each command to a higher level, a higher understanding, and to allow it to bring forward its actions from your Divine Source.

Let us continue. Of course, each of the colors of light has its own sound vibration. It is best, though, that each chela find the sound vibration himself. It is best that each chela begin to meditate upon each of the Ray Forces, and through meditation a sound will be revealed. Why is this so? Each chela is individualized through his differing experiences, through the many choices they have made throughout their travels upon the Earth Plane and Planet. Sound within itself is a harmonizing effect, and seeks its own level. There are certain sounds that can be given to you, and they carry a very high frequency. But if the chela is not prepared or ready to absorb that certain sound energy, it will not, and cannot, bring the Rays into their consummate interplay. So, it is more important for the chela to find the sound vibration that will meet the interplay of his or her own Rays.

The process for this is quite easy. Within meditation, you will begin to hear a sound vibration. Soon, you will identify this sound starting with a consonant. It will contain a vowel sound. Very often these sound vibrations end with the "M" or the "ING" sound—this creates, of course, the vibration within the human to activate the kundalini. This is of vast importance to understand that each find one's own sound vibration to the Ray Force that one is integrating within one's system.

It is also of vast importance to continue to use the Violet Flame, for the Violet Flame will lift the chela to a higher realm, and a higher understanding. Within the time of meditation, there will also be occurrences of hearing mathematical harmonies associated with each sound vibration. Sometimes these sound vibrations are rythmatic, tapping out within the mind their own repeated rhythm. This is an important note for the chela, for these mathematical harmonies work to bring a correction or a harmonization effect for the Ray Forces. I will not give you a set formula on how to activate sound and light to work together as ONE. It is more important that each chela, through the medium of his or her own experience, find this path. As I have stated before, Dear ones, it is most important to know thyself, and this becomes your grand experience, as your time in meditation and the interplay of the Rays become your own laboratory. Through your own practice, you will experience the force of God working within you, and this indeed will give you a new experience, a new evolution, and a greater understanding. Above all, Dear hearts, meditate with a clear intention, with a clear understanding of your own service to that Mighty Light of God that Never Fails.. Do you have questions?

Answer: "Not at this time."

So, Dear hearts, I shall take my leave from you, for this is the discourse of the day, and I shall return at a later time to bring forward more information.

Response: "Thank you very much."

CHAPTER THREE

A New Day

Saint Germain and El Morya present prophecies and teachings on belief.

Greetings, Beloveds, in that Mighty Christ, I AM Saint Germain, and I stream forth on that Mighty Violet Ray of Mercy and Forgiveness. As usual, Dear ones, I ask permission to come forward.

Response: "Dear one, come forth."

HUMANITY'S EVOLUTION AND ASCENSION

Beloveds, the work at hand is indeed important, for I have explained before in previous discourses that the information that is soon to be received is, shall we say, of a finer quality and lies beyond the tip of the iceberg. As I have explained before, the prophetic material, the I AM America Maps, the Freedom Star Map, were all given like an appetizer to a main course. For now, the information must be given to prepare humanity for a greater evolution, and for a greater understanding of their Divine Destiny. For you see, Dear ones, the work that is now in front of the Spiritual Hierarchy is that of raising the vibration through the spiritual evolution of humanity. Those who have the eyes to see, the ears to hear and the hands to do, will now come forward in this New Time, this Golden Age that is indeed the important part of this Prophecy.

For you see, Dear ones, it has long been determined that humanity shall raise its vibration to a greater understanding, and to a greater knowledge of their internal light. This has long been known as the Ascension. There have been those who have raised their vibration, understanding, and consciousness, and who now reside in New Dimensions, in a new understanding of breath, light, sound, thought, feeling, and action. So, Dear hearts, in this New Time it is important that you understand so that you may prepare yourself for the great opportunity that now awaits. This great opportunity is one that many have prayed for, sought after, lusted after and now thirst for, for many embodiments, and they now wait for this most especial time.

SHATTERING OLD BELIEFS

This is a time when mankind will be adjusted in many ways. Frequencies will change, not only in the electromagnetic field, which is the Human Aura, but there will be an understanding, a telepathic Oneness, a union between all of humanity. We have explained this before as Unana. You know this now as Unity Consciousness. Prior to any significant change, there must be changes that happen inside. Today, we see dissent among humanity— Brother against Brother, Sister against Sister, strife among families, but this is just a greater preparation for the understanding of Unity Consciousness. The old ideas, the old beliefs, must first be shattered. Beloved Sananda has said in previous discourses that in order for new wine to be poured, a new wine skin must be structured. This, too, is the process of Ascension. It is indeed structuring a new wine skin, a new belief, a new concept.

DOWN WITH DEATH

The first of these beliefs is, as I have said before, "Down with death; conscious immortality arise." You see, Dear hearts, beloveds, your consciousness is indeed immortal, your thoughts stream forth lifetime through lifetime, ready for you to access at any moment so that you may understand in full knowledge and in full light all circumstances in front of you. The idea of a Shroud of Darkness over your consciousness is one you have instilled through your present beliefs. The information may not be carried from lifetime to lifetime. But you see, Dear one, this an old belief, and in order to maintain and understand the New Consciousness, one must access information from lifetime to lifetime so that the proper choices are made. When one begins to understand that they are consciously immortal, that there is a part of them that never dies, but only the physical body, this prepares the new wine skin.

UNIFICATION OF SELF

When thoughts are continuously upon immortality, feelings and actions will soon follow. These feelings and actions create a new body, a body that is not only linked consciously from one to the next in Unana, in Unity Consciousness, but is also linked as ONE to Beloved Babajeran, to the Mother Earth. For you see the dramas, the tears, the fears in each lifetime with its own desires, wants and trappings, along with its karma, and with its dharma that has been played out on Mother Earth. Mother Earth has served in essence as a witness, as a witness to all the events that you have staged in your journey here upon schoolroom Earth, learning, loving, and living. She, too, comes forward to bring assistance as the grand teacher that she truly is. This assistance helps you to unify from within and create unity within all experiences. This unification of self is extremely important, for unification of self brings forth the birth of conscience, and it is only when Unity Consciousness is united with conscience, or your chosen course of direction, then and only then may Ascension and the work as a Co-creator come forward in its greatness and in its fullness. So, it is true that at this time the Beloved Babajeran has offered herself to be of assistance.

THE ROLE OF THE GOLDEN CITY

We have explained certain geophysical locations upon the Earth Plane and Planet. These are known as the Golden City Vortices. We have explained these quite thoroughly in other discourses, but we hope through this material to explain exactly and directly their purpose, their manifestation, and the role they will play in the times to come. Each Vortex is an energy source upon Beloved Babajeran—one that has been manifested directly by her to bring forth a cosmic lesson and, therefore, a cosmic unity within each individual.

You realize now that, as a small child when you touched a hot stove, the result was your burned finger. This is the idea of cause and effect. Within a Golden City Vortex, one begins to understand cause and effect in its most simple manner.

ILLUSION AND SPIRITUAL DETERIORATION

Today, with Time Compaction, the speeding up of events and the society that mankind has chosen to live through, and the constant and the steady hammering of this illusion, one is unable to recognize cause and effect. This has caused deterioration within humanity, an inability to recognize the truth that lies within, the truth of their Divine Destiny, and their own immortality.

THE NEW CONSCIOUSNESS

Consciousness and conscience work together as ONE and create a unity to body, mind and soul. So, when one is in a Golden City Vortex, because of the arrangements of energies through the assistance of the Beloved Cosmic Beings—the Elohim of this Earth and Mother Babajeran—these teachings are quickly understood. The individual enters into a New Consciousness through body, mind, and soul, an acceleration that not only brings a telepathic response through Unana but also an immortality of such, an understanding that all is connected as ONE.

RELEASE FEAR

All life is for life, and death is indeed the ultimate illusion. This begins with the removal of fear held at a cellular level—fear that you have held from embodiment through embodiment, lifetime after lifetime. This fear that has kept you trapped within the shell of the physical body. It is a time to release this fear, primarily the fear of physical death. As I have said before in previous work, as the thought continues, the feelings and actions model themselves in the same way a potter's wheel forms clay. The hands of God are indeed your hands upon this piece of clay, and it is through your choice and your will that you begin anew. It is your choice if you begin anew.

Perhaps this shall be the first place we will begin. We will begin with this discourse, "Beginning Anew," "Starting Anew," "A New Day."

I would like to introduce the one who shall start this discourse on "A New Day." He is Beloved Brother El Morya.

Saint Germain steps back and Beloved El Morya comes forth.

"Greetings, chelas. I ask permission to come forward."

Answer: "Please come forward, El Morya."

IDENTIFY INTENTION

Beginning anew is an important concept for those who wish to have a new mind. A new mind begins within the intention. This intention is extremely important. It comes within the depth of the soul. This intention determines the outcome—the outcome of all events, and all of the actions that the chela has come to experience. Many upon the Earth Plane and Planet lay down their best plans. They play them out, and then in anguish and sorrow wonder why such plans did not unfold as they had wished and hoped. The reason is quite simple, for not once did they consider their intention, and intention must be closely aligned to Will. To begin anew, one must identify and understand one's own Will—the Will that runs through him—then you begin to understand the Will that encompasses all choice, the flora of choice that has allowed your creation.

THE INTERNAL SPARK

Choice is the backbone of any person upon this planet. Therefore, choice very often can be seen in the Human Aura. It can be seen as a Vertical Power Current that runs along the spine, and attaches itself to the Mother Earth, and the lines to Father Sun. We have encountered those throughout life who we may judge and say, "He has no backbone." "She has no will." They are those whose will is indeed broken, whose idea of their own choice is no longer theirs, who give their will over to collective illusion, collective thoughts, collective feelings. Their actions mirror only those of the collective mind, caught up in fads, in whimsies and in what only others tell them to do. When one makes the choice to begin anew, he makes the choice within himself through an internal process. It is sparked within himself. It is not sparked from any outer influence, but comes through an inner influence, and this grows in its strength and in its current. This you have seen many times upon the Earth Plane and Planet as electricity crackling down as lightning. This is indeed the entity, Beloved Mother Babajeran making Her choice, aligning Her will to the Divine.

FIRST STEPS

In the beginning, to begin anew, one may not particularly choose to align to the Divine Will. In the beginning, one may choose to align to his own wishes, to his own Heart's Desire. This is perfectly normal, and is a developmental stage. But, as you well know, the result of all action is but education, and soon the chela becomes quite educated and begins to understand a greater working, pulse and magnetic pull.

BIRTH OF CONSCIENCE

One begins to understand that beginning anew is not a selfish action, but their intention becomes aligned to conscience. And there is the true birth of Divine Will, where one begins to understand the purpose, the direction, and the flow and that all must contain within it the Divine Plan as a plan Co-created among all God forces.

"EQUAL TO"

Unity Consciousness does not see one God force as greater than another. It sees all God force equal to. This allows for a greater understanding of cooperation and of harmony. The concept of "equal to" is again a step in beginning anew. In beginning anew, one prepares the body, the mind and, inevitably, the consciousness to start fresh. Have you ever heard of a fresh start, a day in which all things seem changed, a day when you can breathe a sigh of relief and begin anew?

DECLUTTER YOUR CONSCIOUSNESS

This is the same consciousness that must be utilized to gain your Ascension. You must discard and throw away the old beliefs, old choices, old collective illusions that will not serve your movement into the ONE. What is holding you back? What are the things that are holding you back? Ultimately, when you examine each and every one of these, you will find it is fear of death, conclusion, fear of ending, fear of decay and destruction. When one releases such fears, one becomes ready to begin anew. Throw them away. Make the choice from within. Find you own backbone. This is your Will. It is your Divine Gift, given to you so you may become a true Divine Inheritor. Contemplate and meditate upon this concept. Now, I shall turn the podium back to Beloved Saint Germain; of course, if there are no questions.

LIVE LIFE FOR LIFE

Response and Question: "Intention, as you have brought forward, both of you, intention, as you have shared before, determines the outcome. In observing humanity, the fear that drives them forward to want Ascension is truly the fear of death, the fear of aging, the fear of decay. This I have observed in everyone, including myself. However, the great desire to be of service to the upliftment of humanity, the great desire to see humanity come to its Divine Plan, its true design, its entering into the ONE, many times overpowers any of those, oh, doubts. So, if there were a one, two, three process to be described by you for those who will hear this tape and who will read this as a transcribed book, I would assume from your discourse that the first is to determine your intention. Why would you want Ascension? Why would you want immortality thought of as consciousness? Why? And so I ask you, give us the reason Why for this."

The greater union that exists beyond the HU-man is a Body of Light that no longer requires physical incarnation. The drudgery then is released of the physical plane, but it is no longer perceived as drudgery, instead it is embraced as life for life. As I have said before, "Live life for life." When one begins to understand the greater plan Divine, they see the interconnection between all circumstances, and between all situations. This is Unana.

SIMPLICITY AND THE ONE

As a simple program, what would I prescribe? Of all things, Beloved Saint Germain, my Brother in Service to Light and Sound, would call upon that Mighty Violet Ray. Of course, what is contained within the Violet Ray but that Ray of Truth, the Blue Ray that understands the alignment of the Will. When I speak about intention and the alignment of the Will, it is important that one spend time alone, that one spend time in simplicity to allow the unessential to drop away. How long would I prescribe? As long as it takes—as long as it takes—Dear one, to spend your time in solace and reflection. Spend your time in meditation upon the ONE. What is the ONE intention that you hold? What is the ONE will that you are of? What is the ONE choice that is of most importance to you? If this takes but one day, then so be it. If it takes ten years, so be it. Many say time is of the essence, but, in this one particular instance, I would say time must be cast aside. It is more important that you understand and totally embody experience, for there is the ONE unity that exists within you. And it is the connection of you to the All. Of all things that must be understood, first is that the hypnotic illusion living upon the Earth in the temporary encasement of the physical body perceives a separation that exists between that one individual life and the many other individual lives that exist upon the Earth at any given time. To understand a grander plan, to understand the connection between all, one must integrate from inside and feel a unity within. Do you understand?

"WE TAKE FORM AT WILL"

Answer: "So, what you're saying is that your appearance to us as Mahatma El Morya is only for our understanding. The Brotherhood and Sisterhood of Light and Sound are ONE."

This is so, Dear ones. We take on form at Will, so that we are able to convey particular and certain focused ideas, focused thoughts, focused vibrations for the work at hand. In this case, it is a preparation of consciousness so that humanity may begin the greater and grander change.

As a second reflection upon your question, I would propose to use that Mighty Violet Ray of mercy and compassion and forgiveness. Of course, this is blended with the Pink Ray of Love. When one develops this greater connection, this greater understanding, transmutation is the end result. If you would like more instruction upon this Violet Ray, Beloved Saint Germain will speak.

Response: "Yes, but I have one other question."

Proceed.

Response and question: "Since all transmutation starts with intention and the redefining of the Alignment of Will, it would seem that your individual existence has now been collectively stuck together so that it is not one will, but it is a unified will. For an individual, such as myself, choosing to join you, you have given reflection and the Violet Flame as the first two steps. The question that I ask is, once we have fulfilled all these desires that we have, all these little magnetic attachments to incarnations repeatedly, and it seems like the same things, new day, I think that humanity gets to the place where it becomes pointless. So, the only thing that is left is the inevitable, and that is to align one's own choices, will and intention to the unified choice for the movement of humanity and the uplifting of consciousness."

SELF-EVALUATION

But the illusion of your thinking is the same things, new day. A New Day does not come forward with the same things. It is the altering of the thoughts. It is the altering of the feelings and the actions that creates a New Day. A New Day comes forward when one has simply stated the intention of one's purpose. It is that simple. It takes a time of release, releasing that which no longer serves the Greater Will Divine. How does one apply such a concept to release that which no longer serves that Greater Plan Divine? You must evaluate your own life and see what is within your life that no longer serves your greater plan. Have the courage to create a greater plan for your life. Have the courage to write it down. Have the courage to meditate upon it. Have the courage to live it, feel it, act it out. Then you will understand what is that that is serving you. What is serving the Greater Plan Divine of your life? Do you understand?

Answer: "Yes, you have answered my question sufficiently."

And now I shall turn this over to Beloved Saint Germain.

Response: "Thank you."

At this moment, I would like to take a brief break.

Response: "As you so choose."

Saint Germain: In that the Mighty Violet Flame, I come forward. Again, I must ask permission to continue this discourse.

Response: "Please come forward. You are most welcome."

COLLECTIVE ILLUSION

As Beloved Brother El Morya has stated, to use the releasing of old energy patterns, old thoughts of disease, old thoughts of decay, all thoughts of death, which can bring forward a greater understanding and a greater unity of the soul, how is this achieved? Of course, in the beginning it is difficult. You have been hypnotized, you see, through collective illusion. Each day in your world when you read a new book, talk to a new person, turn on your television, read a newspaper, what are you participating in? A collective hypnotic illusion of what others think the world must be, reflecting it back to you. You take that unto yourself, digest it as food, assimilate it within your being, and then your cells reflect that thought through feeling and action. How does one begin to embrace the New Day? How does one begin to embrace a new body, a New Consciousness?

THE GIFT OF THE FLAME

One must begin through the gift that was given eons ago through the Lords of Venus, and that is the use of the Violet Flame. As I have said repeatedly, it is only through the use of the Violet Flame that one can begin to release, to let go of, these past patterns that no longer serve, and no longer allow a New Day to emerge. When you become discouraged, when you wonder, will this ever end? That is the time, in that most perfect instant, to call forth the Violet Flame.

> Violet Flame, I AM. God, I AM, Violet Flame.
> Come forward in this instant manifesting perfection,
> in, through and around me.
> Violet Flame, I AM. God, I AM Perfection,
> Violet Flame.

And you see, Dear ones, in that instant the Violet Flame has provided the gift, that one Divine Intervention, in the same way that lightning cracks on Beloved Babajeran. In that instant, the Violet Flame cracks within you, aligning your will, releasing all thoughts, feelings and actions that no longer serve you. When you begin to ponder upon the past through worry and guilt, what is it that you are really engaging in? Fear. The fear of lack or a perceived lack of perfection. These are the things that must be addressed in order for the New Day to come forward in your hearts and in your mind. These are, indeed, the most important key elements. The use of the Violet Flame, may it ever be within you, within your hearts and shared with all of humanity, for the Violet Flame is indeed Divine Intervention— Divine Intervention structured to lift you out of suffering, limitation, death, destruction, and into the New Day.

Violet Flame, I AM. God, I AM, Violet Flame.

Before I proceed with more instruction, are there questions?

Answer: "Yes."

Proceed.

Response and Question: "If we go back to intention, we address that many people, to this day, probably do the Violet Flame, and yet their bodies become old, they decay, they die. And they are still caught in the illusion as we are here in those of us who choose to help you. If the intention were to redirect for personal freedom, to redirect to be ONE with you, to be ONE in the Great Divine Plan, and the Violet Flame were applied to that intention, would that be a much more expedient transmutation?"

BE SPECIFIC

This is quite perceptive, for indeed, the Violet Flame may be applied with a specific idea in mind, a specific focus in mind. If one is practicing Brother El Morya's technique of simplicity and feels that his life is still cluttered, use of the Violet Flame to gain simplicity will only enhance and unencumber the consciousness, the thoughts, to allow the New Day to come forward. To allow a New Day to come forward will allow a new week to come forward. A new week becomes a new month. A month becomes a year. And before long what is it that has been created? But an age, a New Age, a

Golden Age, and an age that is quite different from the time humanity is now experiencing. But we must start with our little steps. We must start with the necessary education that is needed now to begin. Questions?

Response and Question: "Yes. As the intention, we will take me, as an average person, and we will say, "It is now my intention to become ONE with the Great Divine Plan." And I will sit and decree upon that intention. Instead of focusing on the imbalances that I perceive, is it now more expedient to focus upon the unity of the Great Divine Plan?"

FORGIVE YOURSELF

It is expedient to focus upon that which you wish to Co-create, and focus through the use of the Violet Flame on all that would hinder you, or keep you from the fulfillment of that singular intention or focus to be released in a form of transmutation to the Violet Flame of transformation, mercy, compassion, forgiveness. You see, Dear one, until one has truly forgiven oneself, it is almost impossible to move forward into the New Day. This may be compartmentalized into a series of exercises that the chela may then practice. For instance, say that they have decided to embark upon Brother El Morya's lesson of simplicity to find a New Day, but they are still hampered by feelings of guilt concerning an event that happened, perhaps, five years prior. Call upon that Mighty Violet Flame. Transmute the cause, effect, the record and memory of that event, and then one is able to move forward without a harness around one's neck holding him back. When we are held back in this way it is not so much a sin against humanity, but a great sin against the self. It is the little sins of the self that keep us trapped in the ideas of death, delay, destruction and catastrophe. To set yourself free— to truly set yourself free—will require perseverance. But it will only require perseverance in one application, and that is the plea to the Violet Flame for Divine Intervention to allow its Ray of Light to come forward into your life. Do you understand?

Answer: "Yes, I understand that it transmutes."

Questions?

Response: "But I still haven't figured out, even for myself, what the specific intention would be to move myself forward, which now requires immense meditation."

KNOW THYSELF

Know thyself, Dear chelas of my heart. Know thyself, and there shall be the first component of your freedom. To create your New Day, you must indeed know thyself.

Answer: "So, truly that is the format that everyone must follow, and I assume it is the one that you, too, followed to reach the place where you are now."

It is true, Dear one, that it was only through Grace and Divine Intervention that I was allowed this experience to be truth for myself. Now, I would like to proceed with further instruction.

CONSTRUCTIVE CHANGE

It is through the consciousness of Unana that humanity can and will move forward. First, this will be achieved through understanding the need for change. When one accepts that things must change, they can accept that the change must happen first within them, and that the change must reflect to the outer, to their family, loved ones, partner, those with whom they may work, their neighbor and onward into their community. These changes are absolutely necessary in order for the New Day to come forward. From there, the change may reflect to a collective level, and then the change becomes collective reality. Do we need Earth Changes in order to create such changes within ourselves? In some respects, some would say it is necessary, for others will not change unless an outer influence is forced upon them. But is this truly the type of change that is needed? As you can see, Dear ones, Dear hearts, Dear chelas, it is the inner change that truly brings about the constructive change. It is the inner change that brings about the New Day, hence the New Age and the New Time. So, how shall this be achieved? The Greater Plan Divine working with all of us is designed first toward forgiveness—forgiveness of all past mistakes, injustices, understandings where one feels inequities, hurts and harms. These must first be released and dropped from a person's life so that he can move forward in the light of a New Day. When the Ray of Light is so firmly planted within one's heart, one begins to reflect upon the alignment of his will to a Divine Purpose. Beloved Babajeran has offered herself at this time to be of service to humanity, to allow an acceleration of understanding, an acceleration into the realms of light, an acceleration into the New Times.

GOLDEN CITY ENERGIES

The five areas known as the Golden City Vortices shall indeed be put forward as locations upon the Earth, specifically now, within the United States, so that people may travel to them. Feel these energies at an experiential level, and, when within them, occurrences will take place through collective thought form. Do you understand?

Answer: "Yes, so it is your recommendation that people move to the Golden City Vortex centers and have an intention for moving there."

Such movement will allow a movement within themselves. If you feel you cannot release injustice, a sense of inequity within your life, it is suggested that you take a trip to assimilate the Vortex of Wahanee. There, the energies of the Violet Flame, if they cannot be felt, will be absorbed. As I have said before, to drink the water, breathe the air, raise vegetables and to ingest them in an area such as this will increase the Vibration of that single focus within yourself. You see, Dear hearts, Beloved El Morya has put forward to bring forward the ONE, to bring forward truth, harmony and inevitably cooperation; and to bring forward feelings of peace within oneself. One would then travel to the Vortex of Gobean, for that will instill and insight this action within the chela who is seeking to understand, who is seeking to gain a knowledge of Unana. You see, Dear hearts, this is the Greater Plan Divine. Questions?

Question: "Similarly, for each of the Ray qualities that are represented and brought to life in the Golden Cities, if that truly is the intention for the person to experience and to transmute, and in some instances just to absorb, then at the very least, a trip to these areas and at the very most, a new residence?"

UNION OF BODY, MIND, AND SOUL

Whatever one would choose. When one feels he has assimilated these energies, he may move on, move back to where he lived prior, or move on to another Vortex. You see, Dear ones, these energies have been presented so that one may gain a greater understanding of the ONE—a greater union with Mother Earth, a greater union within the Self and his own God, I AM; a greater union with the Hierarchy. It is this union that is sought, a union of body, mind and soul, so that the New Day may begin. One may not perceive a New Day until one has released the past, which holds him from the future. One may not live in the present until the past is no longer in front of him, tripping him up much as a block that one might stumble over. To live fluidly in the now is to release all that has kept you from your Ever Present Now, from your ever-present Oneship. These are the teachings that we will elaborate on, each of the Golden Cities, so that chelas and students will understand what they are present for at this time and the great gift they can bring in a grander service.

THE INNER CHANGE

You see, Dear ones, the Prophecies were given to tantalize those to see the need for change, and now we must move within the greater context of that teaching. It is change that must be made inside. There will be those who will not need to travel to a Golden

City to take in the energies. It may not be necessary, but they are brought at this time to bring a greater acceleration: a greater acceleration vibrationally, electro magnetically; an acceleration of thoughts; an acceleration of feeling. In fact, there will even be an acceleration of the concept of time when one is within a Golden City. That is why the physical body requires less sleep when one first enters a Golden City. These are all concepts that we hold to lay down one by one in the next few weeks and months, as we spend our time releasing this information for humanity.

WORKING WITH THE MASTER

Now, I would like to lay down a template for the way in which we shall work together. As you well know, Dear chelas, I, along with those who work with me, prefer to build an energy. In building energy around a project, it allows a greater harmony and a greater clarity to be brought forward in the works. This we taught with the I AM America Map. Do you remember when we instructed you to place your left hand over your heart, your right hand to project it outward and to bring that visualization into its fullness? We were building an energy, and we shall do the same within that context in releasing the teachings of Gobean. It would be best if we selected a time each day to meet, one in which we can comfortably provide the information and not interfere with your day, yet dispense the information so that it may help all of humanity.

Question: "What was the time that you used previously?"

Early morning hours are always best for the collective consciousness. However, if this is impossible, we can work with other times. However, it is our suggestion that we work at 6 a.m. each morning.

Response: "We will do that, then."

We will instruct on the days we will come forward. We will take frequent breaks. This will allow rest and relaxation, but a more important aspect for the assimilation of the information, so that it may be organized and then utilized.

Now, some visualizations. Bring out the template of the Gobean Vortex, and each day I ask you in your meditation and your visualizations to perform the same technique of the left hand over the heart and projecting the energies out of the right hand toward the Gobean Vortex. Is this understood?

Answer: "Yes."

Then proceed every day until completion of these teachings. Master El Morya will serve as the Master Teacher instructor. I shall serve as Master of Ceremony and will provide an interface. Do you understand?

Answer: "Yes."

Are there any questions, Dear heart?

Answer: "Not about the process and the project."

Then, let us proceed in Grace and Divine Intervention. Let us proceed in the light of a New Day and the hope of a New Age. OM Manaya Pitaya Hitaka. So be it, Beloveds.

Response: "So be it. Hitaka."

CHAPTER FOUR

Golden City Rays

Saint Germain gives instruction on Ray Forces, and the Golden Cities.

Greetings, Beloveds, in that Mighty Christ, I AM Saint Germain, and I stream forth on that Mighty Violet Ray of Mercy and Forgiveness.

As usual Dear hearts, I request permission to come forward.

Response: "Please, Saint Germain, come forward. You're most welcome."

SPIRITUAL EVOLUTION AND THE RAYS

Today, Dear ones, we shall focus on a teaching of the Rays and Ray Forces and their interaction with the Golden Cities, how they work through the Golden Cities, and how this information may be used to move humanity forward into the New Times

The Rays, as you see, Dear ones, are a coalescing of life force, a singular focus of light and sound that come forward to lift humanity in evolution. In this sense, a Ray can allow a person to move forward to become a new being clothed with a new body.

Ray Forces work in such a manner, prodding and moving the person along the path of evolution, spiritual evolution, and begin to move that person onward into greater understanding, knowledge, intuition, and Mastery of the force of his life.

THE RAYS AND THE HUMAN AURA

As I have said before, it is important for you to know thyself first, and to know thyself is to understand how the Rays work within the being, the aura and the electromagnetic field.

The Human Aura is comprised of many such Ray Forces coming together and working, coalescing, one arcing among the other. The

Chakra System is also influenced by the different Ray Forces, each of them coming forward and moving each chakra in a different vibration and through a different sound. It is indeed true that a Ray Force influences each of the chakras, even though there may be a coalescing of the various life forces.

GOBEAN, THE BLUE CITY

The chakras work alongside the light forces, and alongside each light force is also a sound; these work together, Dear ones. The light forces are determined at the moment of birth, and, as you have studied, it is the Astral Body that determines the predominance of a Ray Force or the predominance of a sound force. The two work together, as an Elohim of light and sound, in an Absolute Harmony and absolute cooperation, moving the individual to greater understanding and to greater evolution.

As we understand that there is a predominant light force, and a predominant Ray Force, a predominant sound force within the individual, there is also a predominant light force or Ray Force and a predominant sound force in each of the Golden Cities. As you have known, Gobean is known as the Blue City. It is working toward the qualities of harmony and cooperation. The Blue Ray brings one toward this. First, it holds one's consciousness steadfast unto the idea of a unifying force of cooperation of the Oneship of all things, so steadfastly one holds to this Blue Ray. It is known as Will, or Power, or Force. This, of course, then aligns the Vertical Power Current, which you know as the kundalini of the spine. It works with many of the chakras in different combinations, but, of course, it is most identified with the Throat Chakra and upon occasion with the Third Eye, or pineal gland. This allows one to make the choice in an expression and allows the choice to be expressed through the Will, for the Blue Ray is also at times known as a Ray of Will. This, of course, must be developed within the being to allow evolution. It is only through choices that one begins to evolve in a greater understanding, knowledge, and power of their own Godship.

THE BLUE RAY

You see, Dear ones, the Blue Ray is of vast importance and, of course, is always known as the First Ray. For it is only through Will and the development of choice, and the expression of those choices that one is able to understand one's *own* cause and effect. Cause and effect, of course, has been known as karma, but it is only through karma, or cause and effect, that one begins to learn and to grow through one's choices. So, you see, Dear ones, the Blue Ray is of vast importance. And it is, of course, the first Blue Ray that serves in the Golden City of Gobean.

The Ray Force enters through the apex of each Golden City. It is directed through the Great Central Sun. The Great Central Sun is a source of order in your Universe of collective thought, feeling, and action. Each Ray Force enters into the apex and radiates out in a circular motion, and when one is working toward integration of a Ray Force, it is important to move closer to the apex of a Golden City. And as one is there physically enjoying the energies, one becomes aligned in assimilating the Ray Force into one's being and purifying that Ray Force within one's being. In the beginning of understanding a Ray Force, such as the Blue Ray, one would feel a bit of purification, a bit of disharmony, in the same sense as when a body enters into disease, which sometimes has the same effect. When the Ray strikes the body, the purity of the Ray Force causes one to begin to discard all which does not align to the force and the working of the Ray. In the same way, when the body enters into disease, it is dispelling what the body will not cooperate with. So, it is in the same manner. When one is closer to the purity of a Ray Force when entering into a Golden City, and in this instance I AM referring to the locations of the Stars, there will first be some discomfort. The body may require larger amounts of rest. There could be disharmony in relationships with others, and there may be some purifying process that the body must go through in order to begin to assimilate the purity of the Ray Force. This you will notice in any Golden City when you are working to align with the Ray Force.

MALTON AND THE RUBY-GOLD RAY

It is the same for all of the other Golden Cities. In Malton, you would be working to align with the Ruby and the Gold Ray. The Ruby and the Gold Ray are Rays of Devotion. This Ray may create desires into manifestation, for it has been stated that in Golden City Vortices desires are instantly manifested. So one begins to understand, through one's choices, the desires that they choose, the desires that they wish to attain and bring to fruition. It is also understood that the Ruby and Gold Rays play important roles at this time in assisting and helping the Elemental Kingdoms of the Earth. For many of the Elemental Kingdoms, the Devas and the little fairies, the gnomes and all those who are there and do exist, are also going through their own type of purification. You see, humanity has created an Earth out of balance through the use of many pollutants, which are affecting the Kingdoms and causing an imbalance in many of the Nature Kingdoms. So, it is through the use of the Ruby and the Gold Rays that these are brought back into a balance.

The Gold Ray also rules the ability to take action, and the ability to take action with force. Sometimes it is only through force that things are achieved. Through the Ruby and the Gold Ray rules such actions that exist on the planet as volcanic eruptions, tidal wave motion, tectonic plates moving. This is the Elemental Force at work, working to bring balance to remove that which has brought about disharmony. In the recent tidal wave that you have had upon the planet, humanity must understand that even though great sorrow was brought for the many who have now crossed over into New Dimensions, a great balance was also achieved. This balance allowed the Elemental Kingdoms to achieve a greater sense of their own harmony. You see, Dear ones, it is Absolute Harmony and balance that is sought at this time upon the Earth Plane and Planet. It is balance that must be held in order for humanity to move into the consciousness of Unana. It is only through balance that this is achieved in the great Oneship.

The Ruby and the Gold Rays enter into the Vortex of Malton at the apex, and it is the alignment to this Ray that, if one is seeking fruition of desires to bring their thoughts into instant manifestation, one may travel to align one's energies and Chakra System to this. The chakra that aligns most evenly with the Ruby and the Gold Rays, even though I would also like to add that all chakras are affected by all Rays, is the lowest chakra (base chakra). The lowest chakra is an action chakra. It is the chakra that allows things to move and to be birthed into existence. When one moves to Malton and allows the activation of these energies into one's being, they will begin to experience a movement of the kundalini forces. Of course, in the beginning, they will notice an increase in sexuality, the creative ability, and the desire capacity. It is important to understand when you are integrating a Ray Force from a Golden City into the being, that you must use a type of breathwork to move the energy through the chakras, to keep the body in balance. Any type of breath-work is recommended, any that the chela finds to bring balance.

Of course, Energy Balancing is also recommended, and we have spent much time upon these techniques, have we not? So, Dear hearts, I would suggest that any technique that balances the energy throughout the system will help.

THE PROCESS OF PURIFICATION

Of course, in the beginning, as in Gobean and the assimilation of the Blue Ray, you will note that nothing seems to go right, that the desires that serve your Divine Purpose seem to not work or manifest correctly. But this is all the process of purification, of bringing this forward into alignment to your plan of the best and the highest good.

So, this beloved Ruby and Gold Ray of Ministration and Service begins to serve in its highest way. There will be those souls that will be attracted in the times to come, in the New Times, the Golden Age, to the different Golden City locations that will align to the Ray Force that is most predominant within their being, their soul force, their Star Seed. You see, Dear ones, different Star Seeds serve along different Ray Forces. Of course, there has been such an intermingling of Ray Forces and genetic mix that it is difficult to say that one is strictly of this Star Seed or that Star Seed. But, you see, there will be one (genetic) that becomes more predominant. This domination comes, through the choice of where you wish to serve. So, you see, the Ray Forces serve and work together to bring a greater harmony and a greater self-knowledge. Questions?

ORCHESTRATION OF THE RAYS

Question: "So, what you are saying about the different Star Seeds is the multiplicity of genetic tribes on the planet was for the integration of the individual or the group for each of the Rays, so we have all had our turn, in a sense, through embodiment after embodiment?"

This is so. It brings about a greater orchestration of self-knowledge, a greater orchestration of knowledge of the Rays and their greater working with light and sound forces.

WAHANEE AND THE VIOLET RAY

I shall continue. In the Golden City of Wahanee is the Ray Force of the Violet Ray. The Ray Force enters into the apex of the Golden City. The apex is located in Augusta, as we have enacted a certain amount of inpouring into that area in terms of consciousness and intention. The Ray Force of the Violet Ray brings forth compassion, mercy and forgiveness, but another value of the Violet Ray is its ability to transmute any situation that is holding you back from your achieving the internal union of the ONE.

In working with the Violet Ray, one first begins to understand the purifying and transmuting fires. As I have always stated:

"Down with death, God I AM. Conscious immortality arise."

It is only through the use of the Violet Ray that one begins to understand that one is indeed immortal. The Violet Ray allows one to release the consciousness of death. It is through the Violet Ray that one can begin to regenerate. When you live in a Star area that is near the apex of Wahanee, you can begin to regenerate yourself. You see, there is such a condensation of the Violet Ray energies now entering into that area that the orgone, or prana, is tightly condensed, and for those chelas who wish to drop the consciousness of death and begin to accept their immortal destiny, this is the place toward which they will gravitate.

There are many other uses of the Violet Ray. Of course, this is one that we are releasing at this time so that humanity may begin to understand the great service that the Golden Cities have to offer. So, healing clinics would be a wonderful location in the Golden City of Wahanee for those who wish to regenerate their perspective. You see, mind is the builder, and one must begin with mind if one is to have the new body. We must start first with the thoughts that we hold. We must transmute the old thoughts to bring in the new thoughts. So, Dear hearts, it is through the use of the Violet Ray that Divine Intervention, grace and mercy are imparted to humanity. At a higher level, these energies will be used for Brotherhood, for bringing all to a greater understanding of the unity of all of consciousness. Once we drop the energies of Cellular Fear, we can begin to move into a greater understanding of love and compassion, but first things first. And let us start with regeneration and purification. It is here in this Vortex where one will, in the beginning, notice harder effects upon the physical body: flu-like symptoms, intestinal upsets. You see, the Violet Ray works, not only with the Heart Chakra, but also with the Solar Plexus. It is a transmutation of the Solar Plexus energies that are needed in order to drop the idea of death.

> "Down with death. Conscious immortality arise."

At the higher levels, the Violet Ray works with the Crown Chakra and moves the kundalini energies to the top of understanding. Are there questions?

Answer: "Not at this time."

SHALAHAH AND THE GREEN RAY

I shall move on to the Vortex of Shalahah. Shalahah is known as the Green City. It is only through the Green Ray that one begins to harmonize the body, mind, and spirit. You see, healing is not just repairing the body; it is repairing the mind. It is repairing the spirit; it is repairing the soul. All of these must come into balance in order for total healing to be sustained. The Ray Force, which is the Green Healing Ray, enters into the apex, located near Lolo Pass. This also has a certain coalescing of energies of Blue Rays and Gold Rays. You see, Dear ones, they work together, bringing forth a greater understanding and a greater harmony. Healing is about accepting the Divinity within yourself. These healing forces will bring such about. Healing, also, is understanding that you are not separated, that you are ONE with all things. When one has accepted healing within oneself, he is ready to move to the New Dimensions.

ASCENSION VALLEY

There are two Vortices that have been outlined, sub-vortices that exist within the Shalahah Vortex. One is known as Ascension Valley, which is a Vortex area where one may go to integrate one's Oneship, one's divinity within, to prepare the body, mind, and spirit to move into the New Dimensions.

INTERDIMENSIONAL TRAVEL

Also, there is that which is known as the Transportation Vortex. The Transportation Vortex is a Vortex that will be developed more as we move into the New Times. This is an interdimensional portal, a place where Mother Earth has allowed her energies to commingle with the energies needed, and the heavenly energies of the other dimensions. More will be understood on the Transportation Vortex as we move on and are attuned with the Ray Forces and how they work. You see, Dear ones, when you enter into Shalahah, because of the commingling of the Blue Ray and the Gold Ray, there are other anomalies that exist. This allows for interdimensional travel that is achieved, of course, through the projection of the mind, but as the body becomes fine-tuned, bi-location is indeed a possibility. In the New Times, this will be an accepted form and mode of travel, but only until the body, mind, and spirit are honed and able to accept this type of acceleration. It is suggested that many health retreats be built in this area in the New Times, but the health retreats should focus primarily upon mind as a builder, and body will follow. Do you understand?

Answer: "Yes, so far."

ABUNDANCE AND PROSPERITY

Now, let us return. When chelas travel, or gravitate, to these areas in Shalahah to bring forth the healing forces, they will notice that abundance and prosperity will enter into their lives. When the body, mind, and spirit are brought into balance in complete and Absolute Harmony, the next result is abundance. Natural prosperity comes forward. We have taught this in the Jurisdictions, and Shalahah will be the physical demonstration of this. So, chelas who are working to bring abundance and prosperity into their lives travel to Shalahah, to the apexes, to align themselves to the Green energy. But, Dear hearts, you must understand that in the integration of such a force there is an unraveling effect in the beginning. This will affect not only Heart Chakra energies, but also the Solar Plexus energies. You see, one begins to feel unsafe, for there is over identification with physical materiality. When one begins to understand that it is the coalescing of all the energies that brings about balance within the body, safety is truly a matter of the heart. Abundance, then, can stream forth with clarity and with beauty.

KLEHMA AND THE WHITE RAY

Now, I shall move on to the last and final Golden City and the Ray Force of Klehma. The White Ray of Purity is a Ray of Cooperation. It is also a Ray of Attainment, for it allows one to enter into the New Dimensions that exist beyond where physical embodiment is not required. In the Golden City of Klehma one of the first Crystal Cities will etherealize in the New Times.

UNITED STATES CAPITOL

It has been said that this will be the new capitol of the United States, and indeed it is so, for the rulership and the guidance of the United States in the New Times will come from this ethereal city, where those who have gone before, leaders such as Abraham Lincoln, John F. Kennedy, Martin Luther King, George Washington, Thomas Jefferson. And those you have known as Native American leaders, Mayan leaders, who have known the Christ as Quetzalcoatl will also serve in this City of Cooperation in Klehma.

VENUSIAN ENERGIES

You see, Dear ones, vibration to the White Ray is a vibration to all the Venusian energies. The Venusian energies are a vibration to a White and Crystal Purity, a purity of intention, a purity of heart and mind united in service. So you see, beloveds, when leadership comes from the highest of intention, it leads the country into a New Time, into a new vision.

COOPERATION AND COMMUNITY

Klehma, itself, is aligned to the Golden Cities that existed at one time in South America and in Mexico. These were the Golden Cities that held the ethereal Crystal Cities that guided the Mayan culture into its dimensional leap. You see, Dear one, there is a purpose and a timing to all things. Klehma, as the White Ray, brings about a purity and a cleansing of intention. As we have said before, scrutinize your intentions, for they are powerful Creators. This creation can move one into greater understanding of community and into greater understanding of cooperation. And those who are seeking to learn of unity through cooperation and community, service to humanity, and the united Brotherhoods and Sisterhoods of this Earth can travel and absorb the energies at the Star of Klehma.

WHITE FIRE OF ASCENSION

This energy also develops the energies of Ascension, which will have similar effect on body as in Shalahah, but it is the quality of White Fire. You see, the White Fire is purity, and the body releases the final death urges. The work that is initiated in Wahanee is completed in Klehma. I have given you a brief outline of how the Golden Cities work along with Ray Forces.

GOLDEN CITY MANTRAS

Now, let us talk about sound, for each of the Ray Forces also vibrates to a sound quality, which is important to understand.

Om Shanti vibrates to the Golden City of Gobean. Om Shanti brings about a sense of peace and a sense of harmony, so chelas who wish to chant this as a sound vibration may do so.

Om Eandra is the mantra vibration to be chanted for Malton. Om Eandra is the Vibration of the Elemental Kingdoms. It creates a harmony and a balance. It is also the mantra, or the sound vibration, that can be chanted to bring something into fruition, into attainment, so that you may own it as a Master of your desires.

Om Hue is the chant for Wahanee. You see, Dear ones, Hue aligns all chakras along that Vertical Core Axis, and allows the Violet Flame to work its Mighty Miracle! Om Hue is a Vibration of the Violet Flame Angels and brings about the most purifying and healing effects to the body.

In Shalahah, the vibration to be chanted is Om Sheahah. Om Sheahah for Shalahah means I AM as ONE. You see, Dear ones, in Shalahah one must become as ONE to find healing. One must become as ONE to find true prosperity.

And the final mantra that is chanted for Klehma is again Om Eandra. Om Eandra is the final capstone placed upon the Golden Cities, Om Eandra. You see, Dear ones, through sound vibration and light Ray Forces, all is brought together in a glory and a conclusion. Are there questions?

Question: "I see, so that's how it's qualified. So, for Gobean, when you say Om Shanti, that's the qualification of the Ray specifically for the use of the Blue Ray in Gobean?"

This is so, Dear one.

Question: "Are each of these specific chants the activating phrases for each of the Rays?"

Indeed they are. The activating phrases for the Rays as they work in a Golden City. Remember, it is the energy of your own electromagnetic field, your own aura, working with that of the Golden City Ray Force.

Question: "Okay, and when we utilize these mantras and chants, are you saying that we can apply them in the same way as the Violet Flame in creating, you know, our intention or bringing something into fruition?"

Yes. This is the purpose. This is the intention of the Golden City forces and the way in which they work with your own electromagnetic force-field. You see, Dear ones, the Golden Cities are indeed force-fields that exist for you to access. These are some of the keys of how you may access them and the results that you may get.

Question: "I see, so its effectiveness is better located within the Star?"

This is so, Dear one. It brings forth the intention, the fruition, the qualification of the energy of the Golden City.

Question: "I see. So even if someone wishes to move to a Golden City and they find it difficult to get to the specific one that they have chosen, this chant would help them to expedite that?"

This is so. However, it is preferred that these chants (mantras) be used within the Golden City, as they are sound vibrations that work with the centrifugal force of that Ray Force in the Star. It can be used throughout the whole Golden City, but the pull of it, as you can see, will work most strongly in the apexes. It can be used, of course, throughout the Golden City.

Response and Question: "Hmm. So, by knowing the qualities of each of the Golden Cities, as stated in this discourse and in previous discourses that show up in the books and the tapes and the maps, and utilizing these specific mantras, the purpose intended by you in your life in a Golden City can then be brought into manifestation more easily?"

This is so, Dear one, for those who feel aligned to move to the Golden Cities, can go forward in alignment, knowledge and the force that they may bring into their lives.

Answer: "I see. Well, this sounds like an extremely valuable tool. Thank you."

Now, Dear one, unless if there are other questions, I shall depart.

Response: "Not at this time. This is more than enough to think about and to put into application."

In that Mighty Christ, I AM!

Response: "Thank you."

CHAPTER FIVE

Blue Illumination
*Teachings on the Golden Cities of Gobi,
Gobean, and Shamballa.*

Greetings, beloveds, in that Mighty Christ, I AM Saint Germain, and, as usual Dear hearts, I ask permission to come forth.

Response: "Please, Saint Germain, come forward."

Today, we will discourse more upon the Gobean Vortex, and I have brought with me Beloved Brother El Morya. He is coming forward.

El Morya steps forward, besides Saint Germain.

Greetings, Dear one, in that Mighty Blue Flame, I AM El Morya. I ask permission to come forward.

Response: "Please do, Brother and Teacher, come forward."

GOLDEN CITY NETWORK

Today, I shall bring forth further discourse on the Vortex of Gobean. We have discussed all the Strategic Points, the doorways and the Star of Knowledge. Now, we shall move forward so that you may understand a bit of the ancient history that surrounds the network of the Golden Cities. [Editor's Note: For more information see *I AM America Golden City Series.*]
   Dear hearts, we have spoken about the idea that many of these Golden City Vortices are aligned to other Vortices throughout the planet. As we have explained before, Gobean aligns to energy in Gobi, which is now the Vortex that covers the ancient City of Shamballa. You see, Dear ones, all of these are connected to the idea of emanation, how energy is built. This enables the (Golden

Cities') demonstration or the physical manifestation. When energy is built according to the principal of emanation, you can begin to understand how manifestation, or physical desire, can manifest. Saint Germain has given you continued discourse upon this principal, and it is important to understand, when studying a Golden City Vortex, its doorways, its points, and how it functions. Each of the Golden Cities that are given in the complete network of Vortices are all connected to other cities, but for now we shall place our emphasis upon Gobean and the work of the Blue Ray.

SHAMBALLA'S PROVENANCE

It is the work of the Blue Ray that brought Shamballa into its physical manifestation. You see, Dear ones, some of the original inhabitants of Shamballa were not only from Venus but from other planets. Mercury played a very large role in its inhabitation, along with other planets that are not in your present star system. These people were known as the Blue Race. Many of you have known them as the Vedic traditions. There they built the ethereal city and manifested it into your Earth Plane. Many of those who lived in Shamballa knew perfection and also understood the work of the Blue Ray as representing truth, harmony, and cooperation as a manifestation upon the Earth.

THE CRYSTAL CITIES

The first city, when it was built, held many Crystal Castles. The Crystal Castles were encrusted with rubies, emeralds, pearls and gems that today would be deemed of great value. It was there that the first Unfed Flame of Love, Wisdom, and Power was kept enshrined, and many celebrations and ceremonies were held in honor of this flame.

THE GREAT IMMORTALS

Many of the people understood the idea that they were indeed beyond physical incarnation; and death, as you now understand, did not exist. The great immortals, those who were the great teachers whom your history has now honored, existed in that first City of Shamballa.

DISHARMONY AND WAR

However, as the Earth was populated from other Star Seeds, that is from other planets, a warring force, or a warring energy of non-cooperation and disharmony, was generated. This brought about a dissent within the city. You see, there were those who would enter into the city and their vibration not able to handle the perfection, and the emanation, or the energy, that was built in Shamballa deteriorated.

SHAMBALLA IS MOVED AND REBUILT

It was then decided that this city shall be moved, and indeed it was, and rebuilt. This time, it was kept hidden, so that those, who at that time upon the Earth sought to find it, but could not. This city held again the same energies of perfection, of longevity, of perfect health, and perfect harmony. Music played throughout the day. The night-time was sweet, and the scent of jasmine filled the air.

PERFECTION IS AN EMANATION

You see, Dear ones, perfection is indeed an emanation. It is an energy that is built and held within the body. When you seek your own perfection, you must idealize it as a perfect crystalline thought in your mind first, and then build the energy through the Principle of Emanation. The Principle of Conductivity then comes into play, and it was through conductivity that the second City of Shamballa began to radiate throughout the Earth.

THE SECOND DEMISE OF SHAMBALLA

The second City of Shamballa grew in such a manner that it affected all the Earth for greater harmony and greater perfection. But materiality began to obsess the population. Materiality was the demise of the second City of Shamballa, and this time the deterioration came from within the city. Many long-term residents, the immortals who first held the focus of Shamballa, also fell in consciousness, and for the most part, required rebirth. But the few remaining, who held the purity of consciousness, rebuilt the city for the third time.

THE ETHEREAL SHAMBALLA

Upon the request of Sanat Kamara, it was decided that this city would not manifest in the physcial planes, or to plainly speak: seek physical incarnation. This time, the city was held in the finer ethreal qualities and the emanation would be detected only by those who had developed the finer subtle bodies (qualities) within the Astral Body. So, those who were trained in different ashrams throughout Eastern Asia were also trained to seek, through higher consciousness, entry into the Golden City of Shamballa. It remains in this same location today.

SHAMBALLA AND THE NEW TIMES

At one time, the consciousness of humanity was raised to such a peak that within the Gobi Desert, directly beneath the ethereal Crystal City of Shamballa, another civilization was built. As above, so below. The law was mirrored, and many traveled to this city seeking healing and the ancient teachings. However, as humanity moved into the time period now known as Kali, the gates of Shamballa were tightly shut to but a few; now, this time period is over, and the New Time period moves Earth forward and humanity develops into a new understanding and into a new evolution. [Editor's Note: We've entered the Golden Age of Kali Yuga. For more information see: *The Ever Present Now.*]
Before I proceed with more information, are there any questions?

Answer: "Yes, there are."

Proceed.

Question: "You spoke of conductivity, and prior to that you spoke of focus in creating perfection. In that step-by-step manner, is there an exercise, or is there a tangible way to take this and utilize it for everyday use for humanity?"

EXERCISE OF THE ONE

To build your energy fields through the Principle of Conductivity, it is important to understand the ONE, the Oneship, unity of all things. Conductivity is based upon this idea. Through the course of emanation and conductivity all energies basically function as ONE. To build this within your own energy fields, practice again the meditation which I gave you years ago of the candle. You must have the singular focus that you and the candle become as ONE. Do you understand?

Answer: "Yes, I do."

This prepares the mind for a greater understanding, a greater illumination. Are there more questions?

Question: "So, the practice of the candle meditation, you would say, is the first step in developing the focus what may be sustained through any distraction or any time period that would allow the conductivity to also be sustained?"

This is true, Dear one. You will receive great results if you practice this in earnest. [Editor's Note: Please see Appendix A for instructions on the Candle Meditation.]

Response: "Thank you. Please continue."

SHAMBALLA AND THE GOLDEN CITY OF GOBI

So, the third and final City of Shamballa, which it was decided should remain in its ethereal state, has kept its position over the Gobi Desert. Of course, of the ancient civilization that existed in a physical state, there are still remnants of it, and those who search for the City of Shamballa may find it if they so choose. The energies of Gobean align to this ancient Golden City, known as Gobi. You see, Dear ones, as above, so below. When Shamballa and the City of Gobi intertwined, it created a force-field. The force-field then created a Vortex. This is how all Vortices come into being, through a relationship of ethereal consciousness and emanation and conductivity. Do you understand?

Question: "I see. It's the basic structure of how the Rays of Light and Sound go together."

HEAVEN AND EARTH

It is indeed as such, a Co-creation of Heaven and Earth. The two exist simultaneously, exist together. It takes the two for such to exist, built upon, as I have explained and Master Saint Germain has explained, through the elements of conductivity and emanation.

GOBI AND GOBEAN ARE ONE

Now, I shall proceed, Dear ones. There is yet another city that aligns its energy to the energies of Shamballa, or the City of Gobi, the Golden City of Gobean. These two Vortices are connected as ONE. So, when you meditate upon the perfection of Shamballa in the City of Gobean, you can be instantly transported there. You see, Dear ones, as the perfection streams forth into your own bodies, your own minds, your own hearts, as you are accelerated in the times to come, the times of the Golden Perfections, you shall then be able to transport your body, through the process of bi-location, to the City of Gobi. You shall also be able to take in the perfected energies of the ancient City of Shamballa. This ancient City of Shamballa is the city where many of the Master Teachers meet on a yearly basis. This I'm sure you are familiar with.

Response: "Yes, absolutely."

THE DEATHLESS BODY

As you integrate these perfected energies, as we have instructed you, as time progresses, or as time compacts, in this grand opportunity that is being offered to humanity, you will note further perfections within your own bodies. As you see, the water and air in a Golden City is of a higher and finer quality. The principal of prahna or orgone, as you have been taught, is much more condensed, It rotates at a higher millisecond. This higher rotation within your body brings about an acceleration. We have spoken of the Cellular Awakening. This acceleration brings you closer and closer to the idea of a deathless body of physical immortality, of Ascension into new realms of understanding. This acceleration is most essential to access the energies that are inherent in a Golden City Vortex.

GOLDEN CITY DOORWAYS

Of course, there are other energies that are apparent. I have spoken already of the ability for miraculous healing in the Southern Doors. I have also spoken of the abilities of Instant-Thought-Manifestations of the Northern Doors. You see, there are other qualities and other gifts that the Cities are here to bring to humanity as the course of Divine Intervention proceeds. This alignment of energy with the ancient City of Shamballa is most important, Dear hearts and Dear ones, for Gobean is the perfect location to extract the ancient records through Thought Projection. I have taught you before about this principle; do you not recall?

Answer: "Yes, I recall."

INFUSION OF TRUTH

To project your thoughts, or your mental body, into another realm to receive information, in Gobean one may travel to receive the ancient knowledge of other times. In meditation, you can access this information much more readily than in any other Golden City. You see, Dear ones, through the Blue Ray of Truth, the truth of the history of the planet comes forward for you now to view. It is not a truth that is given through another one's perspective. It is a truth that is infused directly to you so that each is given his or her own individual understanding of the history of this Earth, the history of this schoolroom and your own individual participation. You see, in truth, it must be received at an individual level, so through the individual experiences of each they can receive. When it is imparted only as knowledge or as belief, it carries less importance. You see, Dear hearts, Dear ones, this is the importance of Gobean for its alignment to the ancient knowledge.

AKHENATEN AND SERAPIS BEY

Historically, Gobean also aligns to another ancient city. In your history, this is known as Giza. Why is this so? The teacher Serapis Bey, who was known as Akhenaten, traveled to the location of Gobean, and there he gave forth his teachings. Many did not understand them at the time, for you see he was able to project through his consciousness a perfect form of himself, ethereally, and there the teachings were brought to the cultures that existed in the ancient areas that are now known as Gobean. This is why you will see there are similarities in the cultures. He was known as a great teacher among many, and yet this was a projection of the (his) consciousness. So, you see, again, as above, so below.

Serapis Bey became one of the first teachers of the Continuity of Consciousness. He taught about the opening of the Third Eye and the Crown chakra, the Star of Knowledge. This was passed down, you see, Dear ones, and the energy and the focus that were held through these teachings created a force-field that is in the location of Gobean. In later years, I was to come under the tutelage of this same teacher, and I, too, was taught the technique so that I could project my consciousness, and there became a series of teachings in Gobean, and many of the cultures gravitated toward this. These appearances had a tendency to raise the energies, and you see now how this has come to be. Do you have questions?

ANCIENT GOBEAN

Question: "Yes. Question one: Was the center of Gobean at that time, when you were projecting into it, in the same exact location that it is in now?"

It was more to the North, and assisted many of the different tribes of people that are now known as Native Americans.

Question: "Would these tribes be the Hopi?"

QUETZALCOATL THE CHRIST

Some of the Hopi were affected by this emanation, as well as Anasazi and Mayan cultures. The work that Akhenaten began was a long-held tradition. Before Akhenaten had begun this type of bi-location projection, there were those from the City of Shamballa who were doing such work. I hope this brings a greater understanding to the location. The reason Egyptian teachings now fill the area of Gobean is because of the work of Akhenaten to bring the energy of the Christ forward. This energy of the Christ was known as Quetzalcoatl. Quetzalcoatl was the first to actually anchor this energy into human consciousness in the geophysical area that is now known as Gobean. Do you understand?

SHAMBALLA'S HALL OF WISDOM

Question: "What you're saying is that if we go back to the City of Shamballa, that is in essence the portal for the upliftment of all of humanity, which is a collection of many Star Seeds?"

This is true, Dear ones. This is also known as the Hall of Wisdom. For this Earth, it is an entry point for many souls who come here to gain higher knowledge. Of course, there are those souls who try to come to schoolroom Earth to disrupt the knowledge process, the learning process that is imparted. But now you can understand that, through Thought Projection and bi-location, the evolution of humanity has largely been brought forward through the work of Shamballa. Do you understand?

Question: "Yes, I understand. One more question."

Proceed.

Question: "Then all the Golden Cities are, in essence, stepping stones at one level on the path of the upliftment, and, on another level, they are also energy points that energize the consciousness of humanity in the upliftment process?"

They serve as Divine Intervention, to bring about higher knowledge, higher understanding. They are indeed a pivotal point of evolution.

CHAPTER SIX

Template of Light

El Morya elaborates on the Star of Gobean and prophecies of change.

Greetings, Beloveds. in that Mighty Violet Flame, I AM Saint Germain, and I request permission to come forward.

Response: "Please, Saint Germain, come forward."

Dear ones the work at hand is indeed important, and I shall not tarry longer, but I introduce you this morning to Beloved El Morya.

Master El Morya steps forward.

Greetings, Dear ones. In that Mighty Blue Flame, I AM El Morya, and I request permission to come forward.

Answer: "Please come forward, El Morya."

THE STAR OF GOBEAN

Dear hearts, Dear ones, the activation of Gobean is complete, and it is important to understand each of the teachings as they have been set forward. We have laid down the template of all the doorways, each of them complete in the teaching that they bring and emit. But it is important to understand the full use of the energies of the Star.

The Star, you see, is not only the coalescing of the energies of each of the doorways, but is also the finer qualities of that Mighty Blue Ray. When you understand the Galactic Web and how each of the star systems is interconnected, it is through the Sun of the solar system that these Rays arc their energies to the intersecting grids known as Golden Cities. Each is then qualified by pure mighty God Force. The God Force is known in Gobean as the Blue Ray, and it brings forth many of its inherent qualities. These qualities are peace, harmony, cooperation and, ideally, transformation of the human into a God State.

THE GOD STATE

There will be those, when they recognize the God State, who will feel a Oneness, a sense of bliss, or Unana, with all creation. There will be those who will mock such a state and will ask how a human can obtain such an ideal consciousness; but it is so, Dear ones. The God State is an understanding of the inherent Mastery that exists within each of you. This has been taught before as the Unfed Flame of Love, Wisdom, and Power. This is the perfection of Divinity that exists within each of you. To align to this Divinity brings forth a natural harmony, a natural cooperation of each of your energy fields. Beloved Saint Germain has brought forth a discourse on the energy fields, their separate purposes and how they may be applied as energy forces in this New Time.

HIGHER FREQUENCY

It is in the work of Gobean, particularly that of the Star, in which the energy bodies are brought into a union and a harmony of understanding. You see, Beloveds, it is in the Stars that the Ray Force is at its strongest point or strongest pitch in auditory sound. It is that place of movement where light and sound work in their greatest movement to bring humanity forth in its evolutions. Naturally, when one retreats or retires to a Star, one is filled with a higher frequency, a higher energy.

These Star areas in all the Golden Cities are considered by the hierarchy to be sacred areas. They are areas that shall be used for the strongest pulse of the energies of each Master Teacher who is assigned. These are also areas that, when defined, are where the Master Teachers of each defined area will manifest a physical body when the energies are in their optimum state. Creation toward the optimum state will be required in order for this to happen, and many will ask of you, "In what time span shall this occur?" But you will know, Dear ones, Dear hearts. When the energies will be ready, for they will not be denied. It is important to know that these energies are pure, and in their purity and innocence they are able to bring forth the higher and finer qualities. You see, as we have explained before, it is the hierarchy of consciousness working with the service of Beloved Babajeran, as Mother Earth, to bring this forward now for humanity. Many will see it and exclaim that it is a Divine Intervention. However, it is a plan that has been held in my focus. It is a plan that has been held in my own heart's desire.

A BECKONING

Gobean will perform a great service for many during the times of great change. It will serve as a beckoning point. Have you not noticed that many are being drawn and called to live in this area?

Answer: "This is very true."

These are due to the energies, and many are being called forward. Many feel a magnetic draw or an electromagnetic pulse drawing them closer and closer. You see, it is a plan that was long held, not only through the service of the hierarchy and through the service of Beloved Mother Earth, Babajeran, but it is also within that longing of the soul to become ONE with, to become atoned, to become ONE in the consciousness of Unana. One may say, yes, this is a genetic pulse, but it is only that inherent Divineship . . . exists within each of you which is now being pulled to its fuller expression. Only in the service of Brotherhood and Sisterhood can the chela move forward to the greater understanding, to the greater work, to the greater knowledge. It is only through merging in cooperation and harmony, and in understanding the ONE body of light, that one can move forward in one's own steps of self-mastery. Through collective consciousness, or the consciousness of Unana, one is able to understand the greater working of the greater law.

LET GO

That is the reason we pull you forward into harmony. Let go of your little misgivings. Let go of the little hurts, for they become major stumbling blocks in moving forward in your own greater understanding. It is in the unity of consciousness that the hierarchy works and is able to bring forward its greater service with Beloved Babajeran. It is only through our understanding of the unity of all of consciousness, the unity of all of life, that we are able to move and experience our light being; so, understand, Dear chelas, how important the work of harmony and cooperation is. It is a greater movement into a greater knowledge, a greater understanding, which ultimately will set you free.

Now, I will continue with more teachings upon the arcing of the Ray energy.

RAY FORCES ENTER THE STAR

Each of the Ray Forces enters in and to the Stars, and this pure energy connects itself to the core of the Earth. It is from there that it radiates out again, out through the center of the Earth, and works as a streamline force of energy.

Now, I shall diagram this so that you will understand exactly how a Ray Force works.

He is first drawing the Great Central Sun and from the Great Central Sun he is drawing a series of lines. Each of these lines works as a Ray Force. And they move toward the center of the Earth.

Now, understand, chelas, that this activity is not peculiar only to Earth itself. This is the same type of pattern as Ray Forces arc to any other planet within your (solar) system.

He is showing now that it moves to the center of the Earth.

THE INNER SUN

It is the core, itself, that attracts light force to light force, for the core of the Earth is also a brilliant Sun. Of course, your scientists would say it is a molten type of rock, but this is not so. It is another Sun in its own evolution. You see, as Earth moves forward in its evolution, it, too, shall become the Sun of its own solar system in its own time and in its own place. But you see the attraction of one light to another.

Now, he is showing how the Ray Forces arc from the Central Sun within the Earth to each of the positions of the Golden Cities.

QUALIFICATION OF LIGHT

It is through the work of the hierarchy that this light is qualified. Each of these Vortices exists in a similar compatibility. Each of these Vortices exists as a template that covers the entire planet. It is the work of the Master Teacher and the Elohim of that Ray that brings forward the qualification of the qualities of that light. It is my presence, along with many other servants of the Blue Ray, that brings forward the qualification of this as a light force. Each of the Golden City Vortices exists as they are, each of them very similar in their working and understanding. But it is the presence of the Master Teacher, and those who wish to follow in the ashram of consciousness of that particular thought, that continues to bring that qualification of light through. Do you understand this diagram?

LIGHT UNTO LIGHT

Answer: "Not completely. I was always of the opinion that our local solar Sun was the window to the Central Sun."

There is indeed a Great Central Sun, but it is through the solar system that this energy is allowed to emit to its finer quality. I could explain that so that you would understand how light is attracting light unto light. It is the Great Central Sun that emits

its own Ray of light to the Sun of this solar system. Do you understand?

Answer: "Okay. I think we're talking about the same thing."

RIPPLES OF LIGHT AND SOUND

Essentially, it is. I'm talking only about your own solar system, so that you may understand exactly how this works within the Golden Cities. You see, each solar system has its own evolutionary cause, its own evolutionary template. So, you understand, only in its own time and place can these forces move forward. We have spoken much in the past about the Lords of Venus, and it was through their own evolutionary process that they were able to take each Ray of light and its own sound vibration and bring them into a higher octave of evolution.

At this time, Earth is being readied for a greater understanding of light and sound. Light and sound move many things forward. History is created. Interactions among humanity and societies change, political systems and economic systems also begin to change. This sets up a ripple effect in the same way as when a pebble is thrown into a pond. The ripples over the water create an effect that is felt by all within the pond. Envision your solar system as that pond, exposed to a the Ray of light and sound, with a small pebble being dropped, and a Source which drops it. The hand that dropped the force is now your Sun. But there is a greater force of consciousness behind the hand. That is the Great Central Sun orchestrating a greater Divine Intervention of the Rays of Light and Sound.

LIGHT JOINS SOUND

Understand, Dear ones, chelas, that even sound works as a Ray. It is through this circular vibration—which we have explained before as the spiral—that light and sound join to one another. And it is when this vibration is consciously applied by the chela, through the work of the Violet Flame or other mantra work, that they engage in that light, which is then bonded to sound. Ultimately, it is the intertwining of consciousness with action. Do you understand?

Question: "The intertwining of consciousness with action—so, by taking the action of the Violet Flame Decree, or a mantra, that starts to imbue into the cells of the body a light frequency?"

EVOLUTION AND THE VIOLET FLAME

This is so, Dear ones. And it brings forth an acceleration within the chelas. That is why, when we explain the work of the Violet Flame and the work of the different mantras that can be utilized in each of these Golden Cities, they are brought forward with a timing and an intent to move evolution forward. It is this cooperation that is created within each of the light bodies, which allows a unionization of each of the fields of light. You see, at this point there are indeed layers of the field of the Human Aura, or different light bodies. These can, and are, at times separated by Will by those who have complete Mastery over each of the light fields. And it is through a type of Mastery that they are brought together or unionized at Will, when the Violet Flame is utilized and mantras are utilized by individuals and the Master for different Ray Forces. This brings about a unionization effect within the aura. Do you understand?

Answer: "Yes, and that also explains, when I have seen your aura, or that of any of the other Masters, that the auras are perfectly arranged and harmonized, and are organized by color and sound."

OM SHANTI

The Mantra, "Om Sham, Sham, Sham or Om Shanti, Shanti, Shanti," sham is the vibrational frequency of the Blue Ray within the solar system. This brings forth a coalescing of energies, a natural cooperation, a natural harmony that is inherent within the individual. As you understand each of these teachings, you first exclaim unto yourself, "a great mystery is now revealed," but that is not so.

MASTERY OF THE PHYSICAL

In its own timing and intent, all, as Universal Mind, is revealed. You see, Dear ones, Dear hearts, you are all Divine. You all carry within you the same Source. You are all equal to one another. It is by this concept of Brotherhood and Sisterhood that the Mastery of the physical is accomplished. That is why dear Sananda has always said, "Simply love one another." To bring forth this work of the Blue Ray in the Golden City of Gobean is my first intent. My second intent is to teach this work and its application, to bring your own energy fields to consciously align them, to consciously unify them, to bring them as ONE to at-ONE-ment, to bring them into a tone. Now, do you understand?

Answer: "Yes."

STEP-DOWN TRANSFORMER

This work brings about a greater harmony, a greater force of electromagnetism. For, you see, the qualification of the Golden City Vortex Ray is magnified in force. As others align to its energy, it grows exponentially. Now do you understand?

Answer: "Yes. It's the way in which the system works."

Each is then treated, when reaching this level of intentional service, as a Step-down Transformer, used to carry forth the work of the Ray Force within that Golden City. Some will feel more aligned to energies other than the Blue Ray, but the Blue Ray is the most perfect place to start, to bring the body into alignment, to bring the energy fields to atonement.

AT-ONE-MENT

Question: "So atonement is also at-ONE-ment?"

They are one and the same. They are brought through the light and sound frequencies, working together as ONE. This is the beauty of the creation of the Rays, and part of the greater plan to bring humanity back into its state, its true state of at ONE.

VIOLET FLAME ASSISTS THE ONENESS

During the Time of Change, many changes are occuring; changes not only upon the Earth, but changes within yourself, within your neighbor, within society. Humanity is changing. Is this a change that is forced upon it [humanity]? Hardly, but one that was planned and one that was long desired. Of course, there are always those who resist such change, and this causes disease, insanity, suicide, all of the death urges. You see, when one encounters higher frequency, if one has not cleared the energy bodies out through the steady and constant use of the Violet Flame, one will not feel comfortable in his Oneness. Now, you understand, in its greater working and greater harmony, why Master Saint Germain has brought forward the work of the Violet Flame.

Question: "So you are saying that, in the evolution of humanity, all of the prayers that have pre-existed before this time, which have brought us to this place—those things we call chants or mantras or intonations—culminate with the use of the Violet Flame to bring humanity to its next place in the evolution of a cycle?"

ELIXIR OF THE HEART

This is so. Now the working of the Violet Flame in the mass collective consciousness first stimulates that which is known as the kundalini. This has another electromagnetic force working itself throughout the human body in that which is known as the First Chakra. Have you not seen the lust and the greed, the climbing for physical security when these energies are not allowed to rise further, and to bring their expression towards the true force they are meant for? It is through this work of the Violet Flame, and the rising of the forces of the kundalini to the Heart Chakra, that brings one to the understanding of love. It is only through love that all may be healed. It is only through love that all may become as ONE. You see, love becomes, as Saint Germain would say, the grand elixir. Love is indeed the energy that all must understand, all must experience. It is one thing for me to mention love, but it is another for you to experience it. Is this not so?

Answer: "This is very true. It is love that has brought me here, and it is love that keeps me here on this path."

FAMILY, LOVE, AND THE ONE

In love, the chela encounters sacrifice at many levels, purification at many levels. That is why love is the energy of all Eastern doors. It is not sacrifice that keeps a family together as ONE; it is only when one overcomes petty selfishness and little hurts that energy is raised to a greater understanding of the ONE. This is not to say that the individual's wants and needs are not important, but this allows for a greater understanding of the higher knowledge of choice. It is when one chooses love as the action that the understanding of the Violet Flame comes forward in its greatest harmonizing effect. This template of energies that is laid down through use of the Violet Flame allows one to work with the Blue Flame.

BLUE FLAME MEDITATION

Now let us talk about the work of the Blue Flame. The Blue Flame, in its highest understanding, is anchored within the Throat Chakra. Of course, this is identified with the higher use of the Will. Then, all expression comes forth in cooperation and in a greater harmony and peace: perfect sounds, perfect creations and perfect light. Are these not the blessings and the wants of paradise? But in order to understand how this works within your own physiology, let us now practice a breathing technique.

Together, let us meditate upon the Violet Flame. Raise [visualize while breathing] the energies from the base of the kundalini, the base of your spine, now purposely raise the energies up to your heart. Meditate upon and experience this flame, and when you feel the burning within your heart, signal me.

Response: "It is done."

Now, do you feel the collection of the energies of the Violet Flame?

Answer: "Yes, they grow."

They emanate. This teaching has been brought forward to you. To bring this into a greater understanding, the Blue Flame now rests within the heart of the Unfed Flame of Love, Wisdom, and Power. Now, the Blue Flame of Power, as an electrical current, moves the rest of this energy up to the Throat Chakra. We are speaking now of the higher use of energy. Do you feel this energy, as you breathe, moving itself, ever so gently, to your throat?

Answer: "Yes, I do."

ALIGNMENT OF THE WILL

This energy is used as a Divine expression. It is the work of this Will—this Will of greater love—to bring a unionization. As these energies travel into their higher expression, an alignment of all systems occurs within the physiology. This alignment of systems encounters Elemental Kingdoms, Mineral Kingdoms, and Vegetable Kingdoms. We have spoken of the harmony of Kingdoms as they exist in the human physiology. Now this harmony moves on into its greater working and a greater alignment, for its source is love, pure love, purified love, the love of sacrifice, the love of purification, the love of choice. This is known as Will. Let it come forward.

In that moment did you feel a chill throughout your body?

Answer: "Yes."

UNION

That was the unionization of your energy fields. Some may say "goose bumps."

Answer: "Goose bumps, yes."

Did you get a chill?

Answer: "Yes."

This is the unionization of all fields moving you to the consciousness of Unana. Now, dear chela, do you understand why I gave you the Candle Meditation?

Answer: "Yes, but this was more simple than I had thought."

REGENERATION

Now, you have another understanding of unity and its purpose, and how it brings about greater harmony. Let us focus on the results of what this work can now bring: a beautiful result in your interaction, right action, with others; an ease of understanding in bringing forth your own God idea, your own God creatorship; a greater understanding in working in harmony with others; and a greater understanding in working with the energies of Gobean. This unionization of the energy fields brings, of course, a type of regeneration to the physical body; greater yet, it brings a greater regeneration of you, with your true inherent Divinity.
Now I shall open the floor for your questions.

Response and Question: "I find this very interesting. In my personal meditations, I have asked for a similar instruction, and, without saying a word to Lori, it has come forward, as usual. It is more verification of the inner workings of the Divine connection and of the telepathic connection in that service. The question I would ask is for anyone who may read or hear this. This type of— we could call it an exercise or meditative action—would this be wise to do several times a day?"

SUGGESTIONS FOR SPIRITUAL PRACTICE

It is best to do after one has completed the Violet Flame and after completing one's work with the Blue Flame. You see, this will bring great assistance in raising the energies throughout the kundalini. Do you understand?

Question: "Yes. In considering that our world is made of light and sound, the Blue Flame does have a frequency and a pitch, is this not so?"

Yes, and that has been explained. Of course, pitches will change as frequency changes in resonance. So you must understand that we start with just the pronunciation of what the sound possibly is, for those who can hear.

Response: "I understand. However, in your world, there are specific pitches that are utilized."

They are not utilized. A better word would be "achieved."

Response: "Achieved and experienced. I understand. So, in doing a Candle Meditation and in doing the Violet Flame Decrees, this next step can be added for the harmonization of the layers of the aura. One of its benefits is that it helps to purify the body and energizes it."

THE HIGHER CHAKRA SYSTEM

It also brings forth the creation of what you have known to be the axiotonal bodies, the higher frequency Chakra System. However, we shall not proceed with that teaching yet.
Let us focus on the work at hand and bring it into a perfect harmony.

Response: "I would agree. At this point, I have no further questions."

In that Mighty Blue Flame, let us all move forward in perfect harmony, cooperation, peace and Unana. And now I turn the floor back to Beloved Saint Germain.

Saint Germain steps forward.

Response: "Thank you."

Dear ones, it was our hope, in bringing this information forward, that you would not only understand a greater working of the Violet Flame but also of the Blue Flame and the Blue Ray and its purpose in the Star of the Golden Cities. You see, these teachings are brought forward to be a template of all the teachings so that there will be a greater understanding and a greater knowledge of how these forces work to bring humanity forward.

Unless there are other questions, I shall take my leave.

Response: "No, but I AM thankful to both of you, for this has been a lesson that I have long desired."

In united Brotherhood and Sisterhood, let peace reign supreme. Hitaka.

Response: "Hitaka. So be it. Thank you."

CHAPTER SEVEN

Time of Testing
Saint Germain prophesies world change.

Greetings, beloved Dear hearts. in that mighty Violet Ray, I AM Saint Germain, and I request permission to come forth.

Response: "Please, Saint Germain, you are most welcome. Come forward."

ACCEPT PERFECTION

In the heart of the mighty logos burns this mighty Violet Flame of Mercy, Compassion, and Forgiveness. When you call upon it in your daily decree, or visualization, or meditation work, you call upon this mighty law in action as it streams forth from its great and mighty power through the Great Central Sun and onward to your own Sun and to the planet. In the same way in which I have explained and described how Ray Forces work, this comes forward in that manner. It comes forward in the same natural laws, as they have been set forth in previous discourse. This is important to understand, for, you see, the Violet Flame is this mighty law in action. When you call upon it, what it does, precisely and exactly, is free your consciousness from any inhibiting doubt or harm. It allows for a focus to come forward so that you can begin to accept the perfection of your thoughts and feelings, the perfection of all action, and the activation of the mighty Will in action.

THE PERFECTED CELL AND ITS LIGHTED STANCE

You see, Dear hearts, Dear ones, it is only the acceptance of the perfection that each of you carries in that mighty Chamber of the Heart. It is this one perfected cell that awakens the other cells into their own perfection and carries this awakening throughout your system. I have spoken about this before as the lighted stance of activating each of these cells within your system, to bring about this perfection—the perfection of your divinity, or your Divineship. Within it lie many of the answers to eternal memory, eternal life and eternal Oneship with the Divine Creator.

THE FORGETTING

You see, beloveds, Dear ones, it was through a collective forgetting that a forgetting occurred within the genetics. This created a masking of the consciousness. Because of the inability to retain information, the memory died down. It is through this collective forgetting that mankind entered into successive cycles of embodiment-upon-embodiment of experience, and never knew its true source with the ONE, with all, in the mighty Divineship.

COMPASSION

Beloveds, Dear hearts, a time now comes upon the Earth Plane and Planet when there will be great testing, a testing not only of the Wills, but a testing also of putting this mighty law of ONE into action. You see, when you call upon the Violet Flame and the opening of the heart, you are led into the understanding that all is one, and all is ONE in an unconditional form of love. Through this mighty unconditional love, you are able to develop the higher aspects or emotions of compassion, gratitude, and Brotherly and Sisterly love. This earmarks the beginning of a greater civilization, of a greater society that can vibrate and understand why indeed it is manifesting itself at this time. You see, other societies have existed before you, many other great civilizations in their rise and their fall, but perhaps the one area where they did fault, the one area that they tripped upon, was the lack of development of compassion. You see, when one understands that one must not judge another, for they do not understand the circumstances that another walks or treads upon—one then enters into a higher resonance and a greater frequency. The idea of Mercy, Compassion, and Forgiveness earmarks always the birth of greater awareness and greater understanding, and allows access beyond the Third Dimension. In perceiving, in an empathetic sort of way, the situation of your Brother or Sister, you are then able to understand at a higher energy level how all life is interconnected as ONE.

It is always through thinking and perceiving the self as being separate that produces more separate realities. Thus we enter into a stream of disharmonies, a stream of miscommunications and a lifestyle that filters through that lens of noncooperation.

SWIFT CHANGES

But, indeed, we (will) enter into a time that is an Age of Cooperation. Among all things, Dear hearts, this is of vast importance. The next seven years shall be a Time of Great Trial and Tribulation; a time that will be best known as a Time of Testing—not only a testing of the mighty Will, but, as I have stated before, a time to put the Law of ONE into action. It is also a time when I assure you, Dear ones, Dear hearts, that I shall always be available to give you guidance and discourse, as needed. This has been my assignment, given to you for this time period, so that we may begin on a more personal note to understand how things may swiftly change. This indeed will be a Time of Swift Change, not only upon the Earth Plane and Planet, but you will see within the minds of men that there will be many who will be called to the task, many who will be called for the great choosing. You see, beloveds, Dear ones, the events upon the Earth will be among the greatest teachers that mankind has yet to see. It will take but one or two jarings of this Earth, a few mighty winds and a few mighty rains, and mankind will begin to see things in a subtle and different manner.

CROSSING THE THRESHOLD

How do we touch the heart? How do we open the heart and allow this Oneship to stream forth? This has long been the question at the pivotal point of evolution for humanity and mankind. This has long been an important barrier that we now have an urging to cross. How do we open up the New Dimensions so that mankind may cross this great threshold and begin to understand that it is this Inner Marriage of thought and feeling that leads to Divine action and Divine Manifestation?

INTERVENTION OF THE GOLDEN CITIES

We have given the locations of the Golden Cities so that a Divine Intervention shall come forward. This Divine Intervention is brought for the grace of humanity. It is brought so that humanity may now come forward in a greater choosing, in a greater understanding. This Divine Intervention comes through the integration of many energies that come from the Northern, the Eastern, the Southern and the Western doors, and onward to that Mighty Star where all energies coalesce and are available for integration. Each of these teachings has been given with its timing and intent so that it can be used as a type of intervention. In the next seven years, these doorways and energies of the Golden Cities will become known to their greatest extent, and more probing into their wondrous knowledge will begin.

AWAKENING

You see, there is enough energy within these Golden City Vortices to blaze mankind into the next level of understanding. But if mankind is unable to choose or unwilling to act, then this Divine Intervention may, or may not, move forward. You see, the time is at hand. The awakening is at hand, but indeed, in terms of your Earth years and understanding, this time is short; yet the awakening is immortal. This awakening is for all and beyond the barrier of time. But the events that come will be marked by time and recorded in your history.

Beloveds, Dear ones, know that I AM here to serve. Know that I AM here and that I offer the Cup of the most refreshing drink. I offer this so that those who have the eyes to see and the ears to hear may now understand in the greater opening of the heart and the greater understanding and alignment of the Will. It will take this mighty alignment of the Will to move humanity into a cooperative group, into this group action.

THE ASSIMILATION PROCESS

We have set forth the locations of the Golden Cities so that a relocation of sort may also begin. The relocation we have described several times, that it shall start first from the outer periphery of the Vortices. Then, as a chela, student or Aspirant carefully observes and integrates these energies, he will be ready to move onward to that star—that mighty Star of Self-knowledge. This may also be engendered from our teachings. We brought you forward to the Vortex of Gobean, but you integrated the energies at a much slower pace on the outside, did you not?

Answer: "This is true."

This is perfect and in great Divine Alignment, for you see it is important that, one by one, the energy is understood and assimilated before you can move on. It is suggested, when there are those who ask in each of the successive movements where they should settle and stay, that they spend a time of close to 16 months to two years in each area. You see, Dear ones, we have found that in the human, this is the time that is needed to begin the assimilation process. If you ask for one to come and live near you or with you, this is the time required for the complete integration process. Do you understand?

Answer: "I understand what you're requesting; I don't understand the complete process."

It is a process that begins on the outer periphery of a Golden City Vortex, a 20- to 30-mile flux to the outer outside fringe area of the Vortex. Of course, it is best to live within the Vortex, but for those who wish to just assimilate energies, they can also live at the outside. It is our request that they stay there in the integration and assimilation mode for sixteen months, twenty months, or twenty-four months, depending upon how quickly the energies are assimilated. Then, they can move a little closer in, not yet to the Star. They can do this in successive motions, until they feel the integration of the energies, and then, in that final motion, move onward to the Star. For you see, Dear ones, that is where the higher knowledge can be given. That is where the greater assimilation of the energies occurs. Questions?

STAR ENERGIES

Question: "Yes. Are you versed in the current cities on the planet that exist in the Star area of Gobean, or towns?"

Let me do a quick scan. Now, I AM following Akashic Records. Proceed.

Question: "Is there a preference in the Star of Gobean that you would ask us to move to? A specific location?"

As always with the entry of the Ray Force is the strongest pulsation of the energy matter. You see, Dear ones, Dear hearts, this is the highest concentration of the energy within itself. Now, even upon the entryway into the Star, for those who are not ready for these higher and finer energies, it may be best to enter first into the Star within a 30- to 40-mile radius and onward to the greater energy force, which is from 20 miles to the central point. Do you understand?

Answer: "Yes."

Within twenty miles is, of course, better. Do you see how this interim instruction works simultaneously with the sound and light force?

Question: "What you're saying is that the inner instruction would be heightened and intensified in that Star area?"

Yes, this is so. But it also allows a greater contact with the next realm of creation, reality and understanding, which is absolutely necessary to birth the New Time, the Golden Age. You see, in the Point of Perception, I outlined the scenario of simultaneous reality. This will be so in the Time of the Great Purification, the Time of Great Change, the Time of the Golden Age. Do you understand?

Question: "Yes. So, what you're saying is that in the Star area there will be access to the Fourth and Fifth Dimension?"

This is so, beloveds, Dear hearts. And it is absolutely essential for the work that you are carrying forward, for it brings forward a contact throughout the whole planet of the consciousness that you are carrying forward. For the location of this consciousness to be located in a 20-mile radius of the Stars allows for a greater sensitivity within the collective consciousness, for this work to stream forward into the whole of humanity. As we have stated before: as above, so below. And we are dealing now with the principle of collective consciousness, that of the mighty Unana.

CHOOSING A STAR

Response: "I see. Then your preference is that we move to the Star of Gobean."

Now, you can choose any Star that you feel the alignment to. Any of these will work for you. But for the sake of alignment to that mighty Blue Ray, it is this force that will change the role of mankind, and that is why this Star has been selected. The work that you carry forward actually impacts the work of the Green Ray [Shalahah] for healing and hope for humanity. And within the Green Ray there are components of the Will and a mighty alignment to wisdom within itself. The Green Ray, of course, brings forward that understanding from a technical perspective, and from a scientific point of view, but it also opens the great chamber in the heart. Now do you understand the relationship of Gobean and Shalahah (Green Ray)?

Answer: "Yes."

This, again, is of your choosing. And for that matter, even if you prefer, you may retreat to the city of Wahanee. Again, it is all within your choice.

Response: "It would be my preference for the Gobean center. However, is the way made clear for us to be able to achieve this?"

The way was made clear for you to gain spiritual evolution through the greater energies. And this is what was being brought forward several years prior. But you reached a level of spiritual knowledge, of spiritual assimilation, and it was time for you to move on, as is the current situation.

ON COMMUNITY

Response: "I understand. Is there any need, at a personal level, for us to help create a community in this area?"

If this is your desire, then so be it. But I caution you not to become diverted from the work at hand, as often times this is the case when you bring those who are of mixed vibration into the work that you are bringing forward. I hope you understand it to its fullest conclusion. However, the application and knowledge of the laws are realized through that mighty Law of Attraction; from those who bring a harmony, those who bring an alignment. But remember, if you bring them only to line your coffers, you may not be exercising this mighty law in action. It is important to understand that it is the Law of Harmony that creates abundance and onward, as set forth in the Twelve jurisdictions. These Laws of New Jurisprudence are based upon the forbearers, the Laws of Light and Sound. So, Dear hearts, Dear ones, remember always the mission that you have been given and its sacred stewardship.

Response: "I understand what you're saying. As far as the type of structure, what type of structure should we actually build? We have several . . . "

It has been noted in the Prophecies of Change, the prophecies designed to change your heart, which may change this world, that there are probabilities of wind forces from 300- to 400-miles per hour with polar shift. Now with just gale forces, these are tornado-type winds, which can exceed, at times, up to 500 miles per hour. But in other areas, and in the area in question, if you would give it to me, I then may answer.

Response: "We are considering Greer."

PROPHECIES OF CHANGE

Now, it is important to understand that there can be touch-down tornadoes, which will have wind forces of 200- to 280-miles per hour in this area, so prepare your structure for these types of weather disturbances. These are caused by electro-magnetic fluxes, huge thunderstorms that will hit this area during the Time of the Great Monsoon. The Great Monsoon will come after the Time of the Great Fire. This we have outlined in Map Number Four. [See: I AM America Six-Map Scenario Map.] Now, I can give you, if you so choose, more specific understanding. Once you make the decision to move into an area, I can give you the records for that area, to bring forth the proper conditions.

A VALLEY

Question: "Is Greer close enough to Mount Baldy for your purposes?"

Now, let me scan. Yes. This will work, for it carries a high vibration, not only from Mount Baldy, but there is another mountain in the area that carries within it a vein of mixed alchemical substances. These mineral substances leak their energies into a valley area, which is channeled through the valley. Do you understand?

Question: "Yes. Do they channel through the river that comes from Mount Baldy?"

Of course, these mineral substances can be found in most rivers and from areas of such a high nature. The water impregnates the area with this Vibration of Gobean and the Master Teacher of that mighty Ray in action, El Morya.

Question: "If there were another parcel of land available closer to Mt. Baldy, would that be more in alignment with the needs?"

As I said in our discussions earlier, one must consider the Prophecies of Map Number Four and this fire zone, for, you see, once upon the entry into the Time of Change, one must understand that these changes will occur then for many, many decades.

So, it is best to deal with water that comes from a pure source. This is why, within twenty miles of the central part of Gobean, within itself, the water sources are kept at a purer level. Do you understand?

Answer: "Yes. There are springs and small creeks coming from the mountain. All right. Then I understand. We will look for a suitable location close to the mountain."

I AM here to serve. Do you have questions?

SACRED ARCHITECTURE

Question: "Yes. As far as a building structure, we have, potentially decided upon personal homes. They would be dome-style structures that would be made of concrete and steel reinforcement. The other thought that crosses my mind is the Golden City structure. Would that be a suitable home structure?"

These structures have been provided to raise consciousness. They are given so that one may gain access to fourth- and fifth-dimensional levels of understanding, to achieve communion with the Master Teacher of that Vortex. Now, this will all depend upon the conditions of the Earth at the time. Gold is suitable to arc the energy from each of the doorways. Do you understand?

Answer: "Yes I do."

However, if it is unattainable at that time, copper can also work to some degree to gain this type of energy momentum. This can be done through a simple lining of each of what you would call meridian points, or a lei-line, within the Vortex structure of the construction. Residential homes, again, must carry the safety measure for winds up to 280 miles per hour. Different areas, of course, will vary with this requirement. There will also be some minor earth movement that will be felt through the impact of a meteor in your area. So, it is important to understand all the different possibilities that may occur. However, the Golden City structure, within itself, has been given to assist and enhance spiritual development and raise consciousness to gain entry into the higher levels of understanding.

Question: "I understand what you are saying, but is it suitable as a home?"

A TEMPLE

For those who have the eyes to see and the ears to hear, it may be suitable, however, it is best to be seen as a temple.

Response: "I see."

There will be those who could live within it to become a caretaker. Do you understand?

Answer: "Yes."

However, for those who do live in this manner, it is important that food is prepared in a certain way and that no food of animal substance be prepared within this type of structure. For, you see, that brings a layering of vibration and it is important to keep the vibration of such a structure at the highest possible potential. This is not to say that this structure will not work; however, it is to keep the energy at a level of purity.

Question: "I see. All right. That answers two questions. The third question is that Greer is extremely expensive and at, present time, is not within our budgetary abilities, considering all our other obligations. Is there something you would suggest so that we may become free of our karma, our debt here, so that we may move on in a very easy and rapid manner?"

REMEMBER THE RHYTHM OF CYCLES

The property that you seek exists upon a ridge, which is a bit lower from that of a property that you have already seen. This would be attainable and usable for your purposes. However, again, I strongly urge and remind you to keep up the work at hand. Keep the message of I AM America moving forward. It is important always to keep this flow of knowledge streaming out into the hearts of humanity, for then this energy can be matched equally. Do you understand?

Answer: "I understand."

This is all built upon the principle of momentum, which we have studied before. It is also built upon, and you know this well, that cycle of rhythm.

Question: "Yes, I understand what you're saying. One other question that I have."

Proceed.

Question: "Lori has been continuing on with additional studies of the Vedic work and with the history of mankind through the origins of Sumeria. Are these truly related to you?"

PLANETARY SCHOOLROOMS

They are all related to all. You see, the Earth, within its own framework, is a mighty schoolroom. There are many different genetic life streams, so to speak, which have come here and impregnated themselves. Each of these, in its own time, has left to move onto other schoolrooms, to achieve other goals. You see, as we have stated before, this is a love-in-action planet. And the various life streams from various planets, when they are ready to bring about their souls to this greater understanding, bring about the process. Do you understand?

Answer: "Yes, I do."

So, when one says there is a great harvest or a great collection of souls, it is so. You see, these souls are then readied to leave the Earth Plane and Planet and move onward to other experiences to bring greater perfection.

SPIRITUAL MEMORY

Question: "Is it that time when the souls actually remember?"

Oh, of course. And in between embodiment the soul truly knows. Memory has been wiped during embodiments because that time is a cycle of complete forgetfulness. Yet, this all works together to serve a greater understanding, to serve a greater collective awakening. But, you see, as Lord Macaw, has outlined, each of the Ray Forces reaches its maturation in its own time and in its own place. Now, when I speak of these as Ray(ces), do you understand?

Question: "You're speaking of Ray Forces functioning through the genetics?"

A FAMILY OF THE RAYCES

This is certain. This is so, Dear one. What I also would like to impart to you is that there were other civilizations that existed way before those in Sumeria, Babylon and Mesopotamia. That is the story of the civilization that is related to Aryan. [See: Points of Perception.] However, there were also those life-streams related to Atlantean, those life streams related to Lemurian, and also to other Kingdoms which existed prior to that. This Earth is a great schoolroom, and periodically, through change within itself, it allows a greater education for the Ray(ces) to come forward in their greater understanding. But indeed, for the time that you are dealing with now, Earth continues to be a great cradle of civilization and school for the Aryans.

Question: "I understand. So in this time period, even you are part of this Aryan time period?"

Yes, it is so. And through the perfection of consciousness, through the use of the Violet Flame, all can raise their consciousness and successive embodiment to another level of understanding, to another dimension of being. And then the soul is readied and taken to a new schoolroom, to a new set of circumstances. Do you understand?

Answer: "Yes, so, in a sense, we belong to a family group."

This is so—in the same way that you belong to a graduating class and to a family. But, in a family, does it not have many cousins?

Answer: "Very true."

So, this Aryan time is, in this essence, a family. There are several cousins who also embodied at the same time, and they may, or may not, leave at the time of graduation. They may stay or they may move on to a total perceiving schoolroom. You see, occasionally one great avatar—one great adept—is brought in to lead the masses as a teacher, to bring an understanding in that collective consciousness.

Response: "I see and we've had, I suppose, several of these."

THE TWELVE ADEPTS

They are always sent in groups of twelve. And there are always twelve present at all times upon the planet.

Question: "There are twelve now?"

There are indeed twelve now; twelve in physical embodiment, bringing their teachings. Now, some are not known to the public, but they radiate their energy from where they are located. But indeed, there are always twelve adepts who are always upon the Earth Plane. Then, there are those such as we who work, and there are indeed always twelve of us who work at one level of consciousness to bring teachings forward from that understanding of ONE, and, again above us, another twelve. Always there are 144 of us, always working to move consciousness further, and so on. Do you understand?

Answer: "Yes I do."

TWELVE SACRED TEACHINGS

This is where that teaching comes from. Now, do you understand why there are Twelve Jurisdictions? These are twelve sacred spiritual teachings.

Question: "Then there truly are twelve planets in our three-dimensional realm?"

Indeed, there are, however, it is important to not get lost in that teaching at this moment. For there will be further teachings that will be given at the right time and at the right place. So let us deal now with the work at hand.

SPIRITUAL LINEAGE

Question: "As you wish. Lord Apollo, he is our sponsor?"

He is a grand teacher, and one of my teachers.

Question: "I see. So he came at a time before us?"

As you have a grandfather, a great-grandfather, or an ancestor who has brought you teachings, this is also the way to understand and regard Lord Apollo.

Question: "But an ancestor always sponsors the progeny. Is this not true?"

Yes, but you do understand that this is the awakening of the heart, as I stated before. There is this vast difference between the progeny and the awakening of the genetic. In this time that we are dealing with, because all genetics are so closely related, as I have stated before, now our focus is upon the awakening of the Chamber of the Heart [Eight-sided Cell of Perfection] and the use of the Seventh Chakra. These two things will allow this larger family to enter at Will into a New Dimensional understanding, a New Dimensional awareness. This, of course, is achieved with greater fluency and accuracy in the Stars. You see, Dear ones, there is a greater pulsation with the vibral core of the Earth.

LOSS, OR A NEW WAY?

The Earth, right now, in its simultaneous realities, is offering a great flora and fauna of lessons. It is through the backdrop of this great flora and fauna that many understandings of how we shall all evolve will be understood. Remember before, Dear hearts, Dear ones, when I said there will be a Time of Great Change and one man will perceive it with great sorrow, one will perceive it as a great change, and one will perceive it with great joy! Each of these is dimensional awareness. One perhaps has his focus on what he has lost in his bank, the home that he has lost—all of these are attachments to the physical world. Then, there is one who perceives it with grief, for loss of love, for loss of all things that he was attached to at an emotional level. Then, there is the man who perceives this only as a change and a new way for him to see things, a new way to have experience. Then, there is the one who sees the opening of the gateway, the spirit world, the true existence, the consciousness of Unana. These I've outlined before in the "Point of Perception." It is an understanding that within you, with the activation of your Chamber of the Heart lies the out-picturing of consciousness for creation.

THE ASCENSION

You see, Dear ones, Dear hearts, it is indeed a Time of Co-creation, a time when the activation of the Will can bring forth the finest results. But understand, too, that with the assistance of beloved Babajeran and through the work of the Brotherhood of Breath, Light and Sound, the Brotherhood of this White Lodge—this "white-light" lodge—we are now able to manifest a Divine Intervention. This will bring forward, at Will, a greater understanding of your true divinity—an upliftment—raising the physical body into Ascension, eliminating the craving for the requirement of that cycle of constant rebirth into the Earth Plane. Do you understand?

Question: "Yes. So the Ascension is really an interdimensional movement?"

Indeed, this is so. This is why we have outlined areas such as Ascension Valley, such as the Transportation Vortex located in Coeur d' Alene, Idaho. Do you understand?

Question: "And these will be achieved without external technology?"

They will be achieved through understanding and opening the self, through awakening the perfection within the heart, through opening the Seventh Chakra.

Response: "I see. I understand."

There are also teachings that will assist this. And they will come at a later date, however, so that you can understand them in general terms.

Response: "This is most enlightening and joyous. I thank you very much. I have no further questions."

In that case my beloveds, I must return to the celebrations at Shamballa. Know that always I AM here at your request. In service to that Mighty Breath of Light and Action of God, I AM Saint Germain.

CHAPTER EIGHT

Memory is Freedom
Teachings on developing true memory.

Greetings, Beloveds. In that Mighty Violet Flame, I AM Saint Germain, and I stream forth on that Mighty Violet Ray of mercy, compassion and forgiveness.

As usual, Dear hearts, I request your permission to come forward.

Response: "Please, Saint Germain, come forward. You are most welcome."

TRANSMUTATION AND TRANSFORMATION

Transmutation. Transmutation of all which brings discord into your life, which brings pain and suffering, which brings ills that seemingly keep you off the path and keep you from understanding the United Brotherhoods and Sisterhoods.

Transformation. May transformation now stream forth into the hearts of all mankind. May transformation guide the Will of men. May transformation now stream forward to this Planet Divine and may this Mighty Freedom Star [Babajeran] now take its position within the universe.

TIME AND PERCEPTION

Dear ones, Dear hearts, there is so little time left, yet at other times it may seem there is so much time. Time drags on, yet the minutes and the seconds tick. The awakening is at hand, yet it seems to drag so. Why are these perceptions of time brought forward in such a way that it is difficult for mankind to understand? You see, Dear ones, time is a matter of perception. It is always a matter of understanding. The moment of when you grasp onto your own reality, you will see, Dear ones, that the truth and treasures of heaven lie not in the illusion of Maya, nor in time, but in the eternal wonderment of understanding true love.

THE LAW OF LOVE

The Law of Love, as dear Sananda has spoken, "how does one bring forth this transformation, where this eternal Law of Love is lived everyday," is brought forward into the human existence, and then allowed to move on into a fuller and a richer understanding. The Law of Love, as we have taught before, is the beginning and the end. The Law of Love is the true Alpha, the true Omega. It is the one law that serves all of humanity at all times, and yet, love itself is the drink that all are questing and thirsting for. All are looking for love to fill their lives, and yet there is not one upon the Earth Plane and Planet, in this moment, who feels that his Cup is filled to the brim with true love and the understanding that brings supreme peace. This great truth and treasure comprise the law that brings forward transformation for all upon the Earth Plane and Planet. It brings forth an understanding that goes beyond time and beyond minutes and the ticking clock. It is an understanding that brings peace supreme and allows countries to put down their arms against one another; allowing seemingly bitter enemies to shake hands, and join in a mutual cause. It is this Law of Love that heals all wounds and brings one to that higher understanding, and yet it is so hard to bring about its implementation. Why is this so?

LAW OF ONE

Lifetime after lifetime, we collect experiences, or that collective memory of experience. It imbeds itself into the Records of Akasha, and the soul then carries the memory of every experience with it through successive embodiments. Wouldn't it be a bright New Day if that tape that is carried, that record that is carried, is erased eternally and replaced only through that Mighty Law of Love—the Law of ONE? Then all that is then carried—the hurts, the wounds—which have caused the need for successive embodiments, the need to remain trapped in the physical—are then removed. Oh, but what a day that would be, Dear ones, Dear hearts. It is that simple.

MEMORY AND LIBERATION

When we call upon that Mighty Violet Flame of Mercy, Transmutation and Forgiveness, essentially at the electromagnetic level, we are erasing all memories of the past—memories that hold you from your eternal freedom. Again, it is a matter of perception for you see, Dear ones, Dear hearts, our memories serve either for our higher understanding and for achieving a higher reality, or our memories hold us prisoner, trapped in the confines of the flesh, in successive rounds of birth and death. How can we achieve this liberation?

REMOVING THE DEATH CONSCIOUSNESS

It is a type of detachment—detaching from outcome, loosening the rope of expectation, but it is even more, my Dear ones, a calling upon that transmutative law, the Mighty Violet Flame.
Decree:
"May freedom ring supreme in the hearts of all mankind.
Mighty Violet Flame, blaze in, through and around all situations of memory that hold me from my eternal freedom,
that hold me from my true self.
Mighty Violet Flame, come forth now and remove such memories that may keep me bound into the rounds of birth and death.
Mighty Violet Flame, come through and set me free.
Mighty Violet Flame let me truly BE."

You see, Dear ones, it is that simple. Removing a death consciousness requires embracing the consciousness of love eternal. Love is that one reality, that one true treasure; the one true vibration. It is ever present. It is as it is. To embrace the true Law of Love in its totality is to be set free. Now, before I continue, are there any questions?

Question: "Yes. This question pertains to memory."

Proceed.

Response and Question: "As you have just stated, memory can be for the higher purpose or for the entrapment in the flesh. It is obvious, in speaking to people and in my own instance, most people have no interest in remembering other lifetimes or embodiments because they feel extremely overwhelmed by the current one they're in. As you have just stated, is it to be understood that when you choose to remember, for the higher purpose of freeing yourself, that the memory will come back in a way in which it will free you? That is my question."

TRUE MEMORY AND IMMORTALITY

Memory is indeed one of the keys to obtaining the treasures of heaven, to obtaining your immortality. It is one of the keys to the prison you're trapped in called "illusion." True memory, seen and viewed from its true context, is what we speak of, a "heavenly treasure" of memory. Now, let me explain.

TIME OF TESTING

Indeed you are all, Dear ones, Dear hearts, living in a Time of Great Testing—a Time of Testing once known as tribulation. Yet we now prefer to call it a Time of Testing, for, you see, you are never given a test that you are not ready for. This test is not given as a punishment; this test is given so you may examine and understand the skills you have gained toward your path of spiritual liberation. There was a time when humanity existed in a purer state. There is not one soul now upon this plane of illusion, or Maya, who does not understand or know the truth of this, for memory is embedded within it. Do you see how memory embeds within?

THE ORAL TRADITION

All who hear these words, all who understand this principle and this concept, know within their hearts that they existed in another time, where their being was ONE with God, ONE with Source, ONE unified to a cause of life.

I refer to God as a source of light, as a source of the Causeless Cause, as the source of desireless desire. All understand and know the purity that lies within themself. All feel the urge within the heart, which is that urge to move forward, to know the truth of that memory embedded within themself. The truth of that memory is the Unfed Flame of Love, Wisdom, and Power; true love, true wisdom and true devoted power, that is the eternal memory. The Divine Spark is within all, and all instantly recognize this great eternal truth. But beyond this ONE memory that we all share, and unify toward is the history of who and what humanity is, where humanity came from and where this great schoolroom is heading. Mankind, at one time, contained a greater capacity to learn and to retain, which was known as memory. Of course, I speak of a time before books were required, before the written word was required, and Oral Tradition flourished. That is why our teachings are always brought forward in the Oral Tradition, for, through this tradition, a consciousness is able to pervail. This all-important consciousness is ever expanding, ever transforming, ever transmuting. Even in this moment, as you listen to my words, your consciousness is being impacted at a memory level. Of course, it is not the words themselves, but the intention of the consciousness that you now feel permeating your memory. It is almost as air feeds the flame, that ember of consciousness and memory existing in all upon the Earth Plane and Planet that must now be allowed to expand so that true memory, like the treasure in heaven, is restored among humanity.

RECALL YOUR DIVINITY

There were those who understood the cycles of time—the cycles of time within illusion—and knew that collectively a challenge would come to the memories of those souls trapped in the prison, and that it would become much more difficult for them to absorb knowledge and to work beyond the memory. They would have to keep a written record in order to understand and grow, in order to transmute and move beyond the schoolroom. This is the time you are now experiencing. Some call it Kali, some call it tribulation, but for those, who begin to understand the true difference of illusion and reality, it is known as a Time of Testing. Remember, Dear ones,

Dear hearts, that you are ready for this test. Know, Dear ones, that your memory is now developed and ready to recall its true divinity.

"LISTEN WITH YOUR HEART"

It has been said to "listen with open ears." What does this mean? When one listens with true open ears, the ears are not only connected to the brain, but they are connected to the true memory, and that true memory is connected to the Law of Love. Have you not heard the saying, "Do not listen with your ears, listen with your heart?" This is what is being said. This great truth eternal, true open memory, true memory that understands, is memory based upon that one law eternal, the Law of Love.

A THOUSAND EYES

Through the open heart, the understanding beyond, one is able to see a situation, not from just one perception, but through the eyes, "the thousand eyes of many." Memory is then recalled. For instance, the murderer may finally see the suffering of the parent, the suffering of the victim, the suffering of the husband or wife and the ripple effect that each action causes. Through the Law of Love, one is able to clearly see the grander purpose that is fulfilled, the grander teaching that comes forward which, in the moment as murderer, only play one small role but yet may prove to be central in instigating many roles through the "thousand eyes." Do you understand?

Answer: "Yes. I understand."

This is perception—true perception and true memory. I have said before, "Things do not happen to (people), things happen with." This is of most importance to understand. To truly open the memory is to truly open the gates for the Law of Love. Now, simple exercises.

THE SEAMLESS GARMENT

How does one obtain a greater memory? First, call upon that Mighty Violet Ray. This will pave the pathway for a clear intention and for all obstructions around you to seamlessly fall away. But it is also important to actually put this into action, in the meditative state, to begin to recall the lifetimes of the past. You see, when the chela begins to recall his former lifetimes, he is able to understand the role that he played, as only one set of the "thousand eyes." The tragedy that happens to humans is that they see themselves, as only individualized egos, and they see the one lifetime as a "king or queen," as the mountaintop of their whole existence. Then they see that one lifetime as the "beggar" as the one lifetime of punishment. Yet, all lifetimes are woven together to create the seamless garment. Each experience is like a thread that weaves that garment that the soul then wears. But how else is each thread brought together into that magnificent seamless garment, than through memory? Woven together and held in the consciousness of memory, each thread is ever important; each experience is part of the garment. Each experience is not woven to, it is woven with one garment.

Dear ones, Dear hearts, recalling each past life is important, and I would suggest that you keep a journal of these experiences brought forth through meditation. Soon you will begin to see how each experience weaves the memory of you. Then call upon that Mighty Violet Ray of Mercy and Forgiveness and see the experiences, not in judgment, but see them as experiences that led you to understand knowledge of the ONE, the knowledge of the Law of Love.

Question: "Could you give us the definition of Maya?"

When I use the term "Maya," I speak of illusion. That is the Point of Perception seen only through duality, through only one set of eyes. But understand, that beyond illusion, is reality, where the eternal truth resides. When I use "Maya," it is to indicate that which is the nonperfected memory. It only contains part of; therefore, it implodes upon itself. It is, and I say this so that you will begin to understand, only a partial truth. How could there be but a partial truth? There are those who see their lifetime here as inconsequential because it is an experience only of illusion, yet, all serve the Plan Divine. Each plays its part in weaving that seamless garment of experience. So even the time that is spent in illusion, while it seems to be fruitless, is the fruit of a magnificent feast.

YOUR JOURNEY

So, Dear ones, never give up hope. Forge forward, even though at times you feel worried, at times you feel tired, and wish only to lay the body aside, to move into the greater understanding. But know that you always carry that greater truth with you. Your journey here, yes, is only temporary, but your memory of this journey is a permanent memory. It becomes one of those experiences that becomes part of the greater you. The Maya, the illusion, is when you hold this experience as being the only you. The Maya, the illusion, is when you hold this moment as being the definition of you, yet it is not. The Law of Love is eternal. That Law of Love is the only truth to set your focus upon. Questions?

"WITHIN THE WAVE"

Question: "Could you give us a list of keys that will bring us freedom when we put them into action?"

I give to you this day the first key to focus on. That is to bring into your conscious memory the experiences of your past that have "created you" in this moment. Do you understand?

Answer: "Yes."

It is that simple. However, the retrieving of such memory is sometimes a very painful process. Why is it painful? Perceptions that you hold of an experience are illusive, for you see these experiences through judgment, or dual perception. You hold these experiences as happening to you, not happening with you. You see yourself as only one molecule instead of one part of a wave. You are included "within the wave." You are not included "without it."

Dear ones, Dear hearts, start to retrieve the memories of being "with," rather than memories of things happening "to you alone." Strive and go beyond a limited perception, and you will begin to see with a thousand eyes, and you will open to the Law of Love. Questions?

Question: "Yes. You've just said something, 'included within.' Are you saying that we, including yourself and other members of the hierarchy, are included within God and that all is here is the illusion?"

THE LIMITLESS I AM

We are but a small portion of that mighty, magnificent I AM. And even to fathom the all inclusiveness of that Mighty I AM, even to fathom but one sweet breath of that, is to touch a limitless motion. Now, Dear ones, Dear hearts, focus upon this that I give to you. Focus upon one step at a time. Yes, you are all included within that mighty heart, that mighty love of the I AM. And as each day that the I AM inhales and exhales, you are within. So be it. Questions?

BEYOND ILLUSION

Question: "Yes. May we take this transmission in its audio form and put it on our website?"

You may share all the teachings that I have given you with those who have the eyes to see and the ears to hear. There are those who mock you, those who say, "How could one ever achieve such communication?" But know this, it does exist beyond the dual eyes. There is a reality that exists beyond the small reality—that illusion that you are experiencing now. There is a time that exists beyond time. There is the eternal truth of love, and it binds us all as ONE to another. Dear ones. Questions?

Answer: "I have no further questions on the discourse you have just presented."

Then proceed with your other questions.

SERVICE AND BLESSINGS

Question: "As you are very well aware, we have made great sacrifice and worked diligently to bring this message to this Plane and this Planet, and in doing so we have incurred great expense, which, on one hand, has enabled us to move forward, but on another has encumbered us in this duality. It has been suggested that we do something in addition to this. Would you have any suggestions?"

Of course, this is all "Maya" again.
This is all illusion, but it is the path that you have chosen.

Response: "I understand, but I now choose a path where we can continue with this work without any encumbrance."

And so you desire to be free. You desire your liberation from illusion?

Answer: "Yes. At all levels."

You see, Dear ones, as I've spoken before of karma, and when I speak of this, I speak only of action and the actions we choose to take in the world. You have shared this message in many forms and, for that, we are grateful for your service. It was a service that was chosen with forethought, yet it was a service that was chosen through your free Will. It is odd for you now to question free Will when you are choosing to align yourself to such a mighty plan and such a mighty work. It is your choice always, Dear one, Dear heart, to bring forward even but one or two words of our transmissions. It is your choice always to share this information in whatever form is available for those to receive. We support all of these fine acts of generosity and kindness and they bring blessings unto you. They free you from other Karmic encumbrances. The work that you have done, the work that has been brought forward, has brought many blessings into your life, has it not?

Answer: "I agree."

And now, at this time, do you not feel more free than you ever have been?

Answer: "Yes."

This is where the focus and the attention must go. You must understand and give thanks for such a blessing within your life. However, the tortures of the world are also there, are they not?

Answer: "Yes, however, I take them much less seriously."

And is this not, again, the freedom that you speak of?

Answer: "Yes, it most certainly is."

It is a matter, again, of perception and how you see either with the "dual eyes" or a "thousand eyes." I do suggest that you look upon the great blessings brought forward in this work, and this will help to lessen the suffering of the debt that you feel, the heaviness of lack that you feel, when you begin to understand the great transmutation and transformation that you have brought forward, not only to yourself but to many, many others. It is important to understand the blessings that are brought forward in this work, the sweetness and the joy that it brings, for that is always the intention; that is always the purpose.

Response: "In my heart of hearts, I feel like I have just begun to get warmed up in bringing this message forward to the world."

It is always important to follow your heart, for when you follow your heart you are living only that Law of Love. That is the Divine Law. That is the Divine Law of the truth and the treasures of heaven. Questions?

"DEBT IS DOUBT"

Question: "Is there a way for us to continue to only do this and to satisfy the responsibilities that we have created in doing this?"

To bring balance forward with those past-due responsibilities, one must diligently call upon the Violet Flame to bring mercy, to bring compassion in all situations. That is most important—to call that forward, so that situations can begin to ease themselves. Situations can then begin to transmute themselves. The karmas, the actions that have been taken in the past, seem to follow us and become part of our present. One then feels chained to the past, feels he cannot move to any sort of present, or even visualize a future, until he is unfettered from the actions of the past. This is truly what you speak of when you speak of debt, for debt is indeed doubt. Debt is the measure of your doubt—your doubt of your divinity and of your service. Your doubt will impact what you give.

Response: "Whoa!"

It is indeed that measurement of a lack of confidence in what you are achieving. Call forth the Violet Ray. Call it forth to transmute all that doubt that you carry. Call it forth, Dear ones, Dear hearts. Questions?

Question: "Yes. It sounds like we need to call it forth daily, more than once a day. Transmute it. You are correct. I have doubted my worthiness to help any of you or the world and yet we have continued to do so. It is my desire to bring all of this to balance, to transmute the doubt and to love, and then all will be brought to balance. Is this not so?"

It is so, Dear one. The actions that you choose today indeed impact the world you will live in tomorrow; therefore, the chelas are often presented with, "Am I making a wise choice? Am I truly serving my path?" Do you see, Dear one? It was never promised to be easy, however, the reward is immeasurable. We are always here to give our assistance to you. Questions?

Answer: "Yes. As we have spoken, I can tell from the answers you have given that it would also be your preference that we stay focused on one mission."

Of course, this is always our first choice. However, we realize that the chelas who we work with still carry their karmas of the past and still create karmas presently that they will fulfill in the future. You see, Dear one, spend time in meditation, spend time looking with a "thousand eyes" and you will then begin to see, you will then begin to hear. It is much more important to understand this. Then, your actions will feel aligned with that great and Mighty Law of Love. The work you have brought forward is a blessing indeed. It cannot be measured at all by the doubt that you feel. May that doubt be a feeling only. When you allow it to pervade all action, it becomes an energy and a force unto itself. Do you understand?

Answer: "Yes. I apologize to you for letting my doubt encumber our work."

Then, let us now move forward in the light of a New Day. Let us now move forward, using the Violet Ray to transmute all sense of lack, all doubt that we feel, and to transmute the little Will to align itself to a greater Plan Divine. Understand, Dear heart, Dear one, that the work you have been given to do is one that you are perfectly prepared to handle. Have I not said before that all tests are for those who are properly prepared?

Answer: "Yes."

CHAPTER NINE

Golden Ray Compassion
Saint Germain on Ascension and the Gold Ray.

Greetings, Beloveds in that mighty Violet Ray. I AM Saint Germain and I stream forth on that mighty Violet Ray of Mercy, Compassion, and Forgiveness. As usual, Dear hearts, I request permission to come forward.

Response: "Please, Saint Germain, please come forward."

Greetings and salutations, Dear chelas, Dear students of mine. It has been some time since our last lesson and there is much information for me to impart to you this day. As stewards of this mighty ray of teaching and understanding, as this information is being dispensed through you, it is important that it is brought forward within a rhythm, or sattva. We realize of course, at times it is important for you to conclude or carry out your daily activities; however, it is also important for you to understand the rhythm and the harmony of the lessons that are being given to you. We ask you to schedule time into your life to bring this information forward in that harmony and absolute rhythm of the spheres.

THE GOLD RAY

Dear ones, Dear hearts, we shall be of assistance to you, so that this important information may be carried forth for the chelas and the students whose ears and eyes are now open. This is most important, as the mighty Golden Ray has opened its vibration upon the Earth Plane and Planet and there are many now who are readied in their vibration to receive this higher information, to receive this higher knowledge. As you understand, the Golden Ray is bringing forth many new discoveries in your scientific community, many new discoveries that are coming forth in the Information Age. This is of course very important to those whose eyes and ears are on the pulse of this information but it is also important for the student, the chela of the Ascended Masters, to understand the importance of the Golden Ray.

Not only does this great alignment force of the Golden Ray bring forth an understanding of the past karmas and the past lives that have now been brought to a conclusion in their understanding, but the Golden Ray readies one to understand a new vibration, a new level. This Golden Ray is being brought forward to bring a higher frequency and vibration to the spiritual awakening.

PREREQUISITE USE OF THE VIOLET FLAME

Dear chelas, now listen, for this is of great importance. Understand that the Golden Ray brings forth its higher frequency vibration within the Stars of all Golden City Vortices. But know this: that if one were to hear this information and try to utilize it for the first time, it would take a great integration of the higher frequency of the Violet Flame to be able to bring the Golden Ray forward. So those who wish to utilize the Golden Ray in its higher frequency must have applied and used the Violet Flame for at least a two-year period, that is a full twenty-four months.

PREPARING THE BODY FOR ASCENSION

Those who are prepared know that they can now move to the Stars in this higher frequency and utilize the energy of the Golden Ray to bring a greater understanding and knowledge of the new dimensions. Now when I say "the new dimensions," understand this, Dear ones, Dear chelas, that there is no such thing as a new dimension, for all dimensions have always existed. Since time was created for your knowledge and understanding, also know that this higher frequency does exist and it is important for you to access it. In accessing this greater knowledge of the dimensions, the soul is then readied to move forward into the completion of the Ascension. This has always been the purpose and the intention of the Stars of the Golden City Vortices, to prepare the body for the Ascension process.

PURIFICATION IN THE STAR

Now that you have brought several of the stalwart chelas to this great center, the Star of Gobean, you will hear reports from them that they will begin an alignment process in their physical, astral, mental, and emotional bodies. This great alignment process is very important to bring a greater purity, to bring a purification forward. Honor and allow this purification process to flow throughout your being, Dear ones, Dear hearts, for this brings one to that alchemy of the true soul. The union with the soul is most important at this time; for you see, the monad in its journey in illusion begins to over-identify with the body, over-identify with the illusion. But understand, in the grand interplay of the rays, that there is more that lies beneath, as you have always known. It is this contact with the soul that is most important, for one begins to understand the consequences of past lives and the consequences of past actions, and then moves them all into the transformation of that burning and alchemizing Violet Ray.

> May the Violet Ray stream forth into the hearts and souls
> of those who are ready to serve the Cause Divine.
> May this Golden Ray, in its greater harmony,
> adjunct to this mighty Violet Ray,
> now bring its own harmony forward.
> May the Golden Ray now initiate the consciousness
> to move into the new dimensions.
> May this new initiation now serve this grand and greater plan.

Dear ones, Dear hearts, the Brotherhoods and the Sisterhoods of Light and Sound eagerly await your arrival . . . eagerly await your presence.

> Mighty I AM Presence, stream forth
> into the heart of the Great Central Sun.
> Mighty I AM Presence, stream forth
> into that mighty service of the Great White Brotherhood.

A DIVINE INHERITOR

Dear ones, Dear hearts, this initiation into this greater consciousness will not only increase your telepathic abilities but you will notice, in your dream states at night, more lucidity coming to your consciousness. A greater understanding of the interplay of past lives and how these journeys now serve this greater cause will unite your soul with an understanding of true compassion . . . of true peace . . . of true united Brotherhood and Sisterhood. You see, Dear ones, Dear hearts, this has always been our cause, to bring peace upon this Earth; to bring a greater understanding, a greater evolution, and the knowledge that the true self is a Divine Inheritor of the Kingdom.

THE PATH OF THE HEART

Beloved Brother Sananda was sent, in his journey to the Earth Plane and Planet, as Jesus the Christ, to bring this teaching and knowledge forward. And Buddha followed this great teaching, to show that these teachings could be internalized, that compassion could truly be felt among one another. You see, Dear ones, this greater compassion is a truth among those who come to the Earth Plane and Planet, even those of the alien consciousness. What they seek is this knowledge of true love, true compassion, and how the heart-felt emotions open and initiate the consciousness into a greater understanding.

Until one enters into the path of the heart, the "true blood that washes the feet," one is not truly and absolutely prepared to understand the higher consciousness. Understand that there is no remote viewer . . . understand that there is no mind control . . . understand that there is no unlawful government out there that can take, steal, or even listen in on any information of this type until they have opened that heart of compassion. It is truly the heart of compassion that opens all to this greater understanding, the greater love, and the journey that awaits within.

Dear ones, Dear hearts, open . . . open to this greater compassion . . . open to this greater understanding. This is only done through that mighty path of experience, is it not? As I have always said, "it is in the laboratory of the self where one truly carries out experience." Test the law for yourself and know yourself. Then and only then will you know the truth that I speak.

COMPASSION AND THE FIRE OF ALCHEMY

The experiences that one has here on the Earth Plane and Planet at times, yes, open terrible horrors and fears that are held lifetime after lifetime. Those terrible karmic connections, however, have woven a handshake through pain and suffering. Where is that drink of refreshment? It lies in that Cup of Compassion. When one has truly suffered, then one truly understands and can offer their hand, a helping hand in understanding and knowledge. But until one opens the soul, until one opens the heart and sees that bank of the past experience of tears, of suffering, one may think, "I shall just move forward for myself this day. I shall only serve my common desire." Beyond the common desire lies the truth of all. Beyond the common self, beyond just this one embodiment, lies the true self, the Divine Inheritor.

One may ask, "How do I open Akasha? How do I open the template, so I may peer within and see this mighty truth in action?" Dear ones, Dear hearts, it is as simple as the use of the Violet Flame. At a scientific level, the alchemizing fires transmute the cause and the effect of all past actions that may keep you from your eternal gift and blueprint of Ascension. For you see, Dear ones, consciousness was never meant to be trapped. Consciousness is meant to unfold, to grow beyond the limits of the flesh, and spring free. From that once seed, eternally it branches onward and upward into greater understanding of unity and the realms of beauty. When one views this true effect, they see the beauty that lies within and without . . . they see, understand, and know the harmony of the great eternal spheres . . . they realize that the journey is not a journey in pain and suffering but the journey is one of joy and ultimate glee. Only in this dance of consciousness can the soul truly then be free to understand its true self, the divinity within.

SURRENDER TO VICTORY

Compassion is truly the way of understanding and relating to another. Develop compassion within and share it among yourselves. Work hard to stay out of the lower vibrations of judging one another, of saying and sharing hurtful thoughts toward one another. For you see, the thought is a vibration. Even to think such a thought brings it forward in a manifestation, as if it were a spoken word. Understand, Dear ones, Dear hearts, that only in harmony, only in true compassion, does the soul then surrender to its ultimate victory. The new dimensions await. The Violet Flame and the Golden Ray are both here now to bring you this glorious assistance. Now I shall open the floor for questions.

"TWO SHALL COME FORTH"

Question: "What is the difference between the Divine Complement, the soul mate, and twin flames?"

There is this desire among humanity to know itself. For you see, within the dual consciousness, the soul is only allowed to take one sex at a time. It is either male or it is female; however, there are those of course who work to embrace the two types of consciousness at once and the body holds on the left and the right hand side, the female and the male consciousness. However, the dominant consciousness expresses itself in the embodiment and, therefore, the lessons are brought forward, are they not? For as we have known, there are those cultures that honor the feminine and then those cultures that honor the male.

The monad, in its great journey and the remembrance of itself, works to bring a greater unity forward, so it may move into that glory and power of the Ascension. Prior to the advent of the Golden Ray coming forward, the soul must meet its other half, its twin half. That other half was brought forward at the time of its first expression into physical embodiment. For, you see, when a soul first enters into the Earth Plane and Planet, it enters not as one but it enters as two: "and two shall come forth from the breath of the holiest of holies." This is the law that is written eternal. This was the law that was brought forth for the embodiment of humanity. These two twin rays or twin souls share that great Garden of Existence (Eden). This is the story of Adam and Eve, as you would know now in your culture. One does not come first but they are brought forward in that one great and mighty breath. They are brought forth from their Mighty Logos, from the Great Creator. All praises to this process. All praises and I bow to it eternally.

COMPLEMENT OF ENERGY

Dear ones, Dear hearts, this is how you have been brought forward into your existence. Now this twin beloved, through the cycles of reincarnation, re-embodiment, and that mighty web of illusion weaving itself over the soul, is brought now to a place perceived as an imbalance. Sometimes, these mighty twin rays or twin flames have not seen one another for millions of years. Now, how are they brought back together? They are brought back together through the Divine Complement of energies, through understanding and knowing that energy of the higher order will ultimately seek its own level. Now, maybe one of these beloveds has called upon this mighty Sacred Fire and used the energies for the highest Will Divine? Then and only then are they able to pull upon the vibrational level of the other, for does not like harmony seek like harmony?

MEETING THROUGH THE ASCENSION

Often there are those who meet one another preparing for that Ascension process. That is the process of moving to the higher levels of understanding ... moving beyond the grasp of illusion ... moving beyond the web of re-embodiment. Sometimes the result is a good one and the work that flows through these two streams of consciousness brings a balance and they are allowed to reunite as ONE. However, if the preparation of the souls is not completed through that mighty alchemizing Violet Ray, continuous disharmonies and conflicts within their webs of karmas, actions, and unfulfilled desires, may cast the souls deeper and farther apart from one another. And yet their unity cries for each other: "my other half . . . my twin . . . my beloved."

REMOVE LIMITATION AND BONDAGE

Now let us understand this at a greater unity of cause. You are all united, as all of you are Brothers and Sisters in the Earth Plane and Planet. You are all ONE within this mighty kernel of great truth and light. Perhaps you seek this energy only through that special one; you seek to know and understand yourself only through the uniting with that mighty soul that is the other half of you. The work of the Golden Ray has been brought forward to complete this process, so limitation is no longer on the Earth Plane and Planet. For those souls that have been trapped in this web of time, the Golden Ray is now brought forward to bring a higher vibration, a higher frequency and understanding. Open your heart to compassion, Dear ones, Dear chelas, and the mirror of illusion cracks and you face your eternal self. Questions?

SEPARATION AND THE WEB OF ILLUSION

Question: "I am still a little confused. The soul comes through into experience as one half and one half and is it only through re-aligning their energies that they are reunited?"

This is true, Dear one, Dear heart. When energy is taken and understood at its higher frequency, the consciousness understands that it was the true sense of separation that parted the two halves in the journey of time. Now, how do we gather forces together but through understanding the unity of all of consciousness. In this greater unity and harmony, the web of illusion is cracked and the soul no longer feels the separateness. It feels the completion. This begins the process of Ascension. This Divine Arcing, this Divine Harmony of the Rays, comes forward now and serves a greater plan. For you see, then that Law of Sympathetic Resonance and Sympathetic Harmonies supersedes the Law of Duality, does it not? Understand, know, and apply these greater laws and the journey continues in its upward ascent of joy.

REUNITING THROUGH THE GOLD RAY

Dear ones, Dear hearts, the work of the Golden Ray is now allowing many souls that have not seen one another for thousands of journeys into the Earth Plane and Planet to reunite with a great joy and understanding of this higher completion. Of course, there will be those brief encounters and perhaps one is not ready to join and move forward. But understand, now the Law of Unity prevails. Unana, a higher consciousness that is brought forward through this Golden Ray, has a greater understanding and will now lead many souls into the path of Ascension.

ASCENSION AND THE GOLDEN CITY STAR

This greater unity and harmony comes forward through the service of beloved Mother Earth, Babajeran as we know her. Babajeran has offered, in the same way that she offered to clothe you in your physical bodies, to release this hold and allow the higher frequencies that come through the Stars of each of the Golden City Vortices to unite the consciousness into a higher understanding of a collective unity and consciousness. As Dear Sananda has said, "the time is at hand, the awakening is here. The seconds and the minutes tick." Make your choice, Dear ones, Dear hearts.

The work of the Golden City Vortices and the work of the Stars of these great focuses of higher energy come to assist in that alignment process. Now realize this: do not take the limitation into your consciousness of meeting your other half before entering into that path of Ascension. Know that your other half awaits there, beyond the web of illusion. Know that your true self is complete within itself. Wait not to find union in the Earth Plane but find that union of Divine Harmonies. Questions?

AN ALIGNMENT PROCESS

Question: "The very fact that the Golden Cities now exist energetically and that we can even communicate with you, is that not a crack in the illusion?"

It is the Divine Order and Timing, as it always has been and always shall be. SO BE IT!

Question: "So are you saying, it is time for the global graduation and moving on from this realm of consciousness to the other realms?"

Only consciousness held at a certain frequency or vibration can limit itself. You see, Dear ones, it is as simple as pouring the consciousness into the Cup. Is this Cup half full or is this Cup half empty? What is the perception of how I see things? Am I complete or am I incomplete? Am I ready to move forward or am I still filled with fears? Is my consciousness blocked? Can it no longer receive? Is my consciousness moving forward? Can I see the Divine Interplay and Harmony? This is the work of the alignment process that I have explained in previous discourse. To understand and accept the past and then use it as a building block, will move you into a greater understanding and knowledge. Then the past will no longer serve as a karmic detriment, as a path of previous action to be stuck in, as muck and mire.

Dear ones, Dear hearts, this alignment process brings us into understanding that the work and the Divine Intervention of that mighty Violet Ray is there at all times to lift you into higher consciousness, to lift you into higher frequency. The Golden Ray comes as a twin ray in service with the Violet Ray, to bring an even greater harmony for those who can embrace such consciousness. You see, Dear ones, consciousness must move forward. Consciousness moves beyond the illusion of the physical and moves into its greater creation. This, Dear ones, is the gift that awaits all.

IT IS VIBRATION AND FREQUENCY

Question: "So, in the ever-expanding consciousness, there must be a Golden City that is more aligned for each individual, maybe even a specific Doorway?"

This, Dear ones, of course shows within the astral body but also it shows within the Chakra System. If one vibrates to lower chakras, then perhaps it is better to work first with the Elemental and Deva Kingdoms, to understand the harmony that exists within the creation of Mother Earth. For those who wish to have sympathetic harmonies through sustenance and abundance, work upon that mighty Green Ray. Go to the Golden City Vortex of Shalahah and work to understand the higher frequency of at-one-ment. Work to understand that greater knowledge leading one to the path of Ascension. The soul will be drawn to where it needs to be.

A GENTLE NUDGE

Know that even in that mighty law, all are where they need to be at any given moment. For as you understand, Dear ones, Dear hearts, all is brought in Divine Order and in Divine Timing. It is important to know, though, when the soul feels uneasy, feels disharmony or dis-ease, these are the feelings that lead one to seek harmony, are they not? This is the little "a-ha" that puts one gently back upon the path, with feet now walking toward that mighty light that it had long forgotten.

Yes, it is true, that there is a better Ray Force . . . a better Master Teacher . . . a better Golden City Vortex for each and every one. But know this: each will be led through the process of seeking the great internal self. One is led through that great journey within. There is no greater way to begin this process, no greater joy that I can share than that moment in time when the voice then whispers to the soul, "It is time for you to move; it is time for you to go here." Those gentle nudges from within are the ones that should be listened to. Those are the gentle nudges that open the eyes and the ears and lead one into the path eternal. Questions?

WHEN THE STUDENT IS READY

Question: "So, would that make it relatively simple for a person to visit at least one Golden City?"

The answers always lie within, Dear one, Dear heart. The Master always awaits in that great softness. When the student is ready, the

Master appears. As above, so below, Dear hearts, Dear ones. Let us honor these laws eternal.

Question: "Yes, I see what you are saying. Then, since we are populated by many Star Seeds, is there a group consciousness or a group karma that exists as a pattern?"

"YOU ARE ALL A ONESHIP"

A group karma, or a group consciousness, comes from the perception of separation ... comes from the perception that only one shall unite me to my true self ... comes from the consciousness of separation from the eternal ONE. You are all as ONE, Dear one, Dear heart. You are all united as ONE. Yes, in the annals of history, there have been those groups that have come in to suffer the consequences of a group karma. There have been those who have come in to celebrate the great dharmic paths that await. There are those who come in higher frequencies of consciousness and we know these as the Seventh Manu, do we not? But know, beyond this, there is that greater law eternal and that is the unity of all. You are all a Oneship, Dear ones, Dear hearts.

DEVELOPMENT OF THE WILL

Question: "There have been discussions about individuals or groups who seem to have the desire to control others or to control the entire group and I would like to know if this is really true and can we do anything about it? Do things like mind control exist?"

This comes from handing over one's will. When one recognizes that the law eternal is within, alignment is to that greater and grander will; there is the truth eternal. As I have stated before, sympathetic resonance is very much the key here. Those who have fears of their own will being subjected to another will are those who have not yet defined their own will, is this not true? Those whose will is developed to an understanding of alignment to the greater will, to the greater harmony, to the greater at-one-ment, truly understand that all control is God control. God control is that ONE mind. The ONE mind that exists among us all is the consciousness of that mighty eternal ONE, Unana. How could one force control over that mighty all force? Again, this is the greater understanding of that mighty Violet Ray of Mercy, Compassion, and Forgiveness. The Violet Ray brings forth a development of the will, does it not? For within the Violet Ray is that mighty Blue Flame.

Response: "Yes."

Use of that mighty Violet Ray and alignment to the mighty Golden Ray will bring one into a greater harmony and frequency of alignment. Yes, there are those dark frequencies, those dark forces that play at will with scripted or ended laws, but there are the laws eternal . . . the laws that exist within . . . the law that brought you here . . . the law that shall return you to the heart of God and to that all-encompassing embrace and breath of love. Know the law eternal supersedes. Questions?

ONE MIND

Question: "Yes, do you have a decree that could be shared for the sense of apprehension about the subject of mind control?"

> I AM as ONE mind.
> I AM as ONE heart.
> I AM the mind of God complete.
> I AM the love of God eternal.

Repeat this as seven times seven, then invoke that mighty Violet Ray about you.

> Mighty Violet Ray come forth in the eternal Heart of the Logos.
> Mighty Violet Ray come forth and unite my mind as ONE.
> SO BE IT!

Response: "Thank you."

CHAPTER TEN

Ascension Valley
In Shalahah with Saint Germain.

Greetings, Beloveds and chelas of that mighty Violet Ray. I AM Saint Germain and I request permission to come forward.

Response: "Please Saint Germain, come forward."

UNITY AND HEALING IN SHALAHAH

Before we proceed Dear ones, a slight adjustment of all energy fields is needed.

> May the Violet Ray stream forth
> From the great purity of the Heart of God.
> May this Violet Flame of the Beloved Sacred Fire
> Now burn, blaze, transform, and transmute.
> May it now bring all to the greater harmony
> That serves the greater ONE of Unana.

Dear chelas, I come forward this morning to give you discourse about the process of Ascension and also, to answer questions that you have about your journey. Welcome to that mighty Vortex of Shalahah. Here Dear ones, you shall know the Divine True Self. Here, you shall meet the true unity and cause of all being. In that great eternal fire of the Violet Flame is the cause and effect that brings forward the Divineship, the Divine Human. The process of Ascension brings forward a greater unity ... brings forward a greater harmony ... brings forward that Oneship ... brings forward a greater understanding of true divinity. Yes, it is true, when one enters into the path of Ascension, they are then led to understand a greater Cause Divine. They then begin to understand the reason and purpose of all of their lifetimes, as they begin to unite into a greater journey on the path of life.

> Conscious immortality arise!
> May death no longer be part of my consciousness.

This is the true statement of Ascension. For you see, Dear ones, Dear hearts, it is the consciousness of death, or shall we say, a consciousness that accepts that life has an ending, that then brings forward the need for death and re-embodiment into another cycle, or chain of lifetimes. Within the next lifetime, one is then led again through the cause and effect, record and memory of a death, ultimately of a consciousness that holds a fear that leads one again into the cycle of desires. When I say "cycle of desires," I speak of desire in its lower understanding. Desire itself is truly of the Source. But when it is a desire for only the worldly attachments, it is a desire that is only for the intention of bringing forth a cellular type of fear. This desire of wanting and urging for the world traps one into that world of illusion and leads one only into a cycle of embodiment after embodiment after embodiment. In Shalahah, it shall be known that many shall be led to a higher understanding, into a course of healing those many embodiments.

As you know, with the entry of the great Golden Ray, there have been many opportunities now for the soul to be led into a greater understanding of the interconnectivity of the many lifetimes. Of course, when I refer to a past lifetime, I refer to this only in your understanding of time, for when you begin to understand the greater unity and Cause Divine, you begin to realize that time, within itself, is also limited in the physical, is it not?

Response: "Yes."

ALIGNMENT AND PREPARATION

Time is simultaneous in its greater understanding, all time happening within a great circle of ascent. In this spiral of greater understanding, I now speak of past lifetimes that have led, not only you to this work, but past lifetimes that lead many connected with you and the work that you bring forward. These past lifetimes carry the desires, or the imprinting of the soul, and there we are led to a greater understanding, are we not?

At times, we do not understand what leads or drives us. Instead, we circle in this greater awareness, fulfilling those desires randomly with the desires of the heart. But when one is led truly through the quest of the Divineship, the quest of the Divine Human, then one is led to that greater refreshing drink. One then is prepared, through teachings with the Master Teacher, to bring a greater discipline of the thoughts, the feelings, and the actions. It is there, in that greater preparation, that the alignment then is brought forward.

ENLIGHTENING YOUR CELLS

This alignment prepares first, at the cellular level through the Eight-sided Cell of Perfection, that grade of perfection and harmony that exists within the cells. It is indeed a Cellular Awakening, as I have spoken of before. The Cellular Awakening enlightens each of the cells and brings consciousness permeating the physical. For you see, the physical is permeated with its own consciousness of lifetime after lifetime after lifetime. This is what is known as the genetic code and it is carried forward, trapped in the cycles of death and rebirth, death and rebirth. To enliven the cells of the body with conscious immortality, command and demand to the mighty I AM Presence.

> I AM a beam of conscious immortality.
> I AM a beam of the Divine Oneship.
> Conscious immortality arise within me.
> Conscious immortality within me,
> Take command,
> I AM.

When you call forth this energy, when you call forth the true enlightenment of your being, consciousness then begins to permeate every cell within your physical body. We are addressing what is known as true memory. As you have known that there is memory that exists within the rings of a tree when fallen, there is also memory that exists within your cells. This memory of course permeates even at the spiritual level. But this memory must be clarified and purified in order to be brought into its greater understanding and working, to begin the process of the Ascension.

HIERARCHY OF CONSCIOUSNESS

The Ascension brings forward a greater understanding, a greater consciousness, and a greater unity of ONE heart and ONE mind. For you see, know, and understand, that even the work that I bring forward is linked with thousands of others in physical incarnations, and thousands of others who no longer require the use of the physical. You have sensed and known this and brought forward much information from my Brothers and Sisters of this Lodge that we are affiliated through. This is understood as a Hierarchy of Consciousness. For you see, it is indeed a higher arcing of energy. This higher arcing of energy we bring through each of the cells, one to the next. Each one of your cells operates with their own consciousness. Now it is time to bring this link of consciousness throughout your own being.

ATLANTIS AND THE SUN GOD

Let me explain, so you do indeed understand this. In the days of Atlantis, the process of Ascension was accepted widely by those within society. It was always the goal. It was always, shall we say, brought into a greater understanding within the whole cultural system. That is why the Sun God was understood and celebrated for the knowledge that it truly contained. The Sun represented the link of a soul with the True Self and the True Self was linked to the process of Ascension, moving into higher vibration, resonance, and spiritual awareness. This lineage of information was brought through, not only the oral tradition, but it was also brought through the cellular memory where it was contained.

As we prepared to enter into the time of Kali Yuga, it was known and understood that the cells within the body would no longer be able to receive the Divine Communication of the Sun. Of course, when I speak of this Divine Communication, I also speak of the Ray forces that are from the great Galactic Center. When we say "step-down transformer," it is truly meant in that respect, for you become linked again as ONE cell to a greater cosmos and understanding.

THE DARKNESS OF KALI

This teaching was brought through many of the Temples. It was also held in the consciousness of the culture. Not only was it held in a religious understanding, it was held within the political system, and this process was fostered in cultural belief and complete understanding. But as you know, only like vibration can understand like vibration. Even what I speak of in this moment may be difficult to grasp or understand, for the consciousness began to shut down within the cells, one at a time. As this genetic memory was passed further and further as we entered into the depth and darkness of Kali Yuga, it retreated to but one cell within the chamber of the heart.

So now you understand why we focus always upon the Heart Chakra . . . why we focus always upon the element of love . . . why we focus always within the heart, where it is always brought forward in its greater understanding, that there, the true chamber of perfection lies. There is the opportunity for that one link, a leap of consciousness from my heart to your heart. Dear one, Dear heart, this is a leap of consciousness to bring greater understanding and greater awareness. This Unfed Flame of Love, Wisdom, and Power resides within this Perfect Cell, yes, but it also receives the opportunity through the use of a Sacred Fire then to leap in that one conductive moment to adjoining cells. There it penetrates and fills the body, bringing this enlightenment of the true light, of the true divinity throughout all the cells. Through the use of a Sacred Fire, that mighty Violet Flame I AM, and the use of a Tube of Light to contain the Sacred Fire, one then has the opportunity to gain, at an exponential level, the enlightenment of the cells.

CELLS, CITRUS, AND ENERGY

Of course this is why we ask for changes within the diet. As you understand the physiology of minerals, the physiology of your circulatory system, and the physiology of the substance of light, what you are working to achieve is to bring greater light into the cells. This light of course is carried in all food substances to a greater or lesser degree, but as I have stated before, it is indeed at this time the citrus plants which carry in their fruits and rinds this greater enlightenment for the body. This arcing of energy that comes from the Great Central Sun and onward to your Sun then is able to permeate, allowing this process of the removal of fear at the genetic level and bringing the true divinity forward.

In the Times of Great Changes, many will begin to understand this process. Not only will it be understood at the scientific and dietary level, but the understanding of higher consciousness will be applied alongside it. There will be many who seek to know and understand. Beloved Babajeran too has offered herself to be of service at this time, to bring a greater enlightenment and assistance in this great Time of Global Ascent.

VORTICES OF ACCELERATION

I pinpointed early in my work with you, Dear ones, Dear hearts, in the I AM America Map, the locations of smaller vortices of energy that may be used to bring greater assistance in this global evolution. Ascension Valley was given, for that is indeed a location where Beloved Babajeran is offering herself to serve in an acceleration process. Many of those who will enter into this Portal of Ascension Valley will first feel a great opening of the heart. Many will notice the scent of roses and Beloved Mother Mary, Beloved Kuan Yin, the feminine principle, will come and merge within the body and bring its greater understanding for the soul to evolve, learn, and rejoice.

THE FEMININE NURTURES OUR PERFECTION

This feminine energy, in its greater opening, serves a greater cause within the cell. It helps to bring a nurturing to the great perfection within. This nurturing is then allowed to begin its expansion process. As you see Dear ones, Dear hearts, as the Earth, in her own evolution, moves humanity forward, there will be those who will decide not to join the journey. Indeed, there will always be those who will be left behind. But there will be those who will join, who will understand the greater working and the greater harmony. There will be those who will, shall I say, sup with me.

LORD SANANDA

The Vortex of Shalahah, within this greater Golden City, brings forward one of the greater teachers and the sponsor of this transition, known as Lord Sananda. He sends his open invitation to those who wish to go and experience the energies of Ascension Valley; for there he shall bring his energy forward and you shall unite as ONE with perfection. And now Dear ones, Dear hearts, I open the floor for your questions.

THE CRYSTAL POINTS OF ASCENSION VALLEY

Question: "The question that comes to mind regarding Ascension Valley is about the two buttes that are within that valley. I have always thought these were important. Would you give a description?"

Within the center of both of these two buttes are huge, shall we say, for lack of a better word or understanding, crystal points. These were submerged there during the ancient times of Lemuria. They were understood and known and their relationship to the Earth's grid could also be clearly seen. For you see, as I have given instruction on lei- lines, they line up to that point within the Amethyst City, which is now located on the Island of Cuba, of a great transmuting energy aligning to the Temples of Luxor. That is why one feels the great Fires of Purification when standing on these two buttes. Of course, they triangulate themselves as an entry point, an energy, into the greater Ascension Valley.

These buttes also serve to bring a purification that will indeed happen to this area on a geophysical level during the great Earth Changes. That is why these energies are only to be utilized for spiritual work. Living within this area may be more difficult for some; for you see, this energy will bring a great purification to the South. But as time moves on, these indeed will be points of global ascent. And there, the Violet Flame shall be seen within this entire valley. Questions?

ASCENSION AND THE SACRED FIRE

Question: "Yes. When you refer to Luxor, are you saying that the great knowledge there was also of Ascension?"

Not only of Ascension, but of the use of the Sacred Fire. However, at that time, consciousness had not fallen into the states of fear that are now part of normal everyday consciousness within the culture and the civilization. For you see, the time that you are experiencing now is within a culture and civilization built entirely upon the premise of fear, is it not?

Response: "Yes, it would seem that it is."

In that time, a greater understanding of the Sacred Fire was practiced in the temples, and, of course, communication with other planets was also achieved through this understanding of unity consciousness and the perfection of the Great Cell within. This Great Cell within was also duplicated in the physical within the Temples of Luxor. There it was given, shall we say, a type of technical assistance. However, what was really achieved was an alignment through the Ray forces entering in at a great pointed entry within the Earth. Questions?

Question: "In achieving this Ascension process, would you say that it would be worthwhile to visit the Ascension Valley on a frequent basis, to help the transitional process and purification?"

THE ASCENSION AREAS

While I can give suggestions, I always lead the student, or chela, to converse with the I AM Presence, the great Source within. There indeed is the true record of consciousness. However, two to three trips per year of course will bring a greater purification...a greater enlightening of the cells . . . a greater understanding of the light that exists within . . . a dropping of the consciousness of fear . . . the understanding of the consciousness of Unana, the Oneship . . . and of course, contact with the Master Teacher. This, of course, is but one small Vortex we have given. There are twenty-two that exist upon the planet. This one was given, not that it is the first, not that it is the last; for you see, they all exist simultaneously upon the Earth Plane and Planet. Dear ones, Dear hearts, it was given so that a model of energy could be understood. It is indeed one of those points where the Earth Mother herself has offered to be of service. Questions?

Question: "I see. At some time in the future, are you saying that you will release the locations of the other Ascension areas?"

It is possible Dear ones, Dear hearts, but there will be those who have the eyes to see and the ears to hear, who will know this within their own heart and mind. While some of these areas are protected, some of them have been used since time immemorial. There have been those who have preserved the integrity of their consciousness and understood the true life of the Divineship within and been led or directed to that great contact. There they have been prepared in the greater working and understanding and the unity to the spheres of the heavens has been achieved. But Dear one, Dear heart, in its time, in its own time, it shall be known.

Response: "I understand. At this point, I do not have any further questions with regard to this subject."

Then Dear one, I will take my leave.

CHAPTER ELEVEN

Ascension of Consciousness
Saint Germain on the heart, mind, and emotions.

Greetings Beloved chelas in that mighty Violet Ray. I AM Saint Germain and I stream forth on that Violet Ray of Mercy, Compassion, and Forgiveness. As usual Dear hearts, I request permission to come forward.

Response: "You have our permission Saint Germain, please come forward."

CAUSE AND EFFECT

There is much work for us to continue with Dear ones, Dear hearts, within this dispensation, not only of that Mighty Violet Ray but also of that Mighty Green Ray. The work that you are bringing forward, while it contains many aspects of that mighty Violet Ray of Transmutation, Alchemy, ultimate Compassion, and Forgiveness, it also contains within it that Green Ray of Understanding. For you see Dear ones, Dear hearts, it was long decided that there would be brought forth a dispensation to bring an understanding of cause and effect to humanity. This has now been brought forth in the teachings of prophecy but also in the teachings of the energetic grids, the layers of the field of the aura and the layers of the field of the Earth. When all of this is brought to a greater understanding, then healing can come forward. This healing that comes forth from the heart of the Central Sun, that mighty logos, aligns to the Divine Plan, to that mighty will. OM MANAYA, PITAYA, HITAKA!

ALIGNMENT AND HARMONY

Dear ones, Dear hearts, this healing work that comes forward brings a greater alignment of that mighty will among the collective consciousness of humanity. It is this alignment of the will that is of most importance and you know that this has been the focus and the intention of the work in Gobean and the work of beloved Master El Morya. This mighty Blue Ray, as it streams forth from the heart of the Central Sun, arcing through the solar system to the core of your own Earth, brings with it an understanding and an intention to bring others to that greater plan . . . to a greater alignment . . . to their own purpose in this embodiment.

When one enters into this path of greater purpose and alignment to that Divine Plan, a greater harmony then ensues. This harmony brings forth an easing in the collective consciousness. The tensions begin to ease and balance begins to come forth from the great heart of compassion. This balance, when it is understood, brings a greater opening of the heart of love and a greater peace and tolerance is the end result. This grand alignment brings a greater energy over the Earth. This energy, when it is understood as a greater cosmic unity, begins to align with greater ease to the solar system. That alignment to the solar system brings forth a greater alignment to the Great Central Sun.

"LOVE, IN ACTION"

As you see Dear ones, these three actual physical locations are always working to bring a greater harmony for the evolution of those on planet Earth. This alignment also brings a greater understanding of the positioning of the Earth as a schoolroom. As it has always been said, "To do, to dare, and to be silent." Those who enter into the Earth Plane understand the great need to bring demonstration into the physical . . . understand the great need to bring forth action . . . understand the great need to put love into complete and total action. As we have always stated before, it is love in action, is it not, that brings about that greater understanding, that greater education?

When one begins to understand the intention of their heart and brings this intention further into its greater plan and awareness, the schoolroom becomes, shall we say, a great flora and fauna of experience. To love brings about a completion, does it not? To love brings about a greater understanding of the emotional fields and a greater understanding of higher intelligence and how this higher intelligence can be brought into greater thinking and arenas of experience. Through this greater plan, the Law of Love, all is brought to greater alignment and to greater harmony and ultimately, a greater abundance. This grand alignment upon the Earth Plane and Planet brings about a graduation of souls upon this schoolroom. This graduation of course is not just a graduation in consciousness but also a graduation that leads one to a greater understanding of the Ascension.

HEALING AND THE ASCENSION

The Ascension, as you see Dear ones, Dear hearts, is the movement, yes, interdimensionally but it is also a greater and higher awareness of experience. The Ascension of consciousness brings a greater understanding of the purpose of the Law of Love and the inter-connectivity of all in your path. Compassion, which is an element and an aspect of that mighty Violet Ray, brings forward a greater understanding of the Law of Love. One then is readied and able to see that great inner working in all situations and circumstances. As I have said before, there is never a mistake, ever, ever, ever. When one enters into that mighty Law of Compassion, one is then able to see how this mighty law works in the Earth Plane and Planet and brings one into a higher awareness, into a higher experience of consciousness. This of course is the path of Ascension and many who work on that mighty White Ray understand and know that the healing of many wounds is always essential in order to bring one to a higher consciousness. But this healing, does it not come forward through the letting go of past experience?

SPIRITUAL EDUCATION

This letting go is not forgetting the lesson but forgetting the pain and moving beyond the experience that is encoded in the memory. The memory is then viewed with the end result, as I have always said, of education. This grander education exists for all upon the Earth Plane and Planet. It is the purpose of life here ... it is the purpose that one is moving towards ... moving to a greater education ... having a greater knowledge of the inter-connectivity that exists within that mighty Law of Love. When you call upon that mighty Violet Flame, it leads you into a greater awareness, a greater tolerance of experience, and expands one in that mighty heart of love into the consciousness of Unana, into the consciousness of that all and mighty ONE.

KARMIC PATTERNS

In the consciousness of the all and mighty ONE, lies the memory eternal, lies the true memory that exists in all situations and circumstances. This is important to understand as one enters into that focused path of Ascension, that all experiences are inter-connected, each to the next. Yet, all experiences are seen for the unity that they contain, seen through that one thread or path of demonstration that they hold. This path of course is the path of love, for one then sees the tolerance, the open giving. The open door, as Dear Sananda has always expressed, is contained in all experiences. When the soul is non-detached from these experiences, it is very hard to let go of the wounds of the past and the soul is held back in its own evolution. The soul is then called upon to repeat the experience over and over again. While some might see this as a punishing effect of karma, know Dear ones, Dear hearts, it is no punishing affect at all but only the exercise of your will and your choice. These repeat performances, shall we say, of experiences are seen at a point in evolution as a pattern.

"THE REWARD IS IMMEASURABLE"

These patterns of course are very important for the development of the will and the soul. Through this experience and demonstration of end results, one is then able to align through choice to a higher experience. This higher alignment and the use of that mighty Blue Ray brings transformation. This transformation is always essential Dear ones, Dear hearts, in order to move to a greater understanding of a pattern. These patterns of past experience are held by all who tread the spiritual path. All will begin to understand through that end result, education. Being led through the experience of a painful existence, education always comes to the forefront, does it not? For we have always stated, it is never promised to be easy but the reward is immeasurable. That is why those who tread the path to higher knowledge . . . who seek Ascension of their own consciousness . . . who seek an Ascension of any situation or circumstance are then led into the embrace of the mighty Violet Ray.

REVIEW YOUR PATTERNS

When one reviews, through meditation or in calmness of their day, the past karmas, or actions of that day, one then can see the result of patterns, many patterns of the past that are held at many levels. These patterns are held in the physical body, yes, but they are also held in that most important body of understanding, the mental body. For in that mental body is contained, at all times, the mighty builder of the physical form. It is true Dear ones, when you put your focus there, you shall see the end result. I have taught this many, many times in my precipitation and manifestation techniques.

It is important to understand that thoughts do create physical end results. Of course, this being a primary entry lesson for those upon the path of the Ascension, it is always important to give this great review, to understand that there is always an end result to an action. The action, does it not always come from the mental functions? Does it not come forth through thinking such a thing first? Thoughts must be held to be more sacred, Dear ones, Dear hearts. Thoughts that are held then seek a manifestation through that natural law. All thoughts will contain an end result. Of course, then one says, "How do I capture the mind? How do I keep the mind from traveling and racing into undesired areas? How do I harness the energy of my mind? How do I bring my mind forward into a greater alignment to the Divine Will?"

THE HEART AND SACRED FIRE

The mind itself is always balanced through that mighty heart of love and in that heart of love is the consciousness of the ONE, Unana. The mind is brought to a quietness, is it not, through the use of that Sacred Fire, the mighty Violet Ray? This is why we have brought these techniques forward at this time, Dear ones, Dear heart, so the mind can be tamed as it travels through the experience of illusion. Illusion is indeed a topic to be understood, is it not? For then one sees the temporal illusion of the creation of the mind and the temporal illusion of the experiences of the physical.

BEYOND ILLUSION

Illusion exists, Dear one, to bring the education of the truth . . . to bring you into the alignment of the mighty Law of Love . . . to bring you into the alignment of that Plan Divine. One then begins to peer above illusion, when having the experience of Divine Love. One then begins to have experiences beyond illusion, when seeing the cause of unity demonstrating in all experience. These indeed are the true treasures that await the one who ascends upon the spiritual path . . . who ascends in consciousness . . . who ascends in understanding . . . who ascends to that mighty alignment – the love of all – that guides humanity.

INVOKE THE FLAME

This mighty Violet Ray streams forth too as the Blue Ray comes forward. This mighty Violet Ray streams forth from the heart of the Great Central Sun, arcing itself to the solar sun, then to core of the Earth. As you invoke its substance, it comes forth from the ethers. As it appears, coming from each layer of the field of the Earth, it is contained within its own manifestation. When you command and demand a Ray Force into action, you are calling, not only upon that Law of Love, but also upon a law that exists within the physical. For you see, all the rays in their action come forth at every level, as well as the same level of your experience of mind into physical manifestation.

TAMING EMOTIONS

Then one is led to ask, "What about the emotional field? Is not all thought, then feeling and action?" Of course, Dear ones, it is but the feeling is brought more to bridge the thought and the action. It is always that great impetus that then brings the will to action, does it not? The emotions have always been so important to understand and the taming of the emotions is as important as the taming of the mind. For the mind, when we see with crystal clarity, we can see each individualized thought as it passes through the mind. But it is the nature of the human to get trapped upon occasion in the fields of emotional experience. Why is this so?

Held within the genetic coding is the genetics of the animal in the experience upon the Earth Plane and Planet. This is not to say that the human is animalistic but, at times, can behave and act in an animal behavior or modality. It is always a matter of choice, is it not Dear ones, Dear hearts? Calling upon that Will Divine, raises one to a higher understanding, to a greater knowledge. Then in that greater knowledge, one begins to understand that the travels among the illusions are indeed controlled through the mental out-picturing.

GROWTH THROUGH EXPERIENCE

All experiences come, of course, through the mental conduit of out-picturing. This is the basis Dear ones, Dear hearts, of manifestation and experience. Through this out-picturing, the soul in its sojourn in the Earth Plane and Planet grows, learns, and receives the most precious gem of all – education. Where does this all fit in, one may ask, lifetime after lifetime? The soul, ascending upon the spiritual path, learns that education is the highest reward.

Dear ones, Dear hearts, as you understand, the Earth schoolroom is a place where you grow only by experience, only by demonstration in the physical. The astute student begins to understand, through these experiences, that there is a higher order which brings about the patterns, demonstrating great physical laws. There is indeed a higher intelligence, is there not? There is indeed a higher order, is there not?

When one begins to see this higher order, they begin to understand the Ascension of consciousness and that there is much more that lies beyond physical demonstration and the Maya or illusion. There is the eternal truth that lies behind all such things, even behind that of the mind . . . a Divine Order that is being orchestrated beyond a great central intelligence. Dear ones, Dear hearts, when one begins to seek this great higher order, they are then ready to meet the I AM THAT I AM.

THE MIGHTY I AM PRESENCE

The first of the I AM THAT I AM is the God-self that dwells within. It has always been there but it lies, shall we say, asleep within so many people. It is not yet awakened, not yet put in its proper authority. When one begins their contact with this mighty I AM, one then begins to see the spiritual laws that lie underneath all activity . . . the true realities that lie within all situations and circumstances. When you travel in the physical experience in contact with the mighty I AM Presence, one then is led beyond illusion and into truth eternal. The contact with the mighty I

AM indeed is the Akashic Record . . . indeed is the silent witness . . . indeed is that wellspring of eternal truth. The mighty I AM, Dear ones, Dear hearts, strives in the Ascension of consciousness to gain emotional and ultimate contact. The mighty I AM is contained within all. It contains within it, not only the universal mind but the universal heart of love. It contains within it all experiences, so it can lead you into new experience. Questions?

THE AWAKENING POINT

Question: "Yes. It is my impression that Ascension can only be taught to a mortal person by an already Ascended Being. Is this true?"

It is very difficult for the consciousness to be brought into its ascending order without the guidance of one who has been there before. However, within healing is the ultimate authority. That ultimate authority longs to be awakened . . . longs to be brought to the complete, full podium of consciousness. This awakening is always fostered by one who has been there before. As we have always said: To do, to dare . . . and then that great silence is the mighty witness.

Response: "I see. Then truly, Ascension occurs when the individual soul is sponsored by one who has already ascended."

It is true Dear ones, Dear hearts. As you have understood before, there is always the sponsor who comes forward to begin that awakening process within the human. First, the animal behaviors are taken to the forefront, so that one may then be able to see the action of such. It is only through seeing ones animalistic instincts and behaviors that one is then able to call upon the mighty Divine Nature of choice and the engendering of the will. It is important Dear ones, Dear hearts, that when the sponsor comes forward, it is brought, shall we say, in the silence of a whisper. That awakening point, the birth of conscience, is most important.

BEYOND THE PHYSICAL

Response: "Yes, I understand. So, as I present some of the principles that you have shared with me with others, it will still require someone such as yourself to sponsor them in the Ascension."

It brings one to a higher understanding of unity consciousness. For you see Dear ones, Dear hearts, in the awakening process, one is always at odds with the ego. Of course, the ego works for the greater purpose of presenting the mirror, or shall we say, the duad, to the soul in its educational process. It is important of course to be able to see how all is inner connected to the ONE. When one is not bound through the physical and not bound through time and space, there is an opportunity for a greater intervention. This greater intervention comes forward in its own timing and intention. There is not one, bound in the physical, who could completely understand this in its entirety.

To work beyond physical constraint and beyond time and space, you begin to understand, through the help of your sponsor, your Master Teacher, that relationship of the guru to the chela. Has it not been brought to you Dear ones, Dear hearts, that you can see what exists beyond time and space and what exists beyond the physical? You see these demonstrations brought forth daily and while each is brought with a physical result, you can also understand its intention and purpose behind and beyond the physical. It is important to understand that when one is not bound by these constraints, there is a fresh perspective. One is then allowed, as you so well know, to "hang on to that elephant" in a whole different manner.

THE ASCENSION PROCESS

Question: "Then as I understand it, the Ascension process is ongoing; it is not just from this realm but from the realm that you are residing in, by your sponsors?"

It is indeed, Dear ones, Dear hearts, for consciousness is ever expanding and growing. It moves beyond, even from its point of birth. And while this principle is taught in the physical, it is not a principle from the physical. The physical was given, Dear ones, as a great gift, so you could see each spiritual principle and how it is applied.

ASCENSION AND DIET

Response: "I understand. With regard to the mental body, emotional body, and action body, it's my impression and observation that the emotional body seems to be infinitely more active and overpowering than the mental body or the action body."

As I have said before, the time period that the Earth is in, which is a time of lesser light, the emotions run quite rampant. These emotions are held in animalistic behavior and animalistic activity. That is why we have asked for the chelas, who wish to bring their consciousness to a momentum of Ascension, to limit their intake of animal products. The day-by-day ordered routine of Ascension necessitates the control of animalistic behavior and the animalistic genetic coding, a coding that has occurred through the intervention of other Star Seeds upon the Earth Plane and Planet. You see Dear ones, Dear hearts, this control can be brought about through the simple principle of energy flows where attention goes. Now, how would this relate to the food that you eat? It is very simple when one understands a spiritual principle brought into physical order, is it not?

Response: "This is true. If you are partaking of animal products, then you are going to increase the energy of that within your own system."

As I have explained before Dear ones, Dear hearts, to bring the consciousness to a higher order, to a higher understanding, we have brought this law eternal. Of course there are those who feel a great restriction in this. However, as I have always assured you, often through restriction, one then begins to become fully free. This freedom is one that is not understood until one has had the experience. I have always said Dear ones, Dear hearts, take this into the great laboratory of the self. Bring it into at least a six-week experiment and see for yourself if your consciousness does not have a higher and a finer quality. Is this not true?

DIVINE LOVE

Response and question: "I can attest to this being true in my own life. I have a question in regard to Divine Love. It has been my impression that, though ever present, Divine Love needs to be accepted to be activated in the consciousness. It seems that so many people deny this acceptance or seem to be attached to the concept of being unworthy. Could you comment on this?"

Divine Love always brings forth a greater enlightenment, does it not? For through the experiment and experience of Divine Love, one then is brought to a higher level of acceptance and a higher level of tolerance. This allows the thoughts then to become freed. Thoughts are freed beyond restriction . . . thoughts are freed beyond doubt . . . thoughts are freed beyond superstition . . . thoughts are freed beyond fear. Divine Love brings forward, in its emotional quality, a freeing of the mental body. Creations then can come forward from a higher order and a higher understanding. When one accepts this higher Law of Divine Love, one then begins to expand in their mental characteristics and expand in their day-to-day thoughts and thinking. These day-to-day thoughts then begin to create new experiences, do they not? These new experiences then begin to reflect and mirror back a greater order, a greater understanding beyond the ego, beyond illusion.

It is through Divine Love and the acceptance of Divine Love that all are loved, accepted, and needed . . . that all have their right to be here . . . that all have their right to have this experience . . . that all have their right to come forward in their own evolution. Divine Love sustains, maintains, protects, nurtures, and ultimately qualifies all to a higher order. Only through Divine Love does all then exist, does it not Dear one?

ACTION AND THE VIOLET FLAME

Response and question: "Yes, without a doubt. I have come to accept that the Divine Plan, Divine Will, and Divine Love are always in action. Another question, if one wishes to go forward and create something new, we have talked about the out-picturing process, but if one wants to be released from something, the only process that I am aware of is the utilization of the Violet Flame. Does this work completely with paying a debt or eliminating karmic attachments that you may find unpleasant?"

There are those who are more attached to their experience of pain than to the education contained therein. It is important of course to always call forth that mighty Violet Ray into any situation and circumstance where you wish to be freed. However, there are also many lessons that come forward, do they not, through the physical? Many lessons are able to be shown to you clearly and succinctly. Money or, shall we say, the attachment to money, is one of these. The attachment at the mental level and through the emotional experiences of feeling secure or insecure, are one way that one becomes over attached. Money is given, shall we say, to clarify the emotional body, so that one may become more clear in their intention with the physical.

EMOTIONAL ATTACHMENTS

It is important, when you are working to become free from such emotional attachments, to not only call upon the Violet Ray, but to use all write and burn techniques. The write and burn techniques not only call upon a level of transmutation and Alchemy but they require a physical action to begin to overcome the circumstances and situations brought about through emotional imbalance. When one becomes, shall we say, stuck within this muck and mire of emotion, it is important then to take action at a physical level. This physical activity is focused and directed always through the intention of the mind. Calling forward the higher order of the mind to identify the emotional response can bring a greater level of physical activity. Do you understand?

Question: "It is a form of out-picturing that will then take the life into an action, is what you are saying?"

It is true Dear one. Work first with the Violet Ray to identify the emotional responses, then use the write and burn techniques to eliminate these emotional responses that are overplaying in patterns. Man and money becomes stuck in emotional securities ... stuck in power plays ... stuck in happiness or unhappiness, contingent upon the amount of security contained in the physical world. Now, for the one who is traveling along the path of ascending consciousness, can you clearly see how this would indeed impede and hold one back?

Response: "It most certainly would."

Do this work, Dear chela of mine, and I shall bring forth further assistance.

Response: "Yes."

ENERGY FOR ENERGY

As you have understood Dear one, all comes forward from the Master Teacher energy for energy. It is true indeed through Divine Love that the sponsor comes forward and fans that flame, awakening the I AM to a greater level of understanding. But it is the Master Teacher who comes forward then and helps through this mighty Principle Divine.

EMOTIONS AND THE VIOLET FLAME

Question: "I see. Isn't it the emotional body that brings up memories and keeps us from being lulled into a state of unawareness and non-sensitivity?"

The emotional body plays its role in allowing the patterns to come forward, that then indeed spark the will to greater action and activity. But the emotional body itself can become out of balance with experiences that are judged as negative or positive. As I have stated before, it is important to use the Violet Flame to allow this sense of judgment of good versus bad, good versus evil, or negative versus positive, a greater understanding. That experience is there for the engendering of the will and moving the soul further on the path into the Ascension of consciousness.

Response: "That would make the most sense. At this point, I have no further questions."

I should also like to remind you Dear ones, Dear hearts, that I will bring forward more information upon the Green Ray. For you see, today I have laid a template down which shall explain to you the beginning of the Blue Ray and the ultimate Alchemy of the Violet Ray. We have also introduced the premise of the mind, which is enlightenment brought from the premise of Divine Love. Now, we have the building blocks for that Mighty Green Ray of healing, do we not Dear ones, Dear hearts? In our next discourse, I shall bring further explanation. In that mighty Christ, SO BE IT!

Response: "So Be It!"

CHAPTER TWELVE

Ascension through the Dimensions
Saint Germain explains the Time of Ascension.

Greetings my Beloved chelas in that mighty Christ. I AM Saint Germain and I stream forth on that Violet Ray of Mercy, Compassion, and Forgiveness. As usual Dear hearts, I request permission to come forward?

Response: "Please Saint Germain, you are most welcome and please come forward."

THE SPIRITUAL TRAINING OF THE MIND

There is much work still for us to complete, is there not Dear ones, Dear hearts? Much work for us to complete upon this Earth Plane and Planet. You see Dear ones, we have brought forward the work of Earth Changes Prophecy to reflect the work that is to be done with the planet, that work held in the sacred stewardship for beloved Babajeran. But there is also that work held within that sacred stewardship of the Ascended Masters. That is the work for humanity, for it to gain in understanding, not only at a spiritual level but also at other levels of the mind. The training of the mind will bring it into complete alignment with its own feeling world. This alignment of thought, feeling, and action is understood, not only in your own world, but also extends on into more subtle understandings within the Fourth and Fifth Dimension.

ASCENSION OF SOULS

The process of extending this understanding and how it reflects into your inner world is the process of Ascension. This Ascension process correlates with the changes of the planet herself. For you see Dear ones, Dear hearts, it is a great graduation of souls .

. . it is a great ascent . . . it is a great Rapture. This great Rapture, or Ascension of souls, has been brought forward within its own timing and pure intention. This intention of course was determined long ago but the soul, in its sojourn, is now ready to move forward. A great completion is ready. As Dear Sananda has always said to you Dear ones, Dear chelas of my heart, "The minutes and the seconds tick. The time is at hand. The time has come for man to receive the gift." This gift is the gift of Ascension.

THE OPEN HEART

These higher teachings, as you are ready to understand, as the eyes and the ears are open, come forward to bring you into that process of Ascension. Of course, we also bring this into an alignment with the other densities . . . the alignment of the body . . . the alignment of the mind . . . the alignment of the spirit. All of these come together in their great timing and also intention. For the body, we have given a great focus upon the work of the diet. We give great focus upon the healing of the body; that is, that greater alignment again of the mind, body, and spirit. This always works through that open heart, does it not? For within that open heart, one is then willing to receive healing at an even greater level. It is this opening of the heart that is ever so important in the understanding of this work and preparing the chela to understand the Fourth Dimension and to open a glimpse into a Fifth Dimensional reality.

PREPARATION THROUGH THE GOLDEN CITIES

The Golden Cities serve at a physical level in this capacity. You see Dear ones, they are a Divine Intervention that has come forward at this time to bring a greater preparation to the physical body. This is in the same way that you bring the physical preparation to the body through changing the diet, the thoughts, and the feelings. You are also then affected, are you not, within a Golden City, feeling a higher vibration affecting your physical body? It brings a greater revolution per millisecond. This greater revolution is that high-pitched ring that you hear when you enter into a Golden City. This brings a higher sensitivity to other frequencies of existence. During the great Earth Changes is a great opportunity for many to graduate, to leap into another dimension of understanding, and end one succession of embodiments that are bound by the physical body.

PARALLEL AND PARADOX

The Time of Ascension is when we become unbound by the physical. Although, in its great parallel and paradox, the physical body is brought into a great understanding of perfection. This provides a stable foundation to guide the thought . . . to guide the feeling . . . to guide the spirit . . . and ultimately the soul into this higher understanding and evolution. Many would wonder, "But are these two not separate, the body and the spirit?" Indeed they are Dear ones, Dear hearts, but the body reflects not the spirit but reflects the thoughts and the feelings that the spirit has delved into. These thoughts and feelings, when brought to a greater alignment, assist in this Ascension process as a grounding within a better understanding of this greater knowledge and greater teaching.

A UNIFIED BODY OF LIGHT

Ascension is not only the Ascension of consciousness but it is also the Ascension or ascending motion of the body at will. As you have known, the Ascended Being is always one who has learned through this sometimes arduous but painful process, how to bring this body into a greater alignment . . . to prepare not only the physical body but the emotional body, the mental body, the Causal body, and onward into other layers of expression which comprise the whole, having greater and lighter awareness. This lighter awareness that I speak of, is a lighter awareness related to immortality. Immortality is always prepared first through the immortality of the consciousness. As I have always said to you, "Down with Death. Conscious Immortality Arise!" This statement of course speaks to the continuity of thought and speaks to the continuity of feeling and therefore, creating a timeless and deathless action. These actions of course, playing one upon the other, become as one unified body of light. It is through this unified body of light that the physical body is then transmuted into a finer substance, which vibrates at the Fourth Dimension.

THE UNSEEN KINGDOMS

Now many of the elementals, the salamanders, undines, gnomes, fairies, and others of the unseen kingdoms - that do exist - understand this greater teaching, this greater knowledge. Therefore, they exist always in this Fourth Dimensional understanding. However, they have not moved into a more unified understanding, which exists at the Fifth Dimensional capacity. I give this to you Dear ones, Dear hearts, so you have at least a beginning understanding of dimensions and how they do relate to physical matter.

TRANSLATION BETWEEN THE DIMENSIONS

You see Dear ones, Dear hearts, it is a matter of understanding the process of translation from one dimension to the next. Matter translates itself and then is understood, shall we say, as another language, another being, another expression. Now these beings that exist in the Fourth Dimension have the ability to translate between a Third Dimensional expression and a Fourth Dimensional expression. There are of course those who are born with the inner sight and with the inner hearing, their eyes and ears long open; they can hear and see through, in the same manner, as a translation between the Third Dimension and the Fourth Dimension. This translation is an important understanding to gain, especially for those who are seeking an expanded awareness, an expanded understanding.

LIFE BEYOND

Conscious immortality embraces the idea that life exists beyond what is seen . . . beyond what is known . . . beyond what is recorded in your dimensional science. The Fourth Dimension exists beyond the rational mind . . . beyond duality . . . beyond right, wrong, North, South . . . beyond all that is tangible and would be seen as Earthly. Yet, within your own understanding, it is an extremely Earthly experience, for it is the experience of the Earth in terms of its own natural or nature spirit.

GOLDEN CITIES AND THE FOURTH DIMENSION

This Fourth Dimension is very important in understanding Golden City energies, for many, when they first enter them, hear this high-pitched ring, bringing immediately an alignment of thought, feeling, and action. Upon the entry into the Golden City Vortices, many are receiving an immediate adjustment of the light bodies; this is the high-pitched ring of that high millisecond, enabling a greater alignment through the Divine Will. This great alignment brings an understanding of the Fourth Dimension. It immediately brings a great sensitivity and awareness of the Kingdoms that exist in the unseen. They show us a parallel world that exists alongside the world that we have lived in. This parallel world has an understanding of the world that we live in, yet so few participate with it.

THE FOURTH DIMENSION AND EARTH CHANGES

The wizards and the shaman of the past have understood the existence of the Fourth Dimension and they have used it for what would seem to be magic, miracles, and Alchemy. Dear ones, Dear hearts, this is an important understanding for gaining insight into the Fourth Dimension, for it is here that the first major alignment affects Mother Earth and her sojourn into her great change. This will bring about, as you well know, the mighty Earth Changes. These changes will come about through this greater change that is happening within the Fourth Dimension, as many souls enter into this greater understanding. The Fourth Dimension, when understood at this level, has a great impact upon the Animal Kingdom, the Vegetable Kingdom, and also the Mineral Kingdom; each of these Kingdoms of course always interacting in their higher level of understanding.

Now I would like to prepare for you a chart.

He is now showing a chart and it looks almost like a rainbow. It has an arch to it.

AN EXPONENTIAL LEAP

As you see Dear ones, light in its own separation shows the differences that you experience as color. You also know, within this range of understanding, that sound separates as well, giving different tones or qualities. This same experience is within the Third Dimension. The same experience is in within the Fourth Dimension. The same experience is in within the Fifth Dimension. But it is important to understand, as we move through one dimension, or octave, to the next, there is indeed an exponential leap in this range of understanding. So again, let me explain this through a chart.

We will start again with the Third Dimension and let us deal now only in the Third Dimension with seven harmonics of understanding. Do you see this chart?

Response: "Yes."

This first level represents the Third Dimension and its seven harmonics of colors and sounds. This is the experience brought through the five senses of touch, smell, hearing, sight, and taste. Moving onto the Fourth Dimension, we move in an exponential ratio, moving from seven harmonics to fourteen harmonics. This comprises the Fourth Dimension. Moving onto the Fifth Dimension, we would have again an exponential, to a twenty-eight degree harmonic. This may give you some understanding

when relating mathematically to the Third, Fourth, and Fifth
Dimensions.

*This chart show seven, fourteen, and twenty-eight frequencies,
quite distinguishable and visible. Seven are functioning at the Third
Dimensional level, fourteen at the Fourth, and twenty-eight at the Fifth.*

ENERGY FIELDS OF THE FOURTH DIMENSION

   Many people are of the opinion that the move into the Fourth
Dimension, or making that leap of the octave, they are then
moving into an eighth, ninth, or tenth layer of the existing field
of the Third Dimension. This is not true, Dear ones, Dear hearts.
While there are expansions of experiences within the Third
Dimension, there is that great deciding moment - a defining
moment - which can be felt when you move between the octaves.
This is the same as when a sound barrier is broken or when a light
barrier is broken and is as thin a barrier that has then broken. In
the moment that I come forward for instruction, do you not hear,
at the inner level, a barrier that is being broken?

Response: "I can hear the pitch open up as you step through."

   This barrier, as I am now defining for you, is indeed that fine
moment that exists between the Third and the Fourth Dimension.
Now it has always been your opinion that when I come forward
to bring discourse, I am projecting my energy through the Fifth
Dimension, through the Fourth Dimension, and onward; but we
are speaking of consciousness, consciousness as thought. These
thoughts permeate from the Fifth Dimension to the Fourth
Dimensional understanding. There they move again, as I have
stated, through fourteen levels of differentiation. From there,
they move onward into the level where they are embraced
through the human senses.

A RANGE OF RAY FORCES

Now, to bring this into a greater understanding: a molecule exists and is protected through the physical structure of the neutron, the proton, and the electron; these physical structures allow mass and matter to exist in your physical world. Similarly, if the consciousness were to move from a different understanding through the Fifth, to the Fourth, and onward to the Third Dimension, there would be the elemental life force which would come forward and bring great service in that motion. You have understood the elemental life force and how it exists on your planet only at a primary level, relating to wind, water, earth, and fire. These primary elements are of course an expression of a higher force that exists from the Fourth Dimension. Again, as you hear these words, known to you in a clairaudient manner, are they not indeed words that come from the Fifth Dimension, arcing through this Fourth Dimensional range of Ray Forces, and moving again into another range of Ray Forces? Questions?

Response: "Lots of questions."

WHEN THE TIME IS RIGHT

I shall proceed first. Perhaps in this second part of this discussion, I can shed even greater light and greater sound upon the purpose and the reason for this instruction.

The Golden City Vortices exist in their own timing and intention. I say this very often, "timing and intention." It is important always that one is not led too early for that drink, for is it then truly appreciated? One should never be forced beyond their time to learn something they are not ready yet to learn. We start always in beginning steps and are led one step after another into a greater understanding.

The heart cannot be opened immediately, not until the lessons of true love, true compassion, and true mercy can be learned. These of course always come as lessons of the heart, lessons that come in their timing and in their intention. But until those lessons are learned, one is not readied. One is not ready yet to understand a greater instruction. But intention can always be held in its purity. Intention can always be held to bring forward that greater lesson . . . to bring forward that greater Light Divine . . . to bring forward that greater sound, which is indeed the song of God. Intention then is qualified through the proper timing. One then knows that when the time is right, the intention flows forward and all moves with that greater harmony of which I speak. Now, I shall continue on this understanding.

BABAJERAN AND THE ELEMENTAL LIFE FORCE

The great Earth Changes are coming forward to bring a great purification. This has always been known by those who have the eyes to see and the ears to hear. What were they seeing? What were they listening to? But to the inner kingdoms of the Fourth Dimension that are, were, and always shall be. These inner kingdoms exist Dear ones, Dear hearts, bringing their service in even a greater degree to beloved Babajeran. They know the purpose of her heart, the purpose of her mind, and the purpose of her greater will. Of course, it is always difficult for one who comes from a Third Dimensional understanding, which sees the Earth only as a forest . . . only as a mountain . . . only as a river . . . only as a strata to be conquered. Here lies this mineral; here lies the oil; here lies the coal to be burnt. From the Third Dimensional understanding, the Earth is seen as something to be Mastered, something to be conquered, and something to be understood only through the five senses.

At the Fourth Dimensional level comes a greater understanding. There is a wonderment of creation and of the kingdoms that lie within. Have you ever wondered about the telepathic responses of the Animal Kingdom, their inner connection with nature itself? The songs of the birds, how are they interconnected to the life on Earth and who rides upon their wings? Those who have the eyes to see and the ears to hear know and understand the great service these kingdoms bring forward, this great service of the Elemental Life Force.

THE DIVINE ONESHIP OF NATURE

In entering a Golden City Vortex, one begins this deeper communication, this deeper communion that exists with these kingdoms. This is the ascent of consciousness. This is the ascent of emotion. This is the ascent of higher activity. When one is led naturally to this understanding, they seek the demonstration of natural law. I have given you this understanding of natural law, for within you exists that first Divine Oneship of nature. This indeed is the Eight-sided Cell of Perfection and it is through this Eight-sided Cell of Perfection that you are indeed connected at the Third Dimension, at the Fourth Dimension, and onward to the Fifth Dimension of consciousness. It is this perfected Cell that lies within you, that brings the stream of consciousness forward . . . which becomes that force within that leads you to seek greater harmony, greater divinity, and acceptance of perfection.

OPENING THE DIVINE CELL

The Fourth Dimension is always connected within you, Dear ones, Dear hearts. Through this collective forgetting, understood as the time of Kali Yuga, consciousness has fallen and no longer opens this Cell within at will. But all communion that exists with the Fourth Dimension exists through the opening of this Divine Cell. That is why the work of the Violet Flame has been brought forward at this time. Through calling and invoking its presence, you then begin to understand those great lessons of love . . . those great lessons of compassion . . . those great lessons of mercy and their ever importance in the opening of your heart.

This opening of your heart is not only the opening of the Heart Chakra; it is the opening of this Divine Cell that is connected through these laws of nature to the kingdoms within. These kingdoms that exist in the elementals . . . these kingdoms that exist in the salamanders . . . these kingdoms that exist within the undines . . . these kingdoms that exist between the gnomes and the fairies, they are indeed at a level that knows and understands a greater harmony. They know and understand the great balancing effect that must take place to keep the Earth in its perfected order.

CHANGE AND CHOICE

Now, Dear ones, Dear hearts, this perfected order also includes change. Change allows for a great cleansing to occur, not only a cleansing of what is not wanted, but also a choosing of what is to be kept. Each time you enter a closet ready to clean, discard, and get rid of what is no longer wanted, in that moment, you will also choose what you will keep . . . you will also choose what you value . . . you will choose what is useful to you. In this Time of Great Change, where humanity and beloved Babajeran are bonded in one natural law through the Fourth Dimension, there is a great assistance that is being given by these beloved beings of light, sound, and their fourteen spaces . . . fourteen directions . . . fourteen understandings of balance. This balance brings itself forward Dear ones, Dear heart, to serve a greater Cause Divine.

INTERCONNECTIVITY

In the Golden Cities, there is a great interaction with these kingdoms. For this communing to occur, for this greater harmonization to come forward, one needs to understand its greater service. It is there to serve the greater heart of desire with another way of approaching and understanding. Conscious immortality is indeed the tie that binds all of these dimensions together; for you see, in conscious immortality, you are able to move beyond a barrier or differentiation. You are able to see the interconnectivity of all of life. You are able then to see the Third Dimension, the Fourth Dimension, and the Fifth Dimension existing, not in a hierarchical sense, but existing in their great spiral of life. Now, I shall open the floor for your questions.

SOUND FREQUENCIES

Question: "Yes. The resonance or sound frequencies between the dimensions, is this where one grouping of sound frequencies start and another grouping stops?"

This is so, Dear one.

Question: "These resonances are the pathways with which the light structures are put forward and sent?"

It is true, Dear one. From the Great Central Sun, they come under a grander direction. A direction is then chosen for Third Dimension. A direction then is orchestrated for Fourth Dimension. This direction at the Fifth Dimension is chosen.

PERCEPTION

Question: "I see. In our world, where the atomic structure is electrons, protons, and neutrons and each one of those is relative to a light ray, to move into the Fourth Dimension, must we have another light ray? And into the Fifth, we must have yet another light ray?"

It is not a matter of another light Ray that brings expansion to an understanding of a dimension. It is an orchestration of the light rays in the Fourth Dimension and complete understanding of these light rays in the Fifth Dimension. Do you understand? It has to do again with perception. It is the way that light is understood. It is the way that sound is understood. In this moment, the light and sound Ray of my thought, coming to you, is beyond an understanding within the physical and yet a physical demonstration is now being given to you, is it not?

Answer: "You are standing there."

This perception is of utmost importance. It is important to understand that perception, within itself, is another key in understanding what we would perceive in this moment for this teaching, which is a separation between Third Dimension and Fourth Dimension and a separation between Fourth Dimension and Fifth Dimension. Questions?

Response: "And yet you are still standing there."

So you see, your perception is one where you have the eyes to see and the ears to hear. But your eyes do indeed still see. Your ears do indeed still hear. They are still one in the same and yet they have been developed to understand at another level, or better yet, along the greater spiral of consciousness. The teaching I bring to you this moment pierces through each of these layers of separation perceived through the limiting Third Dimensional understanding of the five senses. But if one expands the senses, taste can be taken to other levels, can it not?

Answer: "Yes it can."

Touch can be taken to other levels, can it not?

Answer: "Absolutely".

This same paradigm can be applied to all of the senses. In this moment, between my words, do you perceive the Great Silence?

Answer: "Of course."

In this moment, within my words, do you hear another high-pitched ring?

Answer: "Yes."

This is my point Dear one, Dear heart. All dimensions bring their demonstration of the mighty Truth Divine.

DIVINE CHAMBER OF THE HEART

Question: "And this is accomplished with the opening of the Eight-sided Cell of Perfection?"

The opening indeed, Dear one, of that Divine Chamber of the heart.

Response: "It has been my understanding that it was only through that undeniable sense of love for you and other members of the Spiritual Hierarchy, for the planet, and for humanity, that the Cell would open."

And so I say, "love will move a mountain," will it not?

Answer: "Yes it will."

Questions?

Question: "I've noticed that when thought, feeling, and action are completely aligned, that the Ray Forces then open. As you come through, may one pass into that Fourth Dimension with that alignment?"

THE ASCENSION PROCESS AND THE MASTER TEACHER

It is so, Dear one. This indeed is the process of Ascension. It is the process of ascending perception, this perception not to be limited to one definition of the senses. Questions?

Response: "Yes. In aligning the senses, it seems all too easy to focus in different directions at one time, instead of staying on one focus and one intention to create a specific outcome."

This is the work of the Master Teacher, you see. The Master Teacher comes forward and allows the chela the opportunity to bring a great focus into a certain area and there the gates of freedom are found. Questions?

Response: "At this point, I have no further questions with regard to this particular topic. This will be much for everyone to contemplate."

Mighty Violet Ray stream forth from the Fifth Dimension
into the hearts of men.
May the Fourth Dimension bring its alignment
for greater purification of the Earth Divine.
May all align and Ascend in thy flame.

I AM Saint Germain.

Response: "Thank you very much."

CHAPTER THIRTEEN

Finer Bodies of Light

*Saint Germain on developing and building
the energies for Ascension.*

Greetings, Beloved chelas in that mighty Violet Flame. I AM Saint Germain and I request permission to come forward.

Response: "Dear Saint Germain, please come forward. You are most welcome."

VIOLET FLAME ANGELS OF PROTECTION

Greetings Dear hearts, Dear chelas, aspirants, students of mine, in that mighty Violet Ray, that mighty Violet Flame of Mercy, Transmutation, and Forgiveness. It is with great gladness that I am here this morning to give you discourse, to give you advice. You see, it has been some time since we have last discoursed. However, it is important to understand that even if we do not enter into formal discussions, discourses or lessons, that I am always there, present, guiding, and directing you.

Throughout the last year, I have sent my presence to be around you at all times. The mighty Violet Flame angels have stood guard over your work and protected your business and your home, as per your request Dear ones, Dear hearts. However, it is important that we continue with our public work. For you see, we have also given you much instructions on the inner planes, this is known as the individual work. But there is also much work that can also be distributed to the public at large and help them gain a momentum in their own Ascension and spiritual process.

EXERCISE THE LIGHT BODIES

At this time, the most important thing to focus upon is your spiritual growth and development, this of course in tandem with the

Ascension process. It is the letting go of the gross, or shall we say, the misconduct of the physical body, so that it can be let go of and you may train your consciousness to understand the finer bodies where the Light of God Never, Never Faileth.

This is not to say Dear ones, Dear hearts, that these finer bodies are not always surrounding you. Indeed they are, but it is like this, for your understanding, the more that you use and exercise a thing, you gain a greater understanding of it. And so it is with the finer bodies of light, the more that you grow and exercise and understand their use, the more then that you can indeed use them.

THE INNER MIND

At night time when you sleep, this is perhaps one of the best times that you begin to understand the finer bodies. The sleeping process is one where the outer mind, for lack of a better word, or shall we say, the grosser, denser body, has a tendency to drop itself, or to lower itself in a circadian rhythm. This then allows the greater, inner mind to come forward. The finer essence of these energy bodies then steps forward for your experience.

DREAM WORLD

In the dream state, one then begins to have contact with other worlds that cannot be seen during the physical waking hours. Now one may say, "how does this dream world exist?" Yes, it does indeed exist to the belief system and some of it also exists just to the essence of your thought. But it is the greater reality from whence you come Dear ones. It is the greater, finer body that someday you will return to and take upon into the glory of light and the Ascension.

THE GREATER SPIRITUAL BODY

But in the beginning, as a small child just begins to walk (toddle), before it can walk, so you too must have this experience of exercising these bodies. Now I would recommend that sleeping more hours is not the solution. It is developing an awareness of these bodies and how these bodies, at all times, can bring your physical world in contact with the other world of the unseen. This unseen exists at many levels. There is of course a greater spiritual body, but just so you may understand, there is first the physical body; then there is the Astral body; we move on then to the Causal body. The Causal body of course will bring the purest instant result. The Astral body at times can also bring a beautiful effect. It is the melding of these two spiritual bodies, the Astral and the Causal that leads one then in the dream states, as you would understand them, to the greater spiritual body. This is the body that combines, as a Master will demonstrate for you, in bi-location and also in the transmigration process.

These bodies of light are essential Dear ones, Dear heart, to carry forward the Ascension process. It is important to understand, at this time of the Earth Plane and Planet, that there is much that is changing but nothing ever happens by mistake, ever, ever, ever. The Earth Changes indeed will happen alongside a great acceleration of energies upon the Earth. These accelerations of energies are due to give a great influence to the spiritual bodies of humanity. This will allow a greater development of Astral and Causal bodies, thus combining into that greater collective body.

CANDLE MEDITATION

There are many different techniques that can be used for the improvement and strengthening of these bodies. Perhaps the best that we teach our chelas and aspirants is that of meditation. It is important in meditation to always focus upon one single element. That is why beloved El Morya has often given you the meditation of the candle. This allows a unity of consciousness to come forward throughout the meditation process.

Meditation itself, you see Dear ones, helps the union of the Astral and the Causal body to meld as ONE, that then the chela can step into. This also happens in the night time hours, or for those who sleep during the day; but of course, what I am referring to is sleep itself. When one goes to sleep, there is that instant where the Astral and the Causal bodies combine. This occurs sometimes as that feeling that you are falling off of a cliff and you instantly jar or jump. This jar or jump is the merging of the two bodies. It is usually felt first in the solar plexus. Sometimes it is felt through the back chakras, but more commonly, it is felt in the solar (plexus) itself. The next technique for merging these two bodies together is working with the Chakra Centers. As you know Dear ones, Dear hearts, it is best to always use a breathing technique, and there are many that open up the chakras. [Editor's Note: Please see Appendix A for instruction on the Candle Meditation.]

OVERLAPPING AND NIGHTMARES

Now, nightmares occur when the merging of the Astral and the Causal bodies occur through the lower chakras. Sometimes this happens because one maybe ill, or in a diseased state, or may be feeling physical pain before they enter into the night time worlds. Sometimes it also happens when one has used drugs or alcohol. Leaving through these lower chakras allows for an overlapping of the Astral and the Causal bodies, making it much more difficult to integrate the two, and experience is not perceived in such a manner that is conducive for the soul.

BREATH TECHNIQUES

Breathing techniques that can be used are those that always open the Heart Chakra, for they are the best. I recommend breathing techniques that integrate the solar plexus and the heart, for this allows for a greater integration of energy along the kundalini. For with the kundalini energies, inner development is also related to this development of the light fields and forces.

Now before I proceed with more information, I sense your question.

NATURE AND THE PHYSICAL BODY

Question: "Yes. The first question I have regarding these finer energy bodies, where there is a merging of the Astral and the Causal, is what system the Masters use to achieve their interaction with Nature?"

The interaction with Nature at the physical level is achieved with the putting on of the gross physical body. However, as one begins to Master the merging of the Astral and Causal bodies, there comes a greater knowledge of the physical itself. For you see Dear ones, as Hermetic Law would state: as above, so below. But not to get into that technique just yet, it is most important that you exercise and develop the merging of the two (light) bodies. Each of these bodies of course has seven (major) layers of the field, in the same way that the physical body has seven layers of its field.

Do you understand?

Response: "Yes, I do."

NEW ENERGETICS

This of course is a much more subtle awareness. And so the physical body, as it would appear, contains within it three times seven; that is, at the first stages of development, as one begins to enter into the merging of the Astral and the Causal bodies, new energetic bodies are added bit by bit, layer by layer. This is of course the process of Mastery. As one is able to develop each of these energy bodies, then they are able to access other dimensions of consciousness and layers of consciousness, into other worlds now unseen. This is one of the understandings of the other dimensions. You see Dear ones, Dear hearts, consciousness must grow. When it is ready to flow, it will grow into the areas that it needs to move into.

ATTENTION AND THE FLOW

Currently today, your scientists work to understand the new dimensions, but what they do not understand, is that they have not yet built the vessels to move into. I know that this is a complex and almost a metaphysical question and understanding, but you see Dear one, energy will go once the attention has flowed. That is the premise behind the statement. Questions?

Response: "If we can visualize it in our attention, then it can be experienced and created."

Yes Dear one, Dear chela of mine. It is through that attention that then the experience begins to flow. Experience becomes even a greater or grander Creator in this process, as one begins to exercise, just at the most elementary steps, this creating of the first integrated light body. One then begins to achieve a greater dominion and Mastery over the physical. For when one begins to notice the nuance and the flow of energy within this subtle light body, one then also begins to notice the nuance and subtleties of the flow of the physical plane. This comes though the silent gestures and the "a-ha," if you will, of noticing through the corner of the eye, the flashing of light, or a sunlit orb that may be hovering. These of course are the beloved Elementals who exist in these planes of consciousness. They too have gained Mastery over their light bodies. For you see, when one begins to vibrate and resonate to a certain dimension or plane of consciousness, one will then begin to notice others who are reciprocating in harmonic resonance at the same field or energy of light and sound.

BUILDING BLOCKS

Yes, it is true Dear ones, Dear hearts, within your universe, or scheme of evolution, the building blocks are light and sound. There are indeed other building blocks that exist in other dimensions that perhaps later we could discourse upon. But for now, let us talk about these principles which are most important.

THE LIGHTS OF CREATION

The first of these is light. And I would like to add, light and darkness. Now, we can speak in metaphor but perhaps it's better if we just speak in a literal stance, of light as physical light that comes from your physical sun. There is also its polarity, which is the spiritual light that arcs from the Galactic Center through your sun, which also creates the body. Both of these are forms of light.

DARKNESS DEFINES LIGHT

There is also darkness, darkness that comes, resonates, and forms, shall we say, the Cup for the light. This is the reason for the presence of the dwarf sun within your sun, so that the polarities are complete. It brings about the darkness and from the darkness, it is the same as the thought that then holds the energy for the light to come forward.

HARMONIC CONCORDANCE OF LIGHT AND SOUND

When we speak of sound, we speak of the resonance of light. Some would say that sound is light at a denser consolidation. However, we see sound as almost a higher frequency, if you will, and of course, its companion is that of silence. Silence, sometimes it is said that it can be deafening, but yet within the silence, if one will truly, truly listen, is contained the Harmony of the Spheres.

This harmonic concordance of light and sound comes forward to fill the void, the void that is created through silence and darkness. Both of these are components of the creation and the creative process. When I speak of this as creation, and I speak of this as creative, I speak that there is the creation as it exists in a natural response to harmonic vibration. When I speak of the Creator or the creative process, I am also speaking of the application of such laws into their natural order. For your see, engendered within each and every one of you Dear ones, Dear hearts, is the ability to bring both of these together and create the world that you wish to live in and experience. This of course addresses the finer principle of thought, for all, as I have said before in these beginning stages, comes from its grander Creator, which is the thought process. You are indeed what you think. However, I wish not to get lost within this, because I understand that you are only in your beginning steps of this understanding.

INSTINCT, FEELING, AND EMOTION

The Astral body, you see Dear ones, is the body of the feeling world. It contains the emotions that have come from the instinct of animal creation. For in your experience of the Earth Plane and Planet, it was deemed sometime ago for this time period upon the Earth, that the souls that are encased at this present time would have more animalistic bodies. This of course gives them the opportunity to sense so much more, to taste, to touch, to hear, to feel, and then to move these emotions into even a greater sensation, that of anger, that of joy, that of passion, lust, and even that of the greater ones, of compassion, of love, of benevolence. All of these Dear ones, Dear hearts, are the qualities that come from the Astral feeling world.

This world, you see, gives a nuance and subtlety to the experience of the Earth Plane and Planet and also brings the vivid colorations of the Astral plane. But in the merging, you see Dear ones, with Divine Thought, the God qualities are expressed in even finer and more brilliant qualities.

Now before I continue, questions?

REINVIGORATION OF THE CHAKRAS

Question: "Yes. In the combination of the Causal body and the Astral body, the breath techniques that you are suggesting are the ones that incorporate the heart and the solar plexus, correct?"

This is correct. This leads to a natural reinvigoration, a movement into the Throat Chakra, the Third Eye, and finally to the Crown Chakra itself.

CONSCIOUSNESS GROWS

Question: "The overlapping of the Astral and the Causal at a sleep level, when exiting through the lower chakras, which is how nightmares occur, is this just an experience of another vibration of consciousness that the combination of these two bodies experience?"

Of course Dear one, it is an experience, but it also shows the vibratory level at which you have developed the merging of the two bodies. This is very important, for the greatest judger, shall we say, of the soul is always the self. But indeed, how can experience be measured? It is important to understand how you are evolving and how you are growing. Now it is not up to the Master Teacher, or up to another fellow companion, to say to you how evolved you are, where you are at on the scale of growth. However, it is important to you to know and understand where you are and where your consciousness may grow and go to.

AWAKENING TO LIGHT

In this process of allowing the consciousness to merge in the night time, is the process of allowing this growth of the light body, a light body that you can then bring into your experience in your waking world. This is what is really known and understood as the Awakening Process. This allows the light body to have its presence throughout the waking time, in full and able consciousness. This is the same body that has its contact with the inner world and the inner workings, where the magic and miracles do indeed occur Dear ones, Dear hearts. However, when one begins to understand the Alchemy that lies within the soul, this is not magic, is it Dear ones? This is not a miracle, but only an understanding and acting of the law.

DARE TO DREAM

Response: "So, in essence, it's a natural course of evolution."

Indeed it is, Dear ones, Dear hearts. However, it is a natural course of evolution for those who dare to dream, for those who dare to see, for those who dare to hear. For you see, it is from this daring, dreaming world that then comes the pure Co-creation into the physical. This leads to an overall leap in consciousness and understanding, for as this light body is developed, it too seeks its own resonance in compatibility and companionship, and like minds find others of like mind.

This is one of the principles working behind the Golden City Vortices, for they function at this higher level of the combining of many, many light bodies. As was taught in the past in so many of our discourses and lessons, these are the inner workings of these vibrations of the Golden City Vortices.

GOLDEN CITIES OF LIGHT

Now you begin to understand the great and grand undertaking that it has been, to coordinate the life energy cycles and forces of so many within those natural worlds, to bring them under a greater command of the unification of a the light body. That is why we have given the instruction for so many to travel to and experience the Golden City Vortices. For these are areas where, not only the techniques can be practiced with greater precision, they are also areas where one may enter into this light body and experience it with a greater fluidity.

THE FIRST SPIRITUAL BODY

Question: "I see. Is there a specific term for the combination of these two bodies, the Causal and the Astral?"

Perhaps the best is to call it the first spiritual body, for it becomes a body which gives an experience, an exercise, and understanding of the fluidity of the spiritual planes. The fact that they work beyond linear time, the fact that they also work beyond the gross physical laws of the physical plane, they contain within them, the higher manifestations of such laws.

Response: "I see. I remember as a child falling asleep and finding myself waking up in the basement, but I wasn't in the basement, and then willing to return to my body. The same with an airplane, falling out of the airplane and finding myself on the ground, watching the airplane continue on, and then I'd have to reenter the airplane."

These of course are metaphors for the solar plexus itself. You see Dear one, even at that time, this understanding was contained naturally within you, was it not?

Response: "Yes."

EMBRACE LIFE

This training is an essential element to begin to understand the Ascension process. There are many who believe that the Ascension process is one of the letting go of the physical plane. And yes, while this is a byproduct, it is also built upon the idea of embracing energies not that of letting them go; it is understanding the working of such energies and how these forces cooperate in timing and intention to bring forth the greater desired result. Yes, it is true that there is an element of renunciation involved in this Ascension, or liberation process, but it is also important to understand that there is an absolute embracing of all of life that is also contained within it. As I have said before Dear ones, Dear hearts, there are no mistakes ever, ever, ever. Each experience that comes to you is an opportunity for your growth, is an opportunity for your evolution, if you but see it that way.

I realize today that I have given you a very valuable lesson. I am open for questions, but it is important that you take this information into the depth of your own experience and there carry out your own laboratory experience of the self and soul. So Be It.

GOLDEN AGE OF KALI YUGA

Question: "I have a particular question now of my own, regarding the Golden Age of Kali Yuga. Does it actually reach the zenith of a true Golden Age?"

It will not reach the true zenith of the times of one hundred percent light. However, through time compaction, it will reach the times of fifty to almost sixty percent light. This of course would give much debate, but it is important to understand the elements of time compaction. When we speak of time, we are really speaking of increased frequencies of light and sound. Of course this also gives increased frequencies of darkness and increased frequencies of silence.

Now that you understand, through this discourse, this expansion of Astral and Causal light, you also will begin to see how consciousness itself will return back at the height of the Golden Age to the times of Dvapara Yugas, that which was the ending times of Lemuria and the beginning of the Atlantean consciousness.

NOURISHING SOUL

Question: "I understand. What is the greatest need to be addressed now?"

First, the greatest needs are the needs of humanity. That first need is not the question of the mind, but that need is to nourish the soul at hand. It is important to understand that we are entering a great time of growth and evolution. This growth and evolution is of the greatest import.

In the beginning of our work, as you well know, it was advised to release all of the information related to the upcoming and possible Earth Changes. It was in that flow of direction that we began our work and in the middle of that flow, we then dispensed the Twelve Jurisdictions. We still would like to see an emphasis placed upon the prophetic work of Earth Change. However, it must always be accompanied by each spiritual remedial measure.

SPIRITUAL PREPAREDNESS

It is important to understand that the Golden Cities have been brought forward at this time to accelerate growth and evolution among humanity and to ensure an interaction with the higher planes. This interaction with the higher planes is the true hope, faith, and preparedness that needs to be taken.

Question: "I understand. Lori has recently had a night of Earth Changes dreams. How significant is this?"

This information is now being flooded, if you will, into the inner mind. It is because certain events are now just destined to happen. Certain events are coming to the Earth Plane and Planet that will change the face of the Earth forever. However, it is important to place an emphasis again upon spiritual growth and development; as Master K. H. has always said, "Within your heart is the gentle revolution which can redirect the course of such events."

What was downloaded was a series of prophetic facts and information of the global warming and catastrophes that could possibly happen within the next ten years. If you wish to explore them, it is certain that we can. However, I also like to place an emphasis upon the growth and direction at a spiritual level. For you see, in the same way that you can build a community that is drought, wind, and earthquake resistant, you can also build your light fields that are just as resistant to all that the physical planes can bring.

Do you understand?

Response: "Now that is a degree of Mastery. Yes, I understand; however, the masses may not."

THE MASSES

This work was never intended for the masses. However, there are many within this Global Awakening who have the eyes to see and the ears to hear. That is why we had directed you so many years ago to move into the Star energies; for you see Dear one, Dear heart, this would give a greater assistance, not only in your own understanding, but in your own experience.

Response: "I see. I have no further questions at this time."

Spiritual Lineage of the Violet Flame

 The teachings of the Violet Flame, as taught in the work of I AM America, come through the Goddess of Compassion and Mercy Kuan Yin. She holds the feminine aspects of the flame, which are Compassion, Mercy, Forgiveness, and Peace. Her work with the Violet Flame is well documented in the history of Ascended Master teachings, and it is said that the altar of the etheric Temple of Mercy holds the flame in a Lotus Cup. She became Saint Germain's teacher of the Sacred Fire in the inner realms, and he carried the masculine aspect of the flame into human activity through Purification, Alchemy, and Transmutation. One of the best means to attract the beneficent activities of the Violet Flame is through the use of decrees and invocation. However, you can meditate on the flame, visualize the flame, and receive its transmuting energies like "the light of a thousand Suns," radiant and vibrant as the first day that the Elohim Arcturus and Diana drew it forth from our solar Sun at the creation of the Earth. Whatever form, each time you use the Violet Flame, these two Master Teachers hold you in the loving arms of its action and power.

 The following is an invocation for the Violet Flame to be used at sunrise or sunset. It is utilized while experiencing the visible change of night to day, and day to night. In fact, if you observe the horizon at these times, you will witness light transitioning from pinks to blues, and then a subtle violet strip adorning the sky. We have used this invocation for years in varying scenes and circumstances, overlooking lakes, rivers, mountaintops, deserts, and prairies; in huddled traffic and busy streets; with groups of students or sitting with a friend; but more commonly alone in our home or office, with a glint of soft light streaming from a window. The result is always the same: a calm, centering force of stillness. We call it *the Space*.

Invocation of the Violet Flame for Sunrise and Sunset
I invoke the Violet Flame to come forth in the name of I AM that I AM,
To the Creative Force of all the realms of all the Universes, the Alpha, the Omega, the Beginning, and the End,
To the Great Cosmic Beings and Torch Bearers of all the realms of all the Universes,
And the Brotherhoods and Sisterhoods of Breath, Sound, and Light, who honor this Violet Flame that comes forth from the Ray of Divine Love—the Pink Ray, and the Ray of Divine Will—the Blue Ray of all Eternal Truths.

I invoke the Violet Flame to come forth in the name of I AM that I AM!
Mighty Violet Flame, stream forth from the Heart of the Central Logos, the Mighty Great Central Sun! Stream in, through, and around me.

(Then insert other prayers and/or decrees for the Violet Flame.)

Glossary

Absolute Harmony: Order and peace permeate throughout.

Age of Cooperation: The age humanity is currently being prepared to enter; it occurs simultaneously with the "Time of Change."

Akashic Records: The recorded history of all created things from time immemorial, and constructed with the fifth cosmic element: ether.

Akhenaten: The ancient king of Egypt (1388 BC) embraced the unfolding consciousness of the ONE, which culturally replaced the polytheistic religion of his Kingdom. A pioneer of monotheistic religion, Akhenaten embraced the Christ Consciousness and some esoteric historians view him as a spiritual forerunner who led the way for the incarnation of Jesus Christ. According to the Master Teachers, Akhenaten is one of the prior lifetimes attributed to Ascended Master Serapis Bey.

Alchemy: A hidden yet transformative and sacred science which bridges the world of chemistry and metallurgy with the spiritual worlds of Mastery and Ascension Process.

Alignment: Balance.

Ascended Master: Once an ordinary human, an Ascended Master has undergone a spiritual transformation over many lifetimes. He or she has Mastered the lower planes—mental, emotional, and physical—to unite with his or her God-Self or I AM Presence. An Ascended Master is freed from the Wheel of Karma. He or she moves forward in spiritual evolution beyond this planet; however, an Ascended Master remains attentive to the spiritual well-being of humanity, inspiring and serving the Earth's spiritual growth and evolution.

Ascension: A process of Mastering thoughts, feelings, and actions that balance positive and negative karmas. It allows entry to a higher state of consciousness and frees a person from the need to reincarnate on the lower Earthly planes or lokas of experience. Ascension is the process of spiritual liberation, also known as moksha.

Ascension Process: The Ascension Process, according to Saint Germain, gathers the energies of the individual chakras and expands their energy through the heart. The Law of Love calibrates the energy fields (aura) to Zero Point—a physical and philosophical viewpoint of neutrality. From there, the subtle and fine tuning of the light bodies is effectuated through the higher chakras, sequentially including the Throat Chakra, the Third Eye Chakra, and finally the Crown Chakra. Zero Point is key in this process and it is here that the energies of all past lives are brought to psychological and physical (karmic) balance. Then the initiate is able to withdraw their light bodies from the physical plane into the Astral Light of the Fourth Dimension. The Ascension Process may take several lifetimes to complete and the beginning stages are defined through the arduous process of obtaining self-knowledge, the acceptance of the conscious immortality of the soul, and the use of Alchemy through the Violet Flame. Intermediate stages may manifest the anomalies of Dimensional Acceleration, Vibrational Shifting, Cellular Awakening and Acceleration, and contact with the Fourth Dimension. Use of the Gold Ray at this level accelerates the liberation process and unites the individual with soul mates and their beloved Twin Ray. Later stages of Ascension include the transfiguration of light bodies and Fifth Dimensional contact through the super-senses as the magnificent Seamless Garment manifests its light. It is claimed that the Golden Cities assist the Ascension Process at every stage of development. According to the Master Teachers diet and fasting will also aid the Ascension Process at various phases.

Ascension Valley: According to the I AM America Prophecies, Ascended Masters appear in physical form in the Golden City Vortices during and after a prophesied twenty-year period. At that time, Mass Ascensions occur in the Golden Cities, at the Golden City Star locations, and in select geophysical locations around the world, which are hosted by the complimentary energies of Mother Earth. A model of this geophysical location is Ascension Valley, located in the Shalahah Vortex. The energy of Ascension Valley prepares students to integrate their light bodies and spiritual consciousness into the Oneship, the divinity within, and further prepares the body, mind, and spirit to experience and travel into the New Dimensions.

Astral Body: This subtle light body contains our feelings, desires, and emotions and exists as an intermediate light body between the physical body and the Causal Body (Mental Body). According to the Master Teachers we enter the Astral Plane through our Astral Body when we sleep, and many dreams and visions are experiences in this Plane of vibrant color and sensation. Through spiritual development the Astral Body strengthens, and the luminosity of its light is often detected in the physical plane. A spiritual adept may have the ability to consciously leave their physical body while traveling in their Astral Body. The Astral Body or Astral Plane has various levels of evolution, and is the heavenly abode where the soul resides after the disintegration of the physical body. The Astral Body is also known to esoteric scholars as the Body Double, the Desire Body, and the Emotional Body.

At-One-Ment: The spiritual practice and state of Unity. This spiritual ideal is philosophically affirmed through the recognition of humanity's innate divinity, equality, and human connection to ONE source of creation. This results in the At-ONE-ment, and the advanced practitioner morphs into a Step-down Transformer of the Seven Rays of Light and Sound as an expression of beauty and creation. The At-ONE-ment facilitates the consciousness of Unana.

Aura: The subtle energy field of luminous light that surrounds the human body.

Axiotonal Bodies: Light bodies of the Human Aura defined by magnetic energy lines, similar to acupuncture lines on the human body and lei-lines on Mother Earth. It is claimed Axiotonal Lines connect our human biology to resonating star systems within our galaxy, affecting human chemistry and genetic change.

Babajeran: A name for the Earth Mother that means, "grandmother rejoicing."

Belief: A conviction or opinion of trust based on insufficient evidence or reality. This confidence may be based on alleged facts without positive knowledge, direct experience, or proof. According to the Master Teachers, beliefs may be negative, positive, or both. Often the unchallenged nature of beliefs form the nucleus of Co-creative activity. The spectrum of individual and collective beliefs can vary from innocent gullibility to unwavering religious faith and conviction.

Blue Flame: The activity of the Blue Ray, based upon the activation of the individual will, manifests the qualities of truth, power, determination, and diligence in human endeavors. The Blue Flame is associated with the transformation of our individual choices, and its inherent processes align the individual will to the Divine Will through the HU-man qualities of detachment, steadiness, calm, harmony, and God-protection.

Blue Ray: A Ray is a perceptible light and sound frequency, and the Blue Ray not only resonates with the color blue, but is identified with the qualities of steadiness, calm, perseverance, transformation, harmony, diligence, determination, austerity, protection, humility, truthfulness, and self-negation. It forms one-third of the Unfed Flame within the heart—the Blue Ray of God Power, which nourishes the spiritual unfoldment of the human into the HU-man. Use of the Violet Flame evokes the Blue Ray into action throughout the light bodies, where the Blue Ray clarifies intentions and assists the alignment of the Will. In Ascended Master teachings the Blue Ray is alleged to have played a major role in the physical manifestation of the Earth's first Golden City—Shamballa and six of fifty-one Golden Cities emanate the Blue Ray's peaceful, yet piercing frequencies. The Blue Ray is esoterically linked to the planet Saturn, the development of the Will, the ancient Lemurian Civilization, the Archangel Michael, the Elohim Hercules, the Master Teacher El Morya, and the Eastern Doors of all Golden Cities.

Breathwork: The conscious, spiritual application of breath, often accompanied by visualization and meditation forms the nexus of Breathwork. Ascended Master teachings often incorporate various breathing techniques to activate and integrate Ray Forces in the Human Aura and light bodies.

Cause and effect: Every action causes an event, which is the consequence or result of the first. This law is often referred to as karma—or the sixth Hermetic Law.

Cellular Awakening: A spiritual initiation activated by the Master Teachers Saint Germain and Kuthumi. Through this process the physical body is accelerated at the cellular level, preparing consciousness to recognize and receive instruction from the Fourth Dimension. Supplemental teachings on the Cellular Awakening claim this process assists the spiritual student to assimilate the higher frequencies and energies now available on Earth. Realizing the Cellular Awakening can ameliorate catastrophic Earth Change and initiate consciousness into the ONE through the realization of devotion, compassion, Brotherhood and the Universal Heart.

Chakra: Sanskrit for wheel. Seven spinning wheels of human-bioenergy centers stacked from the base of the spine to the top of the head.

Chamber of the Heart: The sacred location of the Eight-sided Cell of Perfection, in the human heart. This site is surrounded by a mandala of energy: the Unfed Flame of love, wisdom, and power.

Chela: Disciple.

Chohan: Another word for Lord.

Christ Consciousness: A level of consciousness that unites both feminine and masculine energies and produces the innocence and purity of the I AM. Its energies heal, enlighten, and transform every negative human condition and pave the way for the realization of the divine HU-man.

Closure of Understanding: The completion and release of a Karmic lesson.

Co-creation: Creating with the God Source.

Compassion: An attribute of the Violet Flame is the sympathetic understanding of the suffering of another.

Conscience: The internal recognition of right and wrong in regard to one's actions and motives.

Consciousness: Awakening to one's own existence, sensations, and cognitions.

Conscious Immortality: Awareness, acceptance, and knowledge of the immortal, spiritual soul.

Cup: A symbol of neutrality and grace. The Ascended Masters often refer to our human body as a Cup filled with our thoughts and feelings.

Desire: Of the source; the ninth of Twelve Jurisdictions and states the heart's desire is the source of creation.

Deva: Shining one or being of light.

Dharma: Purpose.

Divine Cell: The Eight-sided Cell of Perfection.

Divine Complement: Each Ascended Master, Divine Being, and Archangel is alleged to be paired with a divine complement of energy. Each divine pair manifests and streams energies into the corporeal worlds through the Hermetic Law of Gender. Hence, one is masculine in quality, while the other is feminine. Similar to a Twin Flame, Divine Complements differ in that they are ascended and purposely divide their efforts to assist Earth and unascended humanity. In the higher realms they are ideally ONE energy, and serve upon one individualized Ray Force.

Dvapara Yuga: The Bronze Period of the cycle of the yugas when fifty to twenty-five percent light from the Galactic Center is available on Earth. During the last Puranic Dvapara Yuga it is alleged that the fabled continent and culture of Atlantis existed.

Dwarf Sun: A companion Sun that orbits with our Solar Sun and has no luminosity of its own. Astrologers speculate its juxtaposition between the Earth and our Sun obstructs, and therefore controls, the flow of this important galactic energy to Earth.

Eight-sided Cell of Perfection: An atomic cell located in the human heart. It is associated with all aspects of perfection and contains and maintains a visceral connection with the Godhead.

Elemental Kingdom: A kingdom comprising an invisible, subhuman group of creatures who act as counterparts to visible nature on Earth.

El Morya: Ascended Master of the Blue Ray, associated with the development of the will.

Emanation: To flow out, issue, or proceed as from a source or origin; especially the path of a Ray as it travels from the Great Central Sun.

Energy Balancing: Also known as Energy Work, Energy Balancing is a healing technique applied by a trained practitioner who balances the Chakra System of an individual through hands-on-healing and energetic adjustment of the energy fields and light bodies.

Energy for energy: To understand this spiritual principle, one must remember Isaac Newton's Third Law of Motion: for every action there is an equal and opposite reaction. However, while energies may be equal, their forms often vary. The Ascended Masters often use this phrase to remind chelas to properly compensate others to avoid karmic retribution; and repayment may take many different forms.

Ever Present Now: Time as a continuous, unencumbered flow without past or future.

Fifth Dimension: A spiritual dimension of cause, associated with thoughts, visions, and aspirations. This is the dimension of the Ascended Masters and the Archetypes of Evolution, the city of Shamballa, and the templates of all Golden Cities.

First Spiritual Body: A light body that forms through the merging of both the Astral and Causal Bodies and allows fluid experience with the spiritual planes. This light body incites the Ascension Process. It is not bound to time or physical laws.

Fourth Dimension: A dimension of vibration associated with telepathy, psychic ability, and the dream world. This is the dimension of the Elemental Kingdom and the development of the super senses.

Freedom Star: The Earth's future prophesied name.

Galactic Center: The great Sun of our galaxy, around which all of its solar systems rotate. The Galactic Center Sun is also known in Ascended Master Teachings as the Great Central Sun, which is the origin of the Seven Rays of Light and Sound on Earth. In Vedic tradition it is known as Brahma, which is the creative force or navel of Vishnu. This great Sun emanates spiritual light that determines life and intelligence on Earth and distributes karma.

Galactic Web: A large, planet-encircling grid created by the consciousness of all things on Earth—humans, animals, plants, and minerals. Magnetic Vortices, namely the Golden Cities, appear at certain intersections. The Ascended Masters often refer to different types of energy points (i.e. Chakra, lei-line, Golden City Vortex, etc.) in the Galactic Web. Since the Angelic Host protects this Web of Creation, the protective web of the Angelic Host is often synonymous with the Galactic Web.

Garden of Existence: The Garden of Eden.

Gobean: The first United States Golden City located in the states of Arizona and New Mexico. Its qualities are cooperation, harmony, and peace. Its Ray Force is blue, and its Master Teacher is El Morya.

Gobi: A Golden City named for the Great Desert of China, *Gobi* in Mongolian means "the waterless place." Ascended Masters claim the Golden City of Gobi is a step-down transformer for the energies of the Earth's first Golden City—Shamballa. Gobi's esoteric definition comes from the Chinese translation of "go—across," and *bi* in Indonesian (Abun, A Nden, and Yimbun dialects) means "star." The Golden City of Gobi means "Across the Star," or "Across the Freedom Star." "Freedom Star" is a reference to Earth in her enlightened state.) Gobi aligns energies to the first Golden City of the New Times: Gobean.

Golden Age: A peaceful time on Earth prophesied to occur after the Time of Change. It is also prophesied that during this age, human life spans are increased and sacred knowledge is revered. During this time, the societies, cultures, and the governments of Earth reflect spiritual enlightenment through worldwide cooperation, compassion, charity, and love. Ascended Master teachings often refer to the Golden Age as the Golden-Crystal Age and the Age of Grace.

Golden Age of Kali Yuga: According to the classic Puranic timing of the Yugas, Earth is in a Kali-Yuga period that started around the year 3102 BCE the year that Krishna allegedly left the Earth. During this time period, which according to this Puranic timing lasts a total of 432,000 years—the ten-thousand year Golden Age period, also known as the Golden Age of Kali Yuga, is not in full force. Instead, it is a sub-cycle of higher light frequencies within an overall larger phase of less light energy.

This Golden Age is prophesied to raise the energy of Earth as additional light from the Galactic Center streams to our planet. This type of light is a non-visible, quasar-type light that is said to expand life spans and memory function, and nourish human consciousness, especially spiritual development. There are many theories as to when this prescient light energy began to flow to our planet. Some say it started about a thousand years ago, and others claim it began at the end of the nineteenth century. No doubt its influence has changed life on Earth for the better, and according to the I AM America Teachings, its effect began to encourage and guide human spiritual evolution around the year 2000 CE.

The Spiritual Teachers say that living in Golden Cities can magnify Galactic Energies and at their height, the energies will light the Earth between 45 to 48 percent—nearly reaching the light energies of a full-spectrum Treta Yuga or Silver Age on Earth. The Spiritual Teachers state, "The Golden Age is the period of time where harmony and peace shall be sustained."

Golden City Vortex: A Golden City Vortex—based on the Ascended Masters' I AM America material—are prophesied areas of safety and spiritual energies during the Times of Changes. Covering an expanse of land and air space, these sacred energy sites span more than 400 kilometers (270 miles) in diameter, with a vertical height of 400 kilometers (250 miles). Golden City Vortices, more importantly, reach beyond terrestrial significance and into the ethereal realm. This system of safe harbors acts as a group or universal mind within our galaxy, connecting information seamlessly and instantly with other beings. Fifty-one Golden City

Vortices are stationed throughout the world, and each carries a different meaning, a combination of Ray Forces, and a Divine Purpose. A Golden City Vortex works on the principles of electromagnetism and geology. Vortices tend to appear near fault lines, possibly serving as conduits of inner-earth movement to terra firma. Golden Cities are symbolized by a Maltese Cross, whose sacred geometry determine their doorways, lei-lines, adjutant points, and coalescing Star energies. Since their energies intensify experiences with both the Fourth and Fifth Dimensions, Golden City Vortices play a vital role with the Ascension Process.

Gold(en) Ray: The Ray of Brotherhood, Cooperation, and Peace. The Gold Ray produces the qualities of perception, honesty, confidence, courage, and responsibility. It is also associated with leadership, independence, authority, ministration, and justice. The Gold Ray is currently influencing the spiritual growth and evolution of the divine HU-man. It is also associated with karmic justice and will instigate many changes throughout our planet including Earth Changes and social and economic change.

Golden Thread Axis: Also known as the Vertical Power Current. The Golden Thread Axis is physically composed of the Medullar Shushumna, a life-giving nadi physically comprising one-third of the human kundalini system. Two vital currents intertwine around the Golden Thread Axis: the lunar Ida Current, and the solar Pingala Current. According to the Master Teachers, the flow of the Golden Thread Axis begins with the I AM Presence, enters the Crown Chakra, and descends through the spinal system. It descends beyond the Base Chakra and travels to the core of the Earth. Esoteric scholars often refer to the axis as the Rod of Power, and it is symbolized by two spheres connected by an elongated rod. Ascended Master students and chelas frequently draw upon the energy of the Earth, through the Golden Thread Axis, for healing and renewal by using meditation, visualization, and breath techniques.

Great Central Sun: The great sun of our galaxy, around which all of the galaxy's solar systems rotate. The Great Central Sun is also known as the Galactic Center, which is the origin of the Seven Rays of Light and Sound on Earth.

Great White Brotherhood (Lodge): A fraternity of ascended and unascended men and women who are dedicated to the universal uplifting of humanity. Its main objective includes the preservation of the lost spirit, and the teachings of the ancient religions and philosophies of the world. Its mission is to reawaken the dormant ethical and spiritual sparks among the masses. In addition to fulfilling spiritual aims, the Great White Lodge pledges to protect mankind against the systematic assaults—which inhibit self-knowledge and personal growth—on individual and group freedoms.

Green Ray: The Ray of Active Intelligence is associated with education, thoughtfulness, communication, organization, the intellect, science, objectivity, and discrimination. It is also adaptable, rational, healing, and awakened. The Green Ray is affiliated with the planet Mercury. In the I AM America teachings the Green Ray is served by the Archangel Raphael and Archeia Mother Mary; the Elohim of Truth, Vista—also known as Cyclopea, and Virginia; the Ascended Masters Hilarion, Lord Sananda, Lady Viseria, Soltec, and Lady Master Meta.

Guru: Teacher.

Hall of Wisdom: Earth's Third Light Body that correlates to the Mesosphere is known as *Eshano*, an etheric Hall of Wisdom. It is associated with the collective consciousness of humanity. It is also the middle layer of atmosphere surrounding the Earth, and this companion energetic light body holds the collective etheric template or pattern for life on Earth. This light body is constantly changing to meet evolutionary needs. Because this ethereal light body holds the Master plan for life on Earth, it is affiliated with divine intelligence and reflects the collective Mental Body of humanity. The Spiritual Teachers refer to this light body as *Eshano*, which means "to have knowledge of Creation and what gives shape to Creation, or knowledge of that which comes from Created forms."

Harmony of the Spheres: A superior form of music, founded on beauty and harmonious combination, heard by those who have developed the ears to hear—clairaudience. The Harmony of the Spheres is an esoteric term that refers to an exacting form of balance and synchronization often realized through the hidden geometric and mathematical perfection of all created forms. The movement of the heavenly bodies is said to be timed to such mathematical precision and perfection that the planets create a celestial music.

Heart Chakra: The location of this chakra is in the center of the chest and is known in Sanskrit as the Anahata. Its main aspect is Love and Relationships; our ability to feel compassion, forgiveness, and our own feeling of Divine Purpose.

Higher Self: Said to reside in the spiritual planes of consciousness, the Higher Self is energetically connected to each individual in the physical plane, and is free from the karmas of the Earth Plane and identification with the material world. Sometimes the Ascended Masters refer to the Higher Self as the I AM Presence, as the Higher Self often bridges vital energies of the I AM Presence. They are however, entirely different from one another. The Higher Self oversees the human development of choice, the development of conscience, and conscious self-correction. Prayers and decrees to the Higher Self act with great efficacy, liberating the I AM Presence from Third Dimensional restraints of time and space. The Higher Self separates the developing human from the lower self (the animal nature) and is sometimes referred to as the Holy Spirit.

HU-man: The integrated and spiritually evolved human; the God Man.

HUE or HU, the: In Tibetan dialects, the word *hue* or *hu* means breath; however, the HU is a sacred sound and when chanted or meditated upon is said to represent the entire spectrum of the Seven Rays. Because of this, the HU powerfully invokes the presence of the Violet Flame, which is the activity of the Violet Ray and its inherent ability to transform and transmit energies to the next octave. HU is also considered an ancient name for God, and it is sung for spiritual enlightenment.

I AM: The presence of God.

I AM Presence: The individualized presence of God.

I AM THAT I AM: A phrase from Hebrew that translates to, "I Will Be What I Will Be." "I AM" is also derived from the Sanskrit *Om* (pronounced: A-U-M), whose three letters signify the three aspects of God as beginning, duration, and dissolution—Brahma, Vishnu, and Shiva. The AUM syllable is known as the omkara and translates to "I AM Existence," the name for God. "Soham," is yet another mystical Sanskrit name for God, which means "It is I," or "He is I." In Vedic philosophy, it is claimed that when a child cries, "Who am I?" the universe replies, "Soham—you are the same as I AM." The I AM teachings also use the name "Soham" in place of "I AM."

Immortality: Everlasting and deathless. Spiritual immortality embraces the idea of the eternal, unending existence of the soul. Physical immortality includes the notion of the timeless, deathless, and birthless body.

Initiation: Admission, especially into secret, advanced spiritual knowledge.

Inner Marriage: A process achieved through the spiritual integration of the masculine and feminine aspects of self, uniting dualistic qualities into greater balance and harmony for expression of self-Mastery.

Instant-Thought-Manifestation: The clear and concise use of thought to Co-create desires. The Master Teachers often refer to this process as Manifest Destiny. Experiences with Instant-Thought-Manifestation are said to prepare our consciousness to enter into the ONE.

Intention: Acts, thoughts, or conceptions earnestly fixed on something, or steadfastly directed. Intentions often reflect the state of an individual's mind which directs their specific actions toward an object or goal.

Judgment: The act of forming negative assumptions and critical opinions, primarily of fellow human beings.

Kali Yuga: The Age of Iron, or Age of Quarrel, when Earth receives twenty-five percent or less galactic light from the Great Central Sun.

Karma: Laws of Cause and Effect.

Klehma: The fifth United States Golden City located primarily in the states of Colorado and Kansas. Its qualities are continuity, balance, and harmony; its Ray force is white; and its Master Teacher is Serapis Bey.

Kuan Yin: The Bodhisattva of Compassion and teacher of Saint Germain. She is associated with all the Rays and the principle of femininity.

Kundalini: In Sanskrit, *kundalini* literally means coiled, and represents the coiled energy located at the base of the spine, often established in the lower Base and Sacral Chakras. Kundalini Shatki (shatki means energy) is claimed to initiate spiritual development, wisdom, knowledge, and enlightenment.

Law of Attraction and Repulsion: Physically, like charges repel; unlike charges attract. Through the Spiritual Law of Allowing, like attracts like.

Law of Love: Perhaps every religion on Earth is founded upon the Law of Love, as the notion to "treat others as you would like to be treated." The Law of Love, however, from the Ascended Master tradition is simply understood as consciously living without fear, or inflicting fear on others. The Fourth of the Twelve Jurisdictions instructs Love is the Law of Allowing, Maintaining, and Sustainability. All of these precepts distinguish love from an emotion or feeling, and observe Love as action, will, or choice. The Ascended Masters affirm, "If you live love, you will create love." This premise is fundamental to understanding the esoteric underpinnings of the Law of Love. The Master Teachers declare that through practicing the Law of Love one experiences acceptance and understanding; tolerance, alongside detachment. Metaphysically, the Law of Love allows different and varied perceptions of ONE experience, situation, or circumstance to exist simultaneously. From this viewpoint the Law of Love is the practice of tolerance.

Law of Rhythm: Everything ebbs and flows; rises and falls. The swing of the pendulum is universal. The measure of the momentum to the right is equal to the swing of the left.

Light: "Love in action."

Lord Apollo: A God of healing, truth, music, and Prophecy. Apollo and Diana serve as the second of the twelve Suns from the lineage of the Alpha-Omega Guardian Suns. The great Apollo is revered as the ancestral father to Saint Germain's heritage of spiritual knowledge and teaching. Additionally, Apollo is a sponsor for the Twelve Jurisdictions.

Lord Macaw or Lord Meru: An Ascended Master of the Ruby and Gold Ray is also known as the great Sage of Ancient Mu. Lord Meru is a teacher of the ancient civilizations of the Earth and considered a spiritual historian of their mythological records. Lord Meru is also known as Lord Macaw—the parrot—a symbol of beauty, wisdom, and spiritual knowledge. Lord Macaw's dark skin is contrasted by a colorful headdress filled with parrot, trogon, and quetzal bird feathers, a symbol of Quetzalcoatl—the Christ Consciousness. In the New Times, Lord Meru is prophesied to steward the Golden City of Gobi.

Lords of Venus: A group of Ascended Masters who came to serve humanity. They once resided on the planet Venus.

Love: "Light in action."

Malton: The second United States Golden City located in the states of Illinois and Indiana. Its qualities are fruition and attainment; its Ray force is Ruby and Gold; and its Master Teacher is Kuthumi.

Mantra: Certain sounds, syllables, and sets of words are deemed sacred and often carry the power to transmute karma, purify the spirit, and transform an individual. These are known as mantras. The mantra is a foundation of Vedic tradition and often treated as a devotional upaye—a remedial measure of difficult obstacles. Mantras, however, are not limited to Hinduism. Buddhists, Sikhs, and Jains also utilize mantras. The Ascended Masters occasionally provide mantras to chelas to improve resonance with certain Golden Cities.

Master Teacher: A spiritual teacher from a specific lineage of teachers—gurus. The teacher transmits and emits the energy from that collective lineage.

Mastery: Possessing the consummate skill of command and self-realization over thought, feeling, and action.

Meditation: Quieting or silencing the mind in order to give focused attention or devotion to one thing.

Mental Body: A subtle light body of the Human Aura comprising thoughts.

Monad: From an Ascended Master viewpoint, the Monad is the spark or flame of life of spiritual consciousness and it is also the Awakened Flame that is growing, evolving, and ultimately on the path to Ascension. Because of its presence of self-awareness and purpose, the Monad represents our dynamic will and the individualized presence of the Divine Father. Ultimately, the Monad is the spark of consciousness that is self-determining, spiritually awake, and drives the growth of human consciousness. The Monad is the indivisible, whole, divine life center of an evolving soul that is immortal and contains the momentum within itself to drive consciousness to learn, grow, and perfect itself in its evolutionary journey.

New Day: The process of seeing or perceiving a problem or an obstacle from a different point of view. This often involves a shift in consciousness.

ONE: Indivisible, whole, harmonious Unity.

Oneness: A combination of two or more, which creates the whole.

Oneship: A combination of many, which comprises the whole and, when divided, contains both feminine and masculine characteristics.

Oral Tradition: According to the Master Teachers and many indigenous teachers, the Oral Tradition, or learning through oral instruction, is the preferred medium to receive spiritual knowledge. This method requires the use of memory and memorization and also instigates the recognition of vital, yet subtle nuances that engender spiritual comprehension and may include the Master Teacher's use of telepathy, clairaudience, and clairvoyance.

Perception: Awareness through the senses, including the super-senses.

Pink Flame: Energy of Divine Love that is held in the consciousness of most Bodhisattvas, primarily Kuan Yin. It is alleged to surround the human heart.

Pink Ray: The Pink Ray is the energy of the Divine Mother and associated with the Moon. It is affiliated with these qualities: loving, nurturing, hopeful, heartfelt, compassionate, considerate, communicative, intuitive, friendly, humane, tolerant, adoring.

Point of Perception: A Co-creation teaching of the Ascended Masters and its processes pivot on the fulcrum of choice. By carefully choosing certain actions, a Master of Choice opens the world of possibility through honing carefully cultivated perceptions, attitudes, beliefs, thoughts, and feelings. This allows the development of outcome through various scenarios and opens the multidimensional door to multiple realities and simultaneous experiences that dissolve linear timeframes into the Ever Present Now.

Prana: Vital, life-sustaining energy; also known as orgone or chi.

Prophecies of Change: Primarily prophecies of Earth Changes, but also include political, social, and cultural change alongside spiritual and biological changes to humanity.

Prophecies of Peace: Prophecies and spiritual teachings aimed toward humanity's spiritual growth, evolution, and entrance into the New Times and the Golden Age.

Prophecy: A spiritual teaching given simultaneously with a warning. It's designed to change, alter, lessen, or mitigate the prophesied warning. This caveat may be literal or metaphoric; the outcome of these events are contingent on the choices and the consciousness of those willing to apply the teachings.

Purification: A clearing process, especially in spiritual practice, which frees consciousness from encumbering or objectionable elements.

Quetzalcoatl: The Quetzalcoatl Energies, as explained and taught by Lord Meru, are akin to the Christ energies when applied in the esoteric Western Christian tradition. Quetzalcoatl, the deity, was an ancient spiritual teacher, predating Christ and his teachings likely had roots in alchemic Atlantean (Toltec) teaching. Quetzalcoatl, in contemporary terms, is the Incan Christ.

Rapture: A form of spiritual liberation, based on sincerity, peace, faith, and acceptance.

Ray: A force containing a purpose, which divides its efforts into two measurable and perceptible powers: light and sound.

Ruby Ray: The Ruby Ray is the energy of the Divine Masculine and Spiritual Warrior. It is associated with these qualities: energetic; passionate; devoted; determination; dutiful; dependable; direct; insightful; inventive; technical; skilled; forceful. This Ray Force is astrologically affiliated with the planet Mars and the Archangel Uriel, Lord Sananda, and Master Kuthumi. The Ruby Ray is often paired with the Gold Ray, which symbolizes Divine Father. The Ruby Ray is the evolutionary Ray Force of both the base and solar chakras of the HU-man; and the Gold and Ruby Rays step-down and radiate sublime energies into six Golden Cities.

Sacred Geometry: Esoteric scholars suggest that diverse universal patterns, geometrical shapes, and geometric proportions symbolize spiritual balance and perfection.

Saint Germain: Ascended Master of the Seventh Ray, Saint Germain is known for his work with the Violet Flame of Mercy, Transmutation, Alchemy, and Forgiveness. He is the sponsor of the Americas and the I AM America material. Many other teachers and Masters affiliated with the Great White Brotherhood assist his endeavors.

Sananda: The name used by Master Jesus in his ascended state of consciousness. Sananda means joy and bliss, and his teachings focus on revealing the savior and heavenly kingdom within.

Serapis Bey: An Ascended Master from Venus who works on the White Ray. He is the great disciplinarian—essential for Ascension—and works closely with all unascended humanity who remain focused for its attainment.

Seven Rays: The traditional Seven Rays of Light and Sound are: the Blue Ray of Truth; the Yellow Ray of Wisdom; the Pink Ray of Love; the White Ray of Purity; the Green Ray of Healing; the Gold and Ruby Ray of Ministration; and the Violet Ray of Transmutation.

Seventh Manu: Highly evolved lifestreams that embody on Earth between 1981 to 3650. Their goal is to anchor freedom and the qualities of the Seventh Ray to the conscious activity on this planet. They are prophesied as the generation of peace and grace for the Golden Age. South America is their forecasted home, though small groups will incarnate in other areas of the globe.

Shalahah: The fourth United States Golden City located primarily in the states of Montana and Idaho. Its qualities are abundance, prosperity, and healing; its Ray Force is Green; and its Master Teacher is Sananda.

Shamballa: Venusian volunteers, who arrived 900 years before their leader Sanat Kumara, built the Earth's first Golden City. Known as the City of White, located in the present-day Gobi Desert, its purpose was to hold conscious light for the Earth and to sustain her evolutionary place in the solar system.

Shroud of Darkness: Inhibiting beliefs that obscure the soul's direct contact with their innate Conscious Immortality.

Simultaneous Reality: A nonlinear perspective of time. It prepares us for potential possibilities in all situations—past, present, and future—and retains the capacity for multiple encounters and outcomes. Each reality exists side by side, so humans can consciously open up to these events to gain insight and self-knowledge.

Solar Plexus: Also known as the Navel Chakra, this chakra is located between the navel and the base of the sternum. It is an intense feeling (intuitive) chakra which is known as the Center of Power and Balance in relationship to everything in life.

Spiritual Awakening: Conscious awareness of personal experiences and existence beyond the physical, material world. Consequently, an internalization of one's true nature and relationship to life is revealed, freeing one of the lesser self (ego) and engendering contact with the higher (Christ) self and the I AM.

Spiritual Liberation: The process whereby the soul gains freedom from the Wheel of Karma, and the need to reincarnate in a physical body on Earth. In Ascended Master Teachings, spiritual liberation is known as Ascension. Depending on the spiritual level and evolution of each soul, after spiritual liberation from the Earth Plane the soul travels onward into higher levels of Astral or Causal Planes, where yet another liberation process ensues. This new level of consciousness and spiritual evolution may include Earth or other planets. In Hinduism, spiritual liberation is known as moksha, which is the release from suffering and the cycle of death and rebirth. It is claimed that the soul is released from duality as the concept of self expands into the sublime realization of the I AM and the soul merges with the I AM Presence. This also includes the realization of the Christ Consciousness or birth of the Quetzalcoatl energies as the soul enters Fourth and Fifth Dimensional Awareness. This perfected state of consciousness realizes the Earthly Plane as illusion or Maya and exists without separation from the God Source, the spiritually free at-one-ment.

Spiritual Preparedness: The practice and application of various spiritual techniques and disciplines that help to increase and leverage spiritual potential alongside the Ascension Process during the Time of Change.

Star (of a Golden City): The apex, or center of each Golden City.

Star Seed: Souls and groups whose genetic origins are not from Earth. Many remain linked to one another from one lifetime to the next, as signified by the Atma Karaka, a Sanskrit term meaning "soul indicator." Star-seed consciousness is often referred to by the Spiritual Teachers as a family or soul group whose members have evolved to and share Fifth-Dimensional awareness. Star Seeds can also contain members who have not yet evolved to this level, who are still incarnating on Earth.

Step-down Transformer: The processes instigated through the Cellular Awakening rapidly advance human light bodies. Synchronized with an Ascended Master's will, the awakened cells of light and love evolve the skills of a Step-Down Transformer to efficiently transmit and distribute currents of Ascended Master energy—referred to as an Ascended Master Current (A.M. Current). This metaphysical form of intentional inductive coupling creates an ethereal power grid that can be used for all types of healing.

Third Dimension: Thought, feeling, and action.

Third Eye: Also known as the Ajna Chakra. This energy center is located above and between the eyebrows. The Third-eye Chakra blends thought and feeling into perception and projection for Co-creative activity.

Thousand Eyes: This term refers to the endless rounds of death and rebirth the soul encounters before entering the Ascension Process of spiritual liberation.

Time Compaction: An anomaly produced as we enter into the prophesied Time of Change. Our perception of time compresses; time seems to speed by. The unfolding of events accelerates, and situations are jammed into a short period of time. This experience of time will become more prevalent as we get closer to the period of cataclysmic Earth Changes.

Time of Change: The period of time currently underway. Tremendous changes in our society, cultures, and politics in tandem with individual and collective spiritual awakenings and transformations will abound. These events occur simultaneously with the possibilities of massive global warming, climactic changes, and seismic and volcanic activity—Earth Changes. The Time of Change guides Earth to a new time, the Golden Age.

Time of Testing: The Time of Testing is a period of seven to twenty years which began around the turn of the twenty-first century, following the time period known as the Time of Transition. According to Saint Germain and other Ascended Masters, the Time of Testing is perhaps one of the most turbulent periods mankind will experience and its first seven years is prophesied as a period of change and strife for many. As its title suggests, the Master Teachers claim this timeframe may challenge students by testing their spiritual acumen and inner strength.

Transportation Vortex: Prophesied to develop as we enter the New Times, a model of this energy anomaly will exist in the Golden City of Shalahah near Coeur d'Alene, Idaho (USA). This interdimensional portal functions through the developed projection of the mind. As our understanding of Ray Forces evolves, our bodies take on a finer quality in light and substance and we are able to bilocate through these energy Vortices. In the New Times this becomes an accepted form of travel.

True Memory: Memory, as defined by Ascended Master teachings, is not seen as a function of the brain, or the soul's recall of past events. Instead, True Memory is achieved through cultivating our perceptions and adjusting our individual perspective of a situation to the multiple juxtapositions of opinion and experience. This depth of understanding gives clarity and illumination to every experience. Our skill and Mastery through True Memory moves our consciousness beyond common experiences to individualized experiences whose perceptive power hones honesty and accountability. The innate truth obtained from many experiences through the interplay of multiple roles creates True Memory, and opens the detached and unconditional Law of Love to the chela.

Twelve Jurisdictions: Twelve laws (virtues) for the New Times that guide consciousness to Co-create the Golden Age. They are Harmony, Abundance, Clarity, Love, Service, Illumination, Cooperation, Charity, Desire, Faith, Stillness, Creation/Creativity.

Twin Flame: The idea that the ONE creative spark of the soul's genesis divides into two distinct parts: one part female, the other part male. The twin aspects of the soul play a number of roles with each other throughout successive lifetimes, and as the soul evolves and spiritually grows, this interaction perfects and expands.

Unana: Unity Consciousness.

Unfed Flame: The three-fold flame of divinity that exists in the heart and becomes larger as it evolves. The three flames represent Love (pink); Wisdom (yellow); and Power (blue).

Vertical Power Current: See Golden Thread Axis.

Violet Flame: The Violet Flame is the practice of balancing karmas of the past through Transmutation, Forgiveness, and Mercy. The result is an opening of the Spiritual Heart and the development of bhakti—unconditional love and compassion. It came into existence when the Lords of Venus first transmitted the Violet Flame, also knows as Violet Fire, at the end of Lemuria to clear the Earth's etheric and psychic realms, and the lower physical atmosphere of negative forces and energies. This paved the way for the Atlanteans, who used it during religious ceremonies and as a visible marker of temples. The Violet Flame also induces Alchemy. Violet light emits the shortest wavelength and the highest frequency in the spectrum, so it induces a point of transition to the next octave of light.

Violet Flame Angels: Legions of Violet Flame Angels are claimed to carry the energies of the transmuting Violet Flame whenever they are called upon. The Angels of the Violet Flame protect the flame in its purity and dispense its transforming vibration.

Wahanee: The third United States Golden City located primarily in the states of South Carolina and Georgia. Its qualities are justice, liberty, and freedom; its Ray Force is violet; and its Master Teacher is Saint Germain.

White Ray: The Ray of the Divine Feminine is primarily associated with the planet Venus. It is affiliated with beauty, balance, purity, and cooperation. In the I AM America teachings the White Ray is served by the Archangel Gabriel and Archeia Hope; the Elohim Astrea and Claire; and the Ascended Masters Serapis Bey, Paul the Devoted, Reya, the Lady Masters Venus and Se Ray, and the Group of Twelve.

Will: Choice.

Write and Burn Technique: An esoteric technique venerated by Ascended Master students and chelas to transmute any unwanted situation or circumstance, primarily dysfunctional life patterns. This technique involves hand-writing and then burning a letter—a petition—to the I AM Presence for Healing and Divine Intervention.

Appendix A

Candle Meditation:
The Candle Meditation by El Morya is one of the first steps to experience the Divine Light within and calm the mind. Use a long tapered candle, not a jarred glass candle. For this exercise a white candle is preferred, but any color should work. Light the candle and establish a constant, stable flame.

First, sit comfortably; you may use a chair for back support if needed. Look and concentrate on the candle and give attention to the different layers of the light of the flame. You will notice these layers: the outer glow; the yellow-white layer of fire; the center of the wick; and the central inner glow, which sometimes contains a blue or violet hue at the base of the flame. Focus on the overall glow of the candle until you identify the layers of light. Breathe evenly and gently as you concentrate on the light.

As you observe the Flame of Light, continue your rhythmic breath as the light begins to expand and absorb the space between you and the flame. Continue this breathing until you have established a large ovoid of light, including the candle and yourself.

Remain focused in the circle of light and you will begin to notice you are in the flame; the light is even, and it flows with your breath. You may notice a pulse in the energy field you share with the flame. At this state you are One with the light.

Individuals who practice the Candle Meditation have reported feeling calm and peace, even in extremely stressful conditions. Sometimes this is accompanied by a high-pitch ring. El Morya asserts the application of the Candle Meditation imparts experience with the consciousness of the One and develops human consciousness into the HU-man. The Candle Meditation can be performed individually or in groups.

Appendix B

Saint Germain, the Holy Brother:
The Lord of the Seventh Ray and the Master of the Violet Flame, Saint Germain lived numerous noteworthy lifetimes, dating back thousands of years, before incarnating as the Comte de Saint Germain during Renaissance Europe. He lived as the Englishman Sir Francis Bacon, the sixteenth-century philosopher, essayist, and Utopian who greatly influenced the philosophy of inductive science. His most profound and well-known work on the restoration of humanity, the *Instauratio Magna* (Great Restoration), defined him as an icon of the Elizabethan era. Research also shows his co-authoring of many Shakespearean sonnets.

According to Esoteric historians, Queen Elizabeth I of England—The Virgin Queen—was his biological mother. Before Bacon's birth, the queen married Earl of Leicester, quieting ideas of illegitimacy. Elizabeth's lady in waiting, Lady Ann Bacon, wife of the Lord High Chancellor of England, adopted him following the stillbirth of her baby. Bacon was, therefore, the true heir to the crown and England's rightful king.[1] But his cousin James I of Scotland succeeded the throne. Sir Bacon described this turn of events in his book, *Novum Organo*, published in 1620: "It is an immense ocean that surrounds the island of Truth." And Saint Germain often reminds us to this day "there are no mistakes, ever, ever, ever."

Bacon's philosophies also helped define the principles of Free Masonry and democracy. As an adept leader of the Rosicrucians (a secret society of that time), he set out to reveal the obsolescence and oppression of European monarchies.

Eventually, Bacon's destiny morphed. He shed his physical form and sought the greatest gift of all: immortality. And that's what placed him in the most extraordinary circumstances throughout history. Even his death (or lack of) evokes controversy. Some say Bacon faked his demise in 1626—the coffin contained the carcass of a dog.

According to the author, ADK Luk, Saint Germain ascended on May 1, 1684 in Transylvania at the Rakoczy mansion. He was 123 years old. Some say Saint Germain spent the lost years—from 1626 to 1684—in Tibet. During this time he took (or may have been given) the name *Kajaeshra*. Interpreted as *God's helper of life* and *wisdom*, it was possibly a secret name and rarely used. Kaja has several interpretations: in Greek it means *pure*; Balinese, *toward the mountain*; early Latin (Estonian), *echo*; Hopi, *wise child*; Polish, *of the Gods*; and Hebrew, *life*. The second part of the name—Eshra (Ezra)—translates into *help* or *aid*.

Indeed, Bacon's work would impact centuries to follow. During his time in Tibet, tucked away in silent monasteries, Germain designed a society that eventually created a United Brotherhood of the Earth: Solomon's Temple of the Future. It's a metaphor used to describe the raising of consciousness as the greater work of democracy. Author Marie Bauer Hall studied the life of Francis Bacon. In her book, *Foundations Unearthed*, she described the legendary edifice: "This great temple was to be supported by the four mighty pillars of history, science, philosophy, and religion, which were to bear the lofty dome of Universal Fellowship and Peace."[2]

But Germain embraced an even deeper passion: the people and nation of America, christening it *New Atlantis*. He envisioned this land—present-day United States, Canada, Mexico, and South America—as part of the United Democracies of Europe and the People of the World. America, this growing society, held his hope for a future guided by a Democratic Brotherhood.

The Comte de Saint Germain emerged years later in the courts of pre-revolutionary France—his appearance, intelligence, and worldliness baffled members of the Court of Versailles. This gentleman carried the essence of eternal youth: he was a skilled artist and musician; he spoke fluent German, English, French, Italian, Portuguese, Spanish, Greek, Latin, Sanskrit, Arabic, and Chinese; and he was a proficient chemist. Meanwhile, literary, philosophic, and political aristocracy of the time sought his company. French philosophers Jean-Jacque Rousseau and Voltaire; the Italian adventurer Giacomo Casanova; and the Earl of Chatham and statesman Sir Robert Walpole of Britain were among his friends.

In courts throughout Europe, he dazzled royalty with his Mastery of Alchemy, removing flaws from gems and turning lead into Gold. And the extent of Germain's ken reached well into the theosophical realm. A guru of yogic and tantric disciplines, he possessed highly developed telepathic and psychic abilities. This preternatural knowledge led to the development of a cartographic Prophecy—the Map of Changes. This uncanny blueprint, now in the hands of the scion of Russian aristocracy, detailed an imminent restructuring of the political and social boundaries of Europe.[3]

But few grasped Germain's true purpose during this time of historic critical mass: not even the king and queen of France could comprehend his tragic forewarnings. The Great White Brotherhood—a fellowship of enlightened luminaries—sent the astute diplomat Saint Germain to orchestrate the development of the United States of Europe. Not only a harbinger of European diplomacy, he made his presence in America during the germinal days of this country. Esoteric scholars say he urged the signing of the Declaration of Independence in a moment of collective fear—a fear of treason and ultimately death. Urging the forefathers to proceed, a shadowed figure in the back of the room shouted: *Sign that document!*

To this day, the ironclad identity of this person remains a mystery, though some mystics believe it was Saint Germain. Nevertheless, his avid support spurred the flurry of signatures, sealing the fate of America—and the beginning of Sir Francis Bacon's democratic experiment.

The Comte de Saint Germain never could shape a congealed Europe, but he did form a lasting and profound relationship with America. Germain's present-day participation in U.S. politics reaches the Oval Office. Some theosophical mystics say Germain visits the president of the United States the day after the leader's inauguration; others suggest he's the fabled patriot Uncle Sam.

Saint Germain identifies with the qualities of Brotherhood and freedom. He is the sponsor of humanity and serves as a conduit of Violet Light—a force some claim is powerful enough to propel one into Ascension.

[1] Marie Bauer Hall, *Foundations Unearthed,* originally issued as *Francis Bacon's Great Virginia Vault,* Fourth Edition (Los Angeles: Veritas Press), page 9.

[2] Ibid., page 13.

[3] K. Paul Johnson, *The Masters Revealed: Madame Blavatsky and the Myth of the Great White Lodge (Suny Series in Western Esoteric Traditions)* (Albany, NY: State University of New York Press), page 19.

Appendix C

El Morya:
El Morya incarnated from a long line of historical notables, including the fabled King Arthur of England; the Renaissance scholar Sir Thomas Moore, author of *Utopia*; the patron saint of Ireland, Saint Patrick; and a Rajput prince. El Morya is even linked to the Hebrew patriarch Abraham. But in spite of his illustrious lifetimes, El Morya is best known as Melchior, one of the Magi who followed the Star of Bethlehem to the Christ infant.

El Morya first revealed himself to the founder of the Theosophical Society Helena Petrovna Blavatasky—also known as Madame Blavatsky or H. P. B.—during her childhood in London; that mid-nineteenth century meeting forged a lifelong connection with her Master and other members of the Spiritual Hierarchy. Some esoteric scholars recount different, more dramatic scenarios of their initial introduction. Blavatsky herself claimed El Morya rescued her from a suicide attempt on Waterloo Bridge.[1] The gracious Master dissuaded her from plunging into the waters of the Thames River. Others say the two met in Hyde Park or on a London street. According to Blavatsky, El Morya appeared under a secret political cover as the Sikh prince Maharaja Ranbir Singh of Kashmir, who served as a physically incarnated prototype of Master M. Singh and died in 1885.

Metaphysical scholars credit Blavatsky's work as the impetus for present-day theosophical philosophy and the conception of the Great White Brotherhood. Devoted disciples learned of the Hindu teacher from Blavatsky's childhood visions, and later on in a series of correspondences known as the *Mahatma Letters*, which contained spiritual guidelines for humanity. El Morya's presence in H. P. B.'s life enriched her spiritual knowledge, and she shared this transformation in a prolific body of texts and writings, namely *Isis Unveiled* and *The Secret Doctrine*.

Master M. is associated with the Blue Ray of power, faith, and good will; the Golden City of Gobean; and the planet Mercury. A strict disciplinarian, El Morya dedicates his work to the development of the will. He assists many disciples in discovering personal truths, exploring self-development, and honing the practice of the esoteric discipline. El Morya passes this wisdom to his numerous chelas and students. The Maha Chohan—El Morya's guru, Lord of the Seven Rays and the Steward of Earth and its evolutions—educated him during his Earthly incarnations in India, Egypt, and Tibet. Declining the Ascension a number of times, it is said that El Morya finally accepted this divine passage in 1888, ascending with his beloved pet dog and horse. (Esoteric symbols of friendship and healing.)

---

[1] Johnson, K. Paul, *The Masters Revealed: Madame Blavatsky and the Myth of the Great White Lodge (Suny Series in Western Esoteric Traditions)* (Albany, NY: State University of New York Press), page 41.

Appendix D

The Violet Flame:
Simply stated, the Violet Flame stabilizes past karmas through Transmutation, Forgiveness, and Mercy. This leads to the opening of the spiritual heart and the development of bhakti—the unconditional love and compassion for others. Our Co-creative ability is activated through the Ascended Master's gift of the Unfed Flame in adjunct with the practice of the Law of Love, and the Power of Intention. But the Violet Flame, capable of engendering our greatest spiritual growth and evolution, is spiritual velocity pure and simple.

Invoking the flame's force often produces feelings of peace, tranquility, and inner harmony—its ability to lift the low-vibrating energy fields of blame, despair, and fear into forgiveness and understanding, paves the path to love.

The history of the Violet Flame reaches back thousands of years before the Time of Christ. According to Ascended Master legend, the Lords of Venus transmitted the Violet Flame as a spiritual consciousness during the final days of the pre-Atlantis civilization Lemuria. As one society perished and another bloomed, the power of the Violet Flame shifted, opening the way for Atlantean religiosity. This transfer of power initiated a clearing of the Earth's etheric and psychic realms, and purged the lower physical atmosphere of negative forces and energies. Recorded narratives of Atlantis claim that Seven Temples of Purification sat atop visible materializations of the Violet Flame. The archangels Zadkiel and Amethyst, representing freedom, forgiveness, and joy, presided over an Atlantean Brotherhood known as the Order of Zadkiel, also associated with Saint Germain. These Violet Flame Temples still exist today in the celestial realm over Cuba.

The Violet Flame benefits humans and divinities equally. During spiritual visualizations, meditations, prayers, decrees, and mantras, many disciples seek the Violet Flame for serenity and wisdom. Meanwhile, the Ascended Masters always use it in inner retreats—

even Saint Germain taps into its power to perfect and apply its force with chelas and students

The Violet Flame, rooted in Alchemic powers, is sometimes identified as a higher energy of Saturn and the Blue Ray, a force leavened with justice, love, and wisdom. Ascended-Master lore explains the Violet Flame's ability to release a person from temporal concerns: Saturn's detachment from emotions and low-lying energies sever worldly connections. That's why the scientific properties of violet light are so important in metaphysical terms. The shortness of its wavelength and the high vibration of its frequency induce a point of transition to the next octave of light and into a keener consciousness.

Discography

This list provides the recording session date and name of the original selected recordings cited in this work that provide the basis for its original transcriptions.

Toye, Lori

Emanation, I AM America Seventh Ray Publishing International, Audiocassette and MP3, © April 10, 1998.

Behind the Interplay, I AM America Seventh Ray Publishing International, Audiocassette and MP3, © April 14, 1998.

A New Day, I AM America Seventh Ray Publishing International, Audiocassette and MP3, © June 26, 1998.

Golden City Rays, I AM America Seventh Ray Publishing International, Audiocassette and MP3, © July 23, 1998.

Blue Illumination, I AM America Seventh Ray Publishing International, Audiocassette and MP3, © July 31, 1998.

Template of Light, from "Golden City Network and Blue Flame of Gobean," I AM America Seventh Ray Publishing International, Audiocassette ℗ No. 07319, 1998, © September 19, 1998.

Time of Testing, I AM America Seventh Ray Publishing International, Audiocassette ℗ No. 092889, 1998, © September 28, 1998.

Memory is Freedom, I AM America Seventh Ray Publishing International, Audiocassette ℗ No. 022400, 2000, © September 22, 2000.

Golden Ray Compassion, I AM America Seventh Ray Publishing International, Audiocassette. ⓟ No. 062200, 2000, © June 22, 2000.

Ascension Valley, from "Ascension Introduction," I AM America Seventh Ray Publishing International, Audiocassette. ⓟ No. 072500, 2000, © June 25, 2000.

Ascension of Consciousness, I AM America Seventh Ray Publishing International, Audiocassette. ⓟ No. 090100, 2000, © September 1, 2000.

Ascension through the Dimensions, I AM America Seventh Ray Publishing International, Audiocassette. ⓟ No.111600, 2000, © November 26, 2000.

Finer Bodies of Light, I AM America Seventh Ray Publishing International, Audiocassette and MP3, © March 13, 2006.

Index

A

Absolute Harmony 84
   definition 223
Age of Cooperation
   definition 121, 223
Akasa 155
Akashic Records 138
   and the Golden City of Gobean 101
   and the I AM 183
   definition 223
Akhenaten
   definition 102, 223
Alchemy
   and the Fourth Dimension 195
   definition 215, 223
alignment
   definition 160, 223
Amethyst City, Cuba
   and Ascension 171
Anasazi
   ancient influences 103
Ancient Golden Cities
   alignment to Golden City of Klehma 90
animal behavior
   in humans 181
apex
   and mantras 93
   of Shalahah 88
Aryan
   ancient civilizations 132
"As above, so below." 98

Ascended Master
   consciousness and metaphysics 197
   definition 191, 223
   role in assisting humanity and the Earth 71
   "We take form at will." 71
Ascension 101, 135
   and Divine Love 180
   and overcoming animalistic behavior 183
   and perception 204
   and personal experience 178
   and review of karmic patterns 179
   and sponsorship through an Ascended Master 183
   and the Amethyst City 171
   and the Earth 191
   and the esoteric history of Atlantis 168
   and the finer bodies 208
   and the Golden City of Klehma 91
   and the Golden Ray 159
   and the preparation of the physical body 193
   and the Stars of Golden Cities 152
   and the Twin Ray 157
   and twenty-two locations 173
   "A new wine skin." 64
   as a "graduation of souls" 177
   beyond the HU-man 70
   definition 65, 224
   "Discard old beliefs, illusions." 69
   global 170
Ascension Process
   definition 209, 224
   training the light bodies 217

Ascension Valley 135, 170
  and Sananda 171
  definition 88, 225
Astral Body
  body
    and specific Golden Cities 160
    definition 82
  definition 225
Astrological Body 47
Astrology 36
Atlantis
  and the Sun God 168
  New 252
At-One-Ment 112
  definition 225
attention and experience 212
aura 41
  and light fields 111
  and Ray Forces 81
  definition 225
auric vision 59
Awakening 135
  and the perfected cell 119
  "Is for all and beyond the barrier of time." 122
axiotonal bodies
  definition 226
  "Higher frequency chakra system." 117

B

Babajeran 33, 57, 159
  and Golden Cities 107
  and Prophecy 191
  and the Ascension Areas 173
  and the inner kingdoms 199
  definition 226
  Time of Change 201

Bacon, Sir Francis 251
Balance
  creating through the Violet Flame 148
belief(s) 58, 64
  definition 226
belief versus experience 102
bilocation 88, 100
birth
  moment of 82
Blavatsky, H. P. 255
Blue Flame 58
  and the Violet Flame 114
  breath technique 115
  definition 226
  within the Violet Flame 163
Blue Race 96
Blue Ray 70, 82, 88, 109
  and the manifestation of Shamballa 96
  definition 226
  for transformation of karmic patterns 179
  Mantra 111
  qualification 43
breathwork 85, 214
  and chakras 210
  definition 227
Brotherhood 87
Buddha
  followed the teachings of Jesus Christ 154
"Build your light fields." 219

C

Candle Meditation from El Morya 99, 116, 209
  instructions 249
cause and effect 65, 165
  definition 227
Causeless Cause 141
Cellular
  Fear 34, 87
Cellular Awakening 101, 167
  definition 227
cellular memory 168
chakra(s)
  and sound vibration 47, 82
  Crown 87
  definition 227
  Heart 89, 113
  movement 40
  Ray Forces 35, 82, 85
  seal 59
  Seventh Chakra 135
  system
    axiotonal bodies 117
  Throat 82, 114
Chamber of the Heart 119
  and awakening 134
  definition 227
change 201
Chela
  and preparation 60
  definition 227
  "Each chela is individualized." 60
chohan
  definition 228
Chohan 38
  Green Ray 38

choice 40
  "Sparked within." 68
  "You begin anew." 66
Christ
  consciousness
    and the Golden City of Gobean 103
Christ Consciousness
  definition 228
circadian rhythm 208
citrus fruits
  and Galactic Light 170
clairaudience 198
Closure of Understanding 45
  definition 228
Co-creation
  and light bodies 215
  and Ray Forces 41
  definition 228
Co-creator 59, 65
Co-creatorship 49
color 60
compassion 52, 59, 155
  and developed societies 120
  and the Law of Love 177
  definition 228
conductivity 97
confidence 148
conscience 65
  definition 228
conscience and consciousness 66
conscious immortality 201
  decree for 167
  definition 228
  fiat by Saint Germain 166
  "Life exists beyond what is seen." 195

consciousness 35, 52
  and Ascension 69, 185, 208
  and decrees 111
  and merging of finer bodies 215
  and oral tradition 141
  and Sacred Geometry of Golden City Structure 128
  and the Violet Flame 48
  collective 107, 176
  definition 228
  ethereal 100
  "Grows beyond the limits of the flesh." 155
  projecting 102
  telepathy and lucid dreaming 154
Continuity of Consciousness 102
cooperation 90
  and harmony 108
courage 72
creation 213
Crown Chakra
  and the Violet Ray 87
Cup 122
  definition 228
cycles of time 141

D

darkness
  and the dwarf Sun 213
death
  and consciousness 64
  and fear 66
  consciousness
    removing 139
  "Down with death." 64, 86
  urge released through the White Fire of Klehma 91

"Debt is doubt." 148
decree
  for apprehension 163
  for the I AM Presence 153
  for Violet and Gold Ray 153
  to adjust energy in a room 165
  to enliven the cells for conscious immortality 167
desire 71, 141
  and Golden Cities 84
  cycle of desires 166
  definition 228
detachment 139
  and spiritual evolution 178
Deva(s) 84
  definition 228
dharma 34
  definition 228
diet
  Ascension and the emotional body 185
Dimensional
  energies and Stars 125
Dimensional leaping
  and the Mayan culture 90
discouragement 73
Divine
  Divine Intervention 107
    and the Golden Cities 122
  Divine Spark 141
Divine Cell
  definition 228
  Eight-sided Cell of Perfection 200
Divine Complement 156
  definition 229
Divine Destiny
  and human evolution 63
  and immortality 66

Divine Inheritor
  the true self 155
Divine Intervention 73, 87
  and the Golden Cities 101
Divine Love 186
  beyond illusion 180
Divine Order 161
Divine Plan 144
  and forgiveness 77
Divine Will
  and the mental body 181
  birth of 68
  releasing to 72
divinity
  "You are all equal." 112
doubt
  overpowering 69
dreams
  and belief systems 208
duality 143
Dvapara Yuga 218
  definition 229
dwarf sun 213
  definition 229

E

Earth
  as a schoolroom 176
  core 109
  evolution 109
  love-in-action 131
Earth Changes
  and acceleration of spiritual energies 209
  and balance 84
  and inner change 76
  and purification 199
  and the Fourth Dimension 195
  and the Ruby and Gold Ray 84
  and Unana 84
  increased light 33
  leap in consciousness 193
earthquake 121
Eight-sided Cell of Perfection
  activation 40
  and the Cellular Awakening 167
  and the Temples of Luxor 172
  connects to the dimensions 200
  definition 229
  "Demonstrates the truth." 204
Elemental Kingdom 212
  and the Fourth Dimension 194
  and the Ruby and Gold Ray 84
  definition 229
  keeps the Earth in perfected order 201
  mantra for 91
Elemental Life Force 84, 199
  and the Fourth Dimension 198
El Morya 128, 176, 255
  definition 229
emanation 36, 38, 42, 95
  definition 229
emotion 181
  and physical activity 187
emotional body
  and diet 185
  and karmic patterns 189
  and money 187
energy balancing
  definition 230
  for integrating Ray Forces 85
energy for energy 188, 230
enlightenment
  of the physical body 167

"Equal to" 68
Ever Present Now 37, 78
  definition 230
evolution
  through the Rays 81
experience 56, 155
  and the soul's education 182
  "The difference is experience." 57
"Eyes to see; ears to hear" 63

F

family 114
fear 34, 170
  and our contemporary culture 172
  cellular
    removal of 66
  genetic 34
  releasing 69
feminine
  and Ascension 170
Fifth Dimension
  definition 230
  harmonic of twenty-eight 196
finer bodies
  and the unseen 209
  merging with breathing techniques 210
First Spiritual Body
  combination of Causal and Astral body 216
  definition 230
five senses
  limitation and expansion 203
Flame of Light
  and the Candle Meditation 249
focus 102
food
  and vibration 129

forgiveness 75
Fourth Dimension 194
  and development of compassion 120
  and Golden City energies 195
  and the Time of Change 201
  definition 230
  harmonic of fourteen 196
  opens through the heart 192
Freedom 144
  Freedom Star 137
  "One is allowed to expand." 47
  through restriction 186
Freedom Star
  definition 230

G

Galactic
  Galactic Center 212
  Galactic Web 105
Galactic Center 169
  definition 230
Galactic Web
  definition 231
Garden of Existence 157
  definition 231
genetics 134
  and animalistic behavior 181, 185
  and the collective forgetting 120
Giza
  and the Golden City of Gobean 102
Gobean 79, 82
  and Great Monsoon 127
  and Mount Baldy 127
  construction perimeters 129
  definition 231
  Golden City of 95, 107
    activation 105

align to the Golden City of Gobi 100
ancient location 103
and Shalahah 125
and the Blue Ray 112
connection to Shamballa 100
to cultivate inner peace 78
integrating Ray Forces 85
Star 105, 124
Time of Great Fire 127
Gobi
definition 231
Desert
ancient civilizations 98
Golden City of 95
God
a source of light 141
within 61
God force 68
Golden Age 63
definition 231
Golden Age of Kali Yuga
definition 232
the zenith 217
Golden City Mantras 111
and centrifugal force of the Ray 92
Golden City Sacred Geometry
raises consciousness 128
Golden City Vortex 43, 65, 77, 105, 109, 232
accelerate spiritual growth 218
and a new consciousness 66
and Babajeran 159
and Elemental Life Force 200
and Master Teacher 109
and the Fourth Dimension 195
and the human energy system 44
and the Star energies 219
and vibrational acceleration 78
apex 83
assimilating energies 78
assist the light bodies 215
development of 43
Divine Alignment 123
dominant Ray and attraction 85
dominant sound 82
doorways 105
 Eastern doors 114
energies 101
for spiritual practice 216
higher energies 33
moving to 93
network 95
of Gobean 78
 definition 231
of Gobi
 definition 231
of Klehma
 definition 237
of Malton 84
 definition 239
of Shalahah 87, 161
 definition 243
of Wahanee 77
 definition 248
qualification of Ray Force 112
relocation to 123
serve the physical aspect of the Ascension 192
Star
 definition 244
the Star
 and Ascension 159
 and the Gold Ray 152
"timing and intention" 198
vibration of water, vegetables 77

Building the Seamless Garment 267

Golden Perfections 100
Gold(en) Ray 84, 88, 166
  and the Twin Ray 158
  decree with Violet Flame 153
  definition 233
  "Many readied in vibration." 151
  use in Golden City Stars 152
Golden Thread Axis 41
  definition 233
Great Central Sun 83
  and Ray Forces 108
  and removal of fear 170
  and the flow of light 56
  and the pathway of sound frequencies 202
  definition 234
  "Is the light that shall free you all." 34
  Ray Forces 36
Great White Brotherhood 135
  definition 234
Green Ray 37, 87
  definition 234
guilt 75
guru
  definition 234
guru and chela relationship 184

H

Hall of Wisdom 103
  definition 234
harmony 36, 37
  and its influence on Collective Consciousness 176
  "Let go of your misgivings." 108
Harmony of the Spheres 213
  definition 235

healing
  and the Green Ray 87
Heart
  lessons of the heart 198
  open 142
  opens Fourth Dimension 192
Heart Chakra
  affected by Green Ray in Golden City of Shalahah 89
  and kundalini 113
  definition 235
  opening through breathwork 210
Heart's Desire 68
Heaven and Earth 100
higher mind
  identifying emotions 188
Higher Self 58
  definition 235
high winds 121
history
  as direct perception 102
Hopi culture
  influenced by the teachings of Akhenaton 103
HU-man 39, 45, 56
  and Ray Forces 35
  definition 235
  developing through the Candle Meditation 249
human aura
  Fourth Dimension 197
humanity
  and evolution 113
human physiology
  and the Nature Kingdoms 115
human senses
  and seven harmonics 197

HU, the 58
   and Violet Flame decrees 59
   definition 236
hypnotism
   "Through collective illusion." 73

I

I AM 145
   and the spiritual awakening 182
   definition 236
   revealed to all 35
I AM America
   dispensation through the Rays 175
I AM America Map 63
I AM Presence
   decree 153
   definition 236
I AM THAT I AM
   and Divine Order 182
   definition 236
illusion 70, 180
immortal consciousness 64
immortality
   definition 236
   of consciousness 193
   physical 101
immortals
   of Shamballa 96
Information Age 151
initiation
   and telepathy 154
   definition 236
inner marriage 121
   definition 236
inner mind
   and sleep 208
instant-thought-manifestation
   and the Golden City of Malton 84
   definition 237
integration 70
   of Ray Forces 83
intention 51, 56, 67, 74, 90, 141, 177, 199
   and money 187
   definition 237
interplay
   of the Rays 57

J

journey
   within 161
judgment
   and developing compassion 156
   and the emotional body 189
   definition 237
   "Exists within yourself." 57

K

Kali Yuga 98, 141, 168, 200
   definition 237
Kamiak and Steptoe Butte
   Ascension Valley 172
karma 57, 146, 148, 178
   and cause and effect 83
   definition 237
   group, or collective karma 162
   release of 47
karma
   past 257
karmic debt 55
karmic patterns 179

Klehma
  definition 237
  Golden City of 89
"Know Thyself"
  through meditation 61
Kuan Yin 221
  definition 237
kundalini 35, 40, 210
  and Blue Flame 117
  and Crown Chakra 87
  and OM 46
  and sound vibration 60
  and the Violet Flame 113
  definition 237

L

Law(s) of
  Attraction 126
  Attraction and Repulsion
    definition 237
  Compassion
    and higher consciousness 177
  Harmony 126
  Light and Sound 126
  Love 138, 147, 177
    definition 238
  ONE 138
  Rhythm 151
    definition 238
  Sympathetic Resonance 158
  Trinity 59
leadership 90
lei-lines
  and Ascension Valley 171
Lemuria
  and Ascension Valley 171
liberation 50

Light
  acceleration 34
  and the Violet Flame 110
  increase 34
  internal 63
Light and Sound
  calibrate historical events 110
  leap in the Fourth and Fifth Dimensions 196
  the building blocks 212
lightning
  as Babajeran's will 68
like mindedness
  and vibration of light bodies 215
"little steps" 75
Lord Apollo 134
  definition 238
Lord Macaw 131
  definition 238
Lord Meru
  definition 238
Lords of Venus 110, 257
  definition 239
love 177
  and healing 113
  and sacrifice 114
  and the opening of the heart 120
  definition 239
  "Will move a mountain." 204
Love, Wisdom, and Power 141
lucid dreaming 154
Luxor
  Temples and Ascension 171

M

Malton 84
  definition 239
  Golden City of
    and kundalini energies 85
mantra
  definition 239
  Golden Cities 91
    centrifugal force 92
Master
  "When the student is ready, the
    Master appears." 161
Master Teacher
  144 133
  and energy for energy 188
  and the "gates of freedom" 204
  definition 239
Mastery 81
  and Ray Forces 111
  definition 239
  of Ray Forces 58
Maya 138, 146
  definition 143
Mayan culture
  and ancient influences 103
  dimensional leap 90
meditation
  and Violet Flame 119
  definition 239
  for alignment 149
  for stengthening light bodies 209
  on the ONE 70
  Ray Forces 45, 60
memory 138
  and immortality 140
  and Law of Love 142
  and oral tradition 141
  and perception 144

Mental Body
  and Divine Love 186
  and karmic patterns 179
  definition 239
Mercury
  and the history of Shamballa 96
merging of finer bodies
  expression of God qualities 214
Mexico
  Ancient Golden Cities 90
mind
  and the Ascension 180
  "As builder, body will follow." 89
mind control 162
  decree for apprehension 163
  overcome through the path of the
    heart 154
mistakes 77
Monad 156
  definition 240
money
  and emotional experiences 187
Mother Earth
  and the Golden Cities 78
  "The witness." 65

N

New Day
  definition 240
  release old patterns 73
New Dimensions 63, 121
  and the White Ray 89
new mind
  and beginning anew 67
nightmares
  and lower chakras 210
Northern Door 101

O

octave
  metaphysical barrier 197
Om Eandra
  Golden City of Klehma 91
  Golden City of Malton 91
Om Hue
  Golden City of Wahanee 91
Om Shanti
  Golden City of Gobean 91
Om Sheahah
  Golden City of Shalahah 91
ONE 107
  and Ascension 168, 184
  and light and sound frequencies 112
  and love 113
  and meditation 209
  and the Candle Meditation 249
  and the group 162
  and the principle of conductivity 99
  definition 240
  "God control is ONE mind." 163
  "Unified to a cause of life." 140
Oneness
  and the Violet Flame 113
  definition 240
  through telepathy 64
Oneship 82, 121
  and Ascension Valley 88
  definition 240
Open Ears, Open Eyes 142
Oral Tradition 141, 168
  definition 240
out-picturing 182

P

pain
  forgetting 178
Peace 138
perception 35
  and karma 147
  and memory 139
  and the dimensions 203
  definition 240
perfection
  and the Ascension 193
  "Is an emanation." 97
perseverance 75
physical activity
  discharges emotion 187
physical body
  and the Ascension 192
Pink Flame 58
  definition 241
Pink Ray 71
  definition 241
planetary systems
  and Ray Forces 56
planets
  are life forces 56
Point of Perception 135, 143
  definition 241
polarity
  and the Suns 213
Pole shift
  and wind force 127
pollution
  and the Elemental Kingdom 84
portal
  interdimensional 88
Portals of Entry 33

prana
- *condensed in Golden City Stars* 86
- *definition* 241

Prophecies of Change
- *definition* 241
- *higher frequencies on Earth* 113

Prophecies of Peace
- *appearance of Master Teachers* 106
- *definition* 241

Prophecy
- *and Babajeran* 191
- *and energies of Stars* 124
- *and the Green Ray* 175
- *changes in Human Aura* 64
- *definition* 241
- *fires in Gobean* 127
- *for a New Day* 76
- *humanity's acceleration into Light* 77
- *Klehma is one of the first Crystal Cities* 89
- *purpose of* 78
- *Time Compaction* 66
- *unconscious fear* 34

prosperity
- *and the Golden City of Shalahah* 89

purification 153
- *and the Earth Changes* 199
- *definition* 241
- *in Golden Cities* 83

Q

Quetzalcoatl
- *definition* 242
- *the Christ energies of Cooperation* 90
- *the first Christ* 103

R

Rapture 192
- *definition* 242

Ray
- *and sound* 110
- *definition* 242

Ray(ces) 132

Ray Force(s)
- *and Golden Cities* 106
- *and Stars* 106, 124
- *and the Fourth and Fifth Dimensions* 202
- *calling into action* 181
- *color* 37
- *qualification* 39

Ray(s)
- *Gold* 84
- *Green* 37, 89
- *interplay* 48
- *lower qualities* 39
- *Ruby and Gold* 84

re-embodiment
- *of historical World Leaders in Golden City of Klehma* 90

regeneration
- *and the Violet Ray* 86
- *and unionization of energy fields* 116

reincarnation 42
- *and desires* 166

releasing the past 78

renunciation
- *and Ascension* 217

responsibilities 148

restriction and freedom 186

Rosicrucians 251

Ruby and Gold Ray 84, 85
- *definition* 242
- *Building the Seamless Garment* 273

S

Sacred Fire
  and the perfect cell 169
  and the Temple of Luxor 172
sacred geometry 44
  definition 242
safety
  "Is a matter of the Heart." 89
Saint Germain
  and the Violet Flame 113, 221
  definition 242
  Holy Brother 251
  Kajaeshra 252
  Map of Political Changes 253
Sananda 138, 178
  and Shalahah 171
  as Jesus the Christ 154
  definition 242
  "Simply love one another." 112
  "The time has come for man to receive the gift." 192
Sanat Kumara 98
saturn 258
Seamless Garment 143
security and emotion 188
separation 121
Serapis Bey 102
  definition 243
service 55, 69
  and detachment 55
seven layers
  Astral and Causal 211
Seven Rays of Light and Sound 48, 59
  definition 243
Seventh Manu 162
  definition 243

Shalahah 165
  definition 243
  Golden City of 87, 91
    and Gobean 125
    and health retreats 88
Shamballa 95
  definition 243
  influence on Ancient America 103
Shroud of Darkness 64
  definition 243
silence
  and sound 213
simplicity 70
simultaneous reality 134
  definition 243
sin
  against self 75
sleep 41, 79
  and the Astral and Causal bodies 209
  and use of the finer bodies 208
Solar Plexus
  affected by energies of Shalahah 89
  and sleep 210, 216
  and transmutation of death consciousness 87
  definition 244
Solomon's Temple 252
soul
  animalistic bodies 214
  group 131
Sound 46, 117
  and harmony 60
  and Ray Forces 58
  and the Great Central Sun 202
  consonants and vowels 60
  vibration 60
    and the Violet Flame 60

South America 90
Southern Door 101
spiritual assimilation
  of Golden City Energies 126
Spiritual Awakening 215
Spiritual Body
  combines Astral and Causal 209
spiritual darkness
  and Kali Yuga 169
spiritual evolution
  and self-knowledge 215
  greatest need 218
Spiritual Hierarchy 168
spiritual liberation 140
  definition 244
spiritual preparedness
  and the higher planes 218
  definition 244
Star 106
  and entry of Ray Force 124
  Golden City 83, 86, 92, 106
  of a Golden City
    definition 244
Star of Klehma 90
Star of Knowledge 102
Star Seed 85, 97
  and animalistic behavior 185
  definition 245
Step-down Transformer 112
  definition 245
strife among families 64
suffering
  "When suffering is lessened." 52
Sun
  and Ascension 168
  and the Great Central Sun 110

T

technology 135
telepathy
  prophecy 64
Temple of Mercy 221
Third Dimension
  and limitation 203
  definition 245
  harmonic of seven 196
Third Eye 82
  definition 245
thought
  and a New Day 72
  and reincarnation 64
  and transforming for Ascension 180
  Projection 101
  "You are indeed what you think." 213
thousand eyes 142
  definition 245
Time 37, 145
  "Must be cast aside." 70
  of Acceleration 35
Time Compaction 66
  and Kali Yuga 217
  definition 245
Time of Ascension
  "We become unbound by the physical." 193
Time of Change 128
  definition 246
  humanity and Babajeran 201
  prophecies 113, 134
Time of Testing 121, 140
  definition 246
"To do, to dare, and to be silent." 183

Transformation 137
Transmutation 71, 137
Transportation Vortex 88, 135
  definition 246
True Memory 178
  and perception 142
  definition 246
tsunami 84
Tube of Light 169
Twelve Avatars of Earth 133
Twelve Jurisdictions 45, 126, 133
  Abundance in Shalahah 89
  definition 247
Twin Flame 156
  definition 247

U

Unana 50, 64, 106, 135
  and Ascension 173
  and Gobean 78
  and interconnectedness 70
  definition 247
Unfed Flame 106, 141
  and the Blue Flame 115
  and the perfect cell 169
  definition 247
  history of 96
unification of self 65
unified body of light
  transmutes the physical body 194
United
  States
    Declaration of Independence 253
United States
  new capitol 90
Unity
  Consciousness 64, 184

V

Venus
  Shamballa's founders 96
Vertical Power Current 67, 82
  definition 247
vibration
  and reciprocity 212
Violet Flame 47, 139, 187
  and fulfillment of intention 75
  and gaining momentum 51
  and mantras 110
  and opening Akashic Records 155
  and the Gold Ray 152
  and the HU 58
  and the Sacred Fire 169
  application for a specific focus 74
  birthed from the Blue Flame 58
  Decree
    use with Gold Ray 153
  decree for the dimensions 205
  Decrees
    and karma 59
    for overcoming difficult karma 46
    for overcoming discouragement 73
    to harmonize the Rays 49
  definition 247, 257
  invocation at sunrise, sunset 222
  overcomes Kali Yuga 200
  Spiritual Lineage 221
  to adjust energy in a room 165
  visible in Ascension Valley 172
Violet Flame Angels 91, 207
  definition 248

Violet Ray 71, 86, 143
  and doubt 149
  and emotional responses 188
  and higher consciousness 160
  and immortality 86
  and the Ascension 179
  and transmutation 87
  and write and burn techniques 187
  for mind control 163
  physical symptoms 87
  to quiet the mind 180
  use to overcome attachments 187
visualization
  technique for Gobean 80
void
  silence and darkness 213
Vortex
  creation of 100

W

Wahanee
  definition 248
  Golden City of 86, 91
    and healing clinics 87
    release injustice 77
White Fire 91
White Ray 89
  and healing for Ascension 177
  and Venusian energies 90
  definition 248
will 67
  alignment 70
  and the collective 67
  and Throat Chakra 114
  definition 248
  unionization 115
Write and Burn Technique 187
  definition 248

Z

Zadkiel
  Order of 257

About Lori and Lenard Toye

Lori Toye is not a Prophet of doom and gloom. The fact that she became a Prophet at all is highly unlikely. Reared in a small Idaho farming community as a member of the conservative Missouri Synod Lutheran church, Lori had never heard of meditation, spiritual development, reincarnation, channeling, or clairvoyant sight.

Her unusual spiritual journey began in Washington State, when, as advertising manager of a weekly newspaper, she answered a request to pick up an ad for a local health food store. As she entered, a woman at the counter pointed a finger at her and said, "You have work to do for Master Saint Germain!"

The next several years were filled with spiritual enlightenment that introduced Lori, then only twenty-two years old, to the most exceptional and inspirational information she had ever encountered. Lori became a student of Ascended Master teachings.

Awakened one night by the luminous figure of Saint Germain at the foot of her bed, her work had begun. Later in the same year, an image of a map appeared in her dream. Four teachers clad in white robes were present, pointing out Earth Changes that would shape the future United States.

Five years later, faced with the stress of a painful divorce and rebuilding her life as a single mother, Lori attended spiritual meditation classes. While there, she shared her experience, and encouraged by friends, she began to explore the dream through daily meditation. The four Beings appeared again, and expressed a willingness to share the information. Over a six-month period, they gave over eighty sessions of material, including detailed information that would later become the I AM America Map.

Clearly she had to produce the map. The only means to finance it was to sell her house. She put her home up for sale, and in a depressed market, it sold the first day at full asking price.

She produced the map in 1989, rolled copies of them on her kitchen table, and sold them through word-of-mouth. She then launched a lecture tour of the

Northwest and California. Hers was the first Earth Changes Map published, and many others have followed, but the rest is history.

From the tabloids to the *New York Times*, *The Washington Post*, television interviews in the U.S., London, and Europe, Lori's Mission was to honor the material she had received. The material is not hers, she stresses. It belongs to the Masters, and their loving, healing approach is disseminated through the I AM America Publishing Company operated by her husband and spiritual partner, Lenard Toye.

Lenard Toye, originally from Philadelphia, PA, was born into a family of professional contractors and builders, and has a remarkable singing voice. Lenard's compelling tenor voice replaced many of the greats at a moment's notice—Pavarotti and Domingo, including many performances throughout Europe. When he retired from music, he joined his family's business yet pursued his personal interests in alternative healing.

He attended *Barbara Brennan's School of Healing* to further develop the gift of auric vision. Working together with his wife Lori, they organized free classes of healing techniques and the channeled teachings. Their instructional pursuits led them to form the *School of the Four Pillars* which includes holistic and energy healing and Ascended Master Teachings. In 1995 and 1996 they sponsored the first Prophecy Conferences in Philadelphia and Phoenix, Arizona. His management and sales background has played a very important role in his partnership with his wife Lori and their publishing company. Other publications include three additional Prophecy maps, thirteen books, a video, and more than sixty audio tapes based on sessions with Master Teacher Saint Germain and other Ascended Masters.

Spiritual in nature, I AM America is not a church, religion, sect, or cult. There is no interest or intent in amassing followers or engaging in any activity other than what Lori and Lenard can do on their own to publicize the materials they have been entrusted with.

They have also been directed to build the first Golden City community. A very positive aspect of the vision is that all the maps include areas called, "Golden Cities." These places hold a high spiritual energy, and are where sustainable communities are to be built using solar energy alongside classical feng shui engineering and infrastructure. The first community, Wenima Village, is currently being planned for development.

Concerned that some might misinterpret the Maps' messages as doom and gloom and miss the metaphor for personal change, or not consider the spiritual teachings attached to the maps, Lori emphasizes that the Masters stressed that this was a Prophecy of choice. Prophecy allows for choice in making informed decisions and promotes the opportunity for cooperation and harmony.
Lenard and Lori's vision for I AM America is to share the Ascended Masters' prophecies as spiritual warnings to heal and renew our lives.

Books by Lori Toye

Books:

NEW WORLD WISDOM SERIES: *Book One, Two, and Three*

FREEDOM STAR: *Prophecies that Heal Earth*

THE EVER PRESENT NOW: *A New Understanding of Consciousness and Prophecy*

I AM AMERICA ATLAS: *Based on the Maps, Prophecies, and Teachings of the Ascended Masters*

GOLDEN CITY SERIES
Book One: Points of Perception
Book Two: Light of Awakening
Book Three: Divine Destiny
Book Four: Sacred Energies of the Golden Cities

I AM AMERICA TRILOGY
Book One: A Teacher Appears
Book Two: Sisters of the Flame
Book Three: Fields of Light

I AM AMERICA COLLECTION
Sacred Fire
Building the Seamless Garment
Time of Change
Classic Teachings of the Ascended Masters

Maps by Lori Toye

Maps:
I AM America Map
Freedom Star World Map
United States 6-Map Scenario
United States Golden City Map

I AM AMERICA PUBLISHING & DISTRIBUTING
P.O. Box 2511, Payson, Arizona, 85547, USA. (928) 978-6435

For More Information:
www.iamamerica.com
www.loritoye.com

I AM America Online Bookstore:
http://iamamericabookstore.iaabooks.com

About I AM America

I AM America is an educational and publishing foundation dedicated to disseminating the Ascended Masters' message of Earth Changes Prophecy and Spiritual Teachings for self-development. Our office is run by the husband and wife team of Lenard and Lori Toye who hand-roll maps, package, and mail information and products with a small staff. Our first publication was the I AM America Map, which was published in September 1989. Since then we have published three more Prophecy maps, thirteen books, and numerous recordings based on the channeled sessions with the Spiritual Teachers.

We are not a church, a religion, a sect, or cult and are not interested in amassing followers or members. Nor do we have any affiliation with a church, religion, political group, or government of any kind. We are not a college or university, research facility, or a mystery school. El Morya told us that the best way to see ourselves is as, "Cosmic Beings, having a human experience."

In 1994, we asked Saint Germain, "How do you see our work at I AM America?" and he answered, "I AM America is to be a clearinghouse for the new humanity." Grabbing a dictionary, we quickly learned that the term "clearinghouse" refers to "an organization or unit within an organization that functions as a central agency for collecting, organizing, storing, and disseminating documents, usually within a specific academic discipline or field." So inarguably, we are this too. But in uncomplicated terms, we publish and share spiritually transformational information because at I AM America there is no doubt that, "A Change of Heart can Change the World."

With Violet Flame Blessings,
Lori & Lenard Toye

For more information or to visit our online bookstore, go to:
www.iamamerica.com
www.loritoye.com
To receive a catalog by mail, please write to:
I AM America
P.O. Box 2511
Payson, AZ 85547

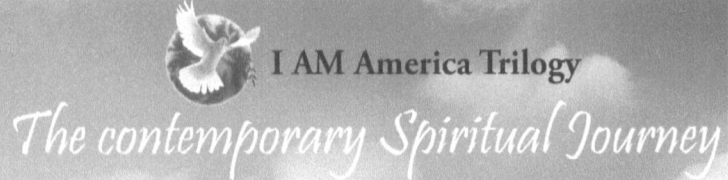

I AM America Trilogy
The contemporary Spiritual Journey

A Teacher Appears
ISBN: 978180050446
254 pages

Sisters of the Flame
ISBN: 978180050262
216 pages

Fields of Light
ISBN: 978180050613
310 pages

This series of insightful books, written by the creator of the acclaimed *I AM America Maps* shares a fresh and personal viewpoint of the contemporary spiritual journey. Lori Toye was just twenty-two years old when she first encountered Ascended Master teaching. The *I AM America Trilogy* takes us back to the beginning of her experiences with her spiritual teachers and includes insights that have never been disclosed in any previous books or writings. In "A Teacher Appears," learn how true wisdom and the inner teacher is within all of us. "Sisters of the Flame," continues an initiatory passage into the feminine with the Cellular Awakening. "Fields of Light," explains how to integrate and Master our spiritual light through soul-transcending teachings of Ascension. Lori's personal story is interwoven throughout the *I AM America Trilogy* in a rich tapestry of spiritual techniques, universal wisdom, and knowledge gained through a life-changing spiritual journey.

I AM America Atlas

Contains all of the
I AM America Maps
Full color
108 pages

New World Wisdom Series

Spiritual Teachings from
the Ascended Masters
Books One, Two, and Three

Spiritual Teaching for the New Times

For more information:
loritoye.com
iamamerica.com
or call (928) 978-6435

Navigating the New Earth

I AM America Map
US Earth Changes
Order #001

Freedom Star Map
World Earth Changes
Order #004

Since 1989, I AM America has been publishing thought-provoking information on Earth Changes. All of our Maps feature the compelling cartography of the New Times illustrated with careful details and unique graphics. Professionally presented in full color. Explore the prophetic possibilities!

Retail and Wholesale prices available.

Purchase Maps at:
www.IAMAMERICA.com

6-Map Scenario
US Earth Changes Progression
Order #022

Golden Cities Map
United States
Order #110

I AM AMERICA
P.O. Box 2511
Payson, Arizona
(928) 978-6435

www.ingramcontent.com/pod-product-compliance
Lightning Source LLC
Chambersburg PA
CBHW021055080526
44587CB00010B/255